Liferay
Beginner's Guide

Quick and easy techniques to build, deploy, and maintain your own Liferay Portal

Robert Chen

Gaurav Barot

Samir Bhatt

Sandeep Nair

Mahipalsinh Rana

BIRMINGHAM - MUMBAI

Liferay
Beginner's Guide

First published: December 2011

Production Reference: 1241111

Published by Packt Publishing Ltd.
Livery Place
35 Livery Street
Birmingham B3 2PB, UK.

ISBN 978-1-84951-700-3

www.packtpub.com

Cover Image by Asher Wishkerman (wishkerman@hotmail.com)

Credits

Authors

Robert Chen

Gaurav Barot

Samir Bhatt

Sandeep Nair

Mahipalsinh Rana

Reviewers

Albert Coronado Calzada

Aritz Galdos Otermin

Jordi Carbonell i Soler

Acquisition Editor

Sarah Cullington

Development Editor

Shreerang Deshpande

Technical Editors

Manasi Poonthottam

Sakina Kaydawala

Ankita Shashi

Copy Editors

Leonard D'Silva

Neha Shetty

Project Coordinator

Jovita Pinto

Proofreader

Aaron Nash

Indexer

Monica Ajmera Mehta

Graphics

Valentina D'silva

Conidon Miranda

Production Coordinator

Shantanu Zagade

Cover Work

Shantanu Zagade

About the Authors

Robert Chen is an Architect for Liferay Portal projects. He was a computer game developer and a software testing engineer. He holds an MS degree in Computer Science from California State University, San Bernardino. His focus was on online banking applications. He also has a bachelor's degree from Wuhan University, China. Mr. Chen was a QA engineer at VMware, Inc. He later led a team in developing four educational computer games for a Florida school district. He worked on Geographical Information Systems (GIS). Mr. Chen has rich experience in J2EE technologies. He has extensive experience in Content Management Systems (CMS) including Alfreso. He is an expert in web portal technologies. Mr. Chen has hands-on experience in 10 Liferay Portal projects.

I would sincerely thank Sarah Cullington (Acquisition Editor), Zainab Bagasrawala (Project Coordinator), Shreerang Deshpande (Development Editor) at Packt Publishing. Thank you for reviewing my chapters. I appreciate your invaluable advice – it has helped me improve the quality of my writing. Thanks also go to Eleanor Duffy, Lata Basantani, and the team at Packt Publishing. It has been a happy experience working together with you!

I would also thank Dr. Munwar Shariff and Dr. Jonas X. Yuan for their support and encouragement along the way.

Gaurav Barot has worked on Enterprise-level portal development projects in various domains such as media, healthcare, and insurance. He has been working on Liferay for more than three years now. Apart from being involved in full lifecycle of portal development projects, he is also a Certified Liferay Trainer and provides Liferay Trainings worldwide. He holds a Bachelor's degree in Engineering in Information Technologies and Post Graduate Diploma in Network Computing. He has more than six years of industrial experience.

Gaurav is working as a Senior Consultant with CIGNEX Datamatics, a global leader in open source technologies.

I would like to thank all my team members at CIGNEX for making this book a reality. I am also very thankful to Munwar Shariff – CTO, CIGNEX Datamatics and Manish Sheladia – Co-founder and Chief Delivery Officer, CIGNEX Datamatics to provide an opportunity to write this book.

I sincerely thank and appreciate the entire team at Packt Publishing for providing continuous support during this project.

Last but not the least, I would like to thank my parents and my two younger sisters – Kinjal and Yogini for their love and encouragement. A special thanks to my wife Kruti and my lovely daughter Twisha – both of them have been very tolerant and understanding during all the time that I've spent on the computer while working on the book.

Samir Bhatt Samir Bhatt has been working on Liferay for more than two years and is a Liferay certified trainer. He is leading Liferay practice at CIGNEX Datamatics. He is also part of architects panel at CIGNEX Datamatics. He has worked as a Liferay Architect in more than 10 projects. He has conducted many Liferay trainings across the globe. Samir has more than 11 years of IT experience. He delivered solutions in various business domains including telecommunication, retail, healthcare, and media. He has also worked on many other technologies including Pentaho BI, Oracle, Java Swing, ICEfaces, and Visual Basic.

I would like to specially thank Munwar Sharif (CTO, CIGNEX Datamatics) and Manish Sheladia (Chief Delivery Officer, CIGNEX Datamatics) for encouraging me to write this book.

I appreciate the whole Packt Publishing team for providing continuous support throughout this project.

Lastly, I want to thank my parents for their encouragement. I specially thank my wife Hetal and my little daughter Shreeya for their support and love.

Sandeep Nair has been working on Liferay for more than two years and has overall more than five years of experience in Java and Java EE technologies. He has executed projects using Liferay in various domains such as Construction, Financial, and Medical fields providing solutions such as Collaboration, Enterprise Content Management, Web Content Management systems. He has created a free and open source Google Chartlet plugin for Liferay which has been downloaded and used by people across 90 countries as per Sourceforge statistics. Besides development, consulting, and implementing solutions, he has also been involved in giving trainings in Liferay in other countries. Before he jumped into Liferay, he has had experience in Java and Java EE platforms and had worked in EJB, Spring, Struts, Hibernate, Servicemix. He also has experience in using JitterBit, which is an ETL tool. When he is not coding, he loves to read books and write blogs.

I would like to thank Munwar Shariff and Manish Sheladia who trusted in me and thought me worthy enough to write this book. I would like to thank Robert Chen for being so supportive from the beginning of the book and leading the team that too very efficiently. I would also like to thank rest of the co-authors Samir Bhatt, Mahipalsinh Rana, and Gaurav Barot, who were there to review and discuss each other's work and make sure we give quality book to the readers. I am also very grateful to Zainab Bagasrawala, who took the pains to co-ordinate the chapters and making sure we deliver the chapter in time, Sarah Cullington and Shreerang Deshpande for reviewing my work and giving right advice as to what should or should not be there in the book. Last but not the least, I would like to thank my parents and my brother for supporting me.

Mahipalsinh Rana's stint with portal server technologies started in Sun Microsystems when he started working with Sun Portal Server 7.2. Later Sun became the technology partner of Liferay for development in 5.2.x and he was part of that team. He looked after Internationalization (I18n) and Localization (L10n) of Liferay across various modules. He then joined CIGNEX Technologies as a Liferay Technical Architect and executed more then 10 projects in various domains such as chemical, media, telecommunications. He also enjoys doing Liferay training from time-to-time being a certified trainer from Liferay. He loves exploring other technologies such as BigData and Internationalization (I18n). He has total seven years of Industrial experience.

Mahipal is a very good speaker and has given speeches at various conferences on technical topics. He also writes blogs (http://mahipalrana.blogspot.com/) occasionally and actively participates in the Liferay Community.

I would like to thank all my colleagues at CIGNEX for their help in various scenarios. I would also like thank Munwar Shariff – CTO, CIGNEX (My Mentor, My Guru) from whom learning never ends. I would like to thank Manish Sheladia – Co-founder and Chief Delivery Officer, CIGNEX – to believe in me and provide opportunity to write this book.

I sincerely thank and appreciate the entire team at Packt Publishing for providing continuous support during this project.

Last but not the least, I would like to thanks my parents for their encouragement. I would also like to give big thanks to my wife Nehal to give me company and tea during my writing hours and my daughter Priyanshi to sleep early in my writing hours.

About the Reviewers

Albert Coronado Calzada is a highly experienced Information Technology professional with more than 12 years of experience in Java EE, high performance web portals, and enterprise software solutions. Albert has studied Information Technology Engineering and has a Master in Economic and Financial Management of companies.

Albert is currently working as a freelance software developer, trainer, and consultant for international customers. Albert is an open source software contributor and has released different applications for Liferay and Android.

Albert lives in Girona(Spain) and maintains a blog at `http://www.albertcoronado.com`.

Aritz Galdos Otermin studied Computer Engineering at UPV / EHU (Euskal Herriko Unibertsitatea) and Coventry University. Aritz has been working as programmer and software architect since 2005 and has specialized in portal development and deployment.

He is especially interested in open source and enjoys developing portlets and integration tools for Liferay with other open source projects, such as video conferencing tools and Android mobile platforms. He releases his developments in his personal projects page `http://sareweb.net`.

I want to thank every single person that has ever contributed to open source in any way.

Jordi Carbonell i Soler after more than eight years working with JEE technologies is currently a JEE Architect specialized in portal environments. His relation with Liferay started in 2007. Since then, he's been working on many Liferay-based portals along all of those projects' stages: from presales and conceptualization to development and installation; usually, integrating them with a wide range of third-party tools, such as Alfresco ECM, Atlassian products, or BPM Engines. Currently, he's working at IN2, one of the first Spanish IT companies who bet on Liferay and Alfresco as trending technologies.

www.PacktPub.com

Support files, eBooks, discount offers and more

You might want to visit www.PacktPub.com for support files and downloads related to your book.

Did you know that Packt offers eBook versions of every book published, with PDF and ePub files available? You can upgrade to the eBook version at www.PacktPub.com and as a print book customer, you are entitled to a discount on the eBook copy. Get in touch with us at service@packtpub.com for more details.

At www.PacktPub.com, you can also read a collection of free technical articles, sign up for a range of free newsletters and receive exclusive discounts and offers on Packt books and eBooks.

http://PacktLib.PacktPub.com

Do you need instant solutions to your IT questions? PacktLib is Packt's online digital book library. Here, you can access, read and search across Packt's entire library of books.

Why Subscribe?

- ◆ Fully searchable across every book published by Packt
- ◆ Copy and paste, print and bookmark content
- ◆ On demand and accessible via web browser

Free Access for Packt account holders

If you have an account with Packt at www.PacktPub.com, you can use this to access PacktLib today and view nine entirely free books. Simply use your login credentials for immediate access.

Robert Chen's Dedication:
I would like to dedicate this book to my eldest sister Xinli Chen, who has always been supporting me behind the scene.

This book would not have been possible without your encouragement.

Thank you from the bottom of my heart.

Mahipalsinh Rana's Dedication:
I would like to dedicate this book to my Late Grandfather
Mr. Vishubha Rana ,who is my constant source of inspiration.

Table of Contents

Preface

Liferay Portal is a leading horizontal portal product, written in Java. It has the power to provide the Intranets and Extranets of large corporations. Liferay will allow you to build your company's portal quickly, efficiently, and in a custom way to suit the needs of your corporation.

Liferay Beginner's Guide will show you how to set up your own site from scratch. Most books assume that you have knowledge of portals before working with Liferay and so include more theory than practice. However, only enthusiasm is required for reading this book as the step-by-step instructions, which follow the creation of a sample community site, will make it easy to install and configure Liferay, set up a Liferay Portal instance, and use the out-of-the-box portlets of Liferay.

By following the logical flow of the chapters and the creation of the sample site, you will set up your Liferay site in several quick and easy stages. You will start by installing Liferay in your application server or servlet container of choice. You will learn how to customize the look-and-feel of the portal, change the URL of the site, and create your own communities and organizations within the portal, then add users to them. By the end of the book, you will have a fully operational Liferay Portal and the confidence to maintain and customize it to meet your needs.

What this book covers

Chapter 1, Planning Your Portal, gives an overview of Liferay Portal– the most popular open source portal framework. It briefly talks about Liferay's features and its portlets.

Chapter 2, Installing a Liferay Portal Instance, teaches you how to deploy Liferay in various application servers from a basic servlet container to an enterprise application server.

Chapter 3, Understanding Portal Basics and Theming, talks about the portal basics and portlet concepts. It also discusses Liferay User interface and use of dockbar to navigate in Liferay. It instructs on how to do basic administration in Liferay using Control Panel and different options of the Control Panel. It provides basic idea about the theme as well.

Chapter 4, Tips and Tricks—Advanced Configuration, discloses Liferay's secrets for tweaking the default behavior of portal by changing a set of properties.

Chapter 5, Building your First Liferay Site, here readers will start developing their first Liferay site. It discusses different components of the site and the approach to design the site. It talks about important concepts of Liferay such as Organization, Community, User Group, and page templates.

Chapter 6, Managing Pages, Users, and Permissions, helps the readers in learning about the concepts related to Liferay's Page, User ,and Permission Management. It will also provide understanding of the various configuration options available for Pages, Users, and Permissions in Liferay.

Chapter 7, Creating and Publishing Content, the content management system and the web content management functionality are two interesting features of Liferay. Liferay's document library portlet allows users to upload documents in various formats. User can set permissions on folders and documents. Users can use the image gallery portlet to manage image files in the Liferay Portal. For web content management, Liferay has a web content portlet and a web content display portlet, which can be used to create and display journal articles.

This chapter will populate the public pages of the Guest community. It will show you how to create the Welcome page, Newcomers page, Lease office hours page, and Swimming pool hours page. We will welcome a user to our neighborhood in this chapter.

Chapter 8, Exploring Communities, helps readers to learn about various useful portlets required to build a site. This chapters covers quite a few out of box portlets such as Bookmark, Chat, OpensSocial, Language, Polls, Search. It also covers some of the custom portlets such as YouTube, SlideShow.

Chapter 9, Setting up an Online Shop, talks about how to set up online shop using the shopping portlet. It instructs reader on how to configure payment terms, shopping items, stock, and so on. It also instructs reader on how to manage orders and discounts. It also talks about end-to-end shopping workflow.

Chapter 10, Liferay Server Administration, instructs reader on how to user liferay's server administration features to maintain Liferay Portal server. It talks about server resource management, logging configuration, virtual host configuration, and so on. It also talks about how to configure staging environment.

Appendix A, PayPal Test Account Configuration, provides step-by-step guide to set up test accounts on PayPal's sandbox environment.

Bonus Chapter, Exploring Social Collaboration, introduces you to the social functionalities of Liferay. Liferay has a blog portlet. A portal user can use it to post articles, which will be shared by the community members. Its calendar portlet can be used to create events, which will show for all community members. The wiki portlet allows a user to post his ideas. Liferay's message board portlet was used as a Liferay forum. This chapter will delve deeper into Liferay organizations. We will configure and use the message board portlet, wiki portlet and blogs portlet in this chapter.

You can download the Bonus Chapter from `http://www.packtpub.com/sites/default/files/downloads/Social_collaboration.pdf`.

What you need for this book

The following are the software that you need for the Liferay Beginners Guide book:

- JDK 1.6
- Liferay Tomcat bundle – `http://sourceforge.net/projects/lportal/files/Liferay%20Portal/6.0.6/liferay-portal-tomcat-6.0.6-20110225.zip/download`
- Liferay JBoss bundle – `http://sourceforge.net/projects/lportal/files/Liferay%20Portal/6.0.6/liferay-portal-jboss-6.0.6-20110225.zip/download`
- Liferay Glassfish bundle – `http://sourceforge.net/projects/lportal/files/Liferay%20Portal/6.0.6/liferay-portal-glassfish-6.0.6-20110225.zip/download`
- Liferay Portal WAR – `http://sourceforge.net/projects/lportal/files/Liferay%20Portal/6.0.6/liferay-portal-6.0.6-20110225.war/download`
- Liferay Portal dependencies – `http://sourceforge.net/projects/lportal/files/Liferay%20Portal/6.0.6/liferay-portal-dependencies-6.0.6-20110225.zip/download`
- Oracle WebLogic 10.3.4 – To be downloaded from the website
- Apache Tomcat 6 – `http://apache.mirrors.redwire.net/tomcat/tomcat-6/v6.0.33/bin/apache-tomcat-6.0.33.exe`
- MySQL 5.1 community server – `http://dev.mysql.com/downloads/mysql/5.1.html`
- OpenOffice – `http://download.openoffice.org/index.html`

Who this book is for

All you need in order to benefit from the Liferay Beginner's Guide is programming experience. No prior knowledge of Liferay is required, although experienced Liferay portal programmers who need to get up to speed with its latest features will also find this book useful.

Conventions

In this book, you will find several headings appearing frequently.

To give clear instructions of how to complete a procedure or task, we use:

Time for action – heading

1. Action 1

2. Action 2

3. Action 3

Instructions often need some extra explanation so that they make sense, so they are followed with:

What just happened?

This heading explains the working of tasks or instructions that you have just completed.

You will also find some other learning aids in the book, including:

Pop quiz – heading

These are short multiple choice questions intended to help you test your own understanding.

Have a go hero – heading

These set practical challenges and give you ideas for experimenting with what you have learned.

You will also find a number of styles of text that distinguish between different kinds of information. Here are some examples of these styles, and an explanation of their meaning.

Code words in text are shown as follows: " It runs the `Liferay.Widget` function, which is defined in the `widget.js` file."

A block of code is set as follows:

```
<script src="http://neiborhood.cignex.com/html/js/liferay/widget.js"
type="text/javascript"></script>
<script type="text/javascript">
    Liferay.Widget({ url: 'http://neiborhood.cignex.com/widget/web/
neighborhood-exchange/special-days/-/8'});
</script>
```

When we wish to draw your attention to a particular part of a code block, the relevant lines or items are set in bold:

```
<script src="http://neiborhood.cignex.com/html/js/liferay/widget.js"
type="text/javascript"></script>
<script type="text/javascript">
    Liferay.Widget({ url: 'http://neiborhood.cignex.com/widget/web/
neighborhood-exchange/special-days/-/8'});
</script>
```

New terms and important words are shown in bold. Words that you see on the screen, in menus or dialog boxes for example, appear in the text like this: "If user has enabled the **Same as Billing** checkbox, then the billing address and shipping address will be same."

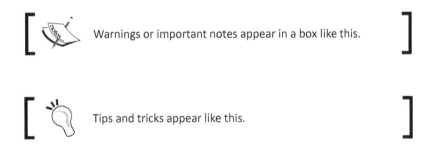

Warnings or important notes appear in a box like this.

Tips and tricks appear like this.

Reader feedback

Feedback from our readers is always welcome. Let us know what you think about this book— what you liked or may have disliked. Reader feedback is important for us to develop titles that you really get the most out of.

To send us general feedback, simply send an e-mail to feedback@packtpub.com, and mention the book title via the subject of your message.

If there is a book that you need and would like to see us publish, please send us a note in the SUGGEST A TITLE form on www.packtpub.com or e-mail suggest@packtpub.com.

If there is a topic that you have expertise in and you are interested in either writing or contributing to a book, see our author guide on www.packtpub.com/authors.

Customer support

Now that you are the proud owner of a Packt book, we have a number of things to help you to get the most from your purchase.

Downloading the example code for this book

You can download the example code files for all Packt books you have purchased from your account at http://www.PacktPub.com. If you purchased this book elsewhere, you can visit http://www.PacktPub.com/support and register to have the files e-mailed directly to you.

Errata

Although we have taken every care to ensure the accuracy of our content, mistakes do happen. If you find a mistake in one of our books—maybe a mistake in the text or the code—we would be grateful if you would report this to us. By doing so, you can save other readers from frustration and help us improve subsequent versions of this book. If you find any errata, please report them by visiting http://www.packtpub.com/support, selecting your book, clicking on the errata submission form link, and entering the details of your errata. Once your errata are verified, your submission will be accepted and the errata will be uploaded on our website, or added to any list of existing errata, under the Errata section of that title. Any existing errata can be viewed by selecting your title from http://www.packtpub.com/support.

Piracy

Piracy of copyright material on the Internet is an ongoing problem across all media. At Packt, we take the protection of our copyright and licenses very seriously. If you come across any illegal copies of our works, in any form, on the Internet, please provide us with the location address or website name immediately so that we can pursue a remedy.

Please contact us at copyright@packtpub.com with a link to the suspected pirated material.

We appreciate your help in protecting our authors, and our ability to bring you valuable content.

Questions

You can contact us at questions@packtpub.com if you are having a problem with any aspect of the book, and we will do our best to address it.

1
Planning Your Portal

In this chapter, we will introduce you to the world's most popular open source portal product. You will get an overview of Liferay's architecture, features, and running environments. You will also learn to prepare the infrastructure for the installation of a Liferay Portal instance.

People use Liferay Portal to set up websites. You can see examples of Liferay Portal in action at the following sites:

- ◆ Cisco site (`http://developer.cisco.com/web/cdc/home`)
- ◆ Sesame Street site (`http://www.sesamestreet.org/`)
- ◆ AutoZone site (`http://www.autozone.com/autozone/`)

By mid-2011, Liferay Portal had been deployed 250,000 times all around the world.

In this book, we will walk through Liferay's functionalities by setting up a website using Liferay Portal. You will learn how Liferay Portal works and how you can take advantage of its features.

In the following sections, we will do some preparation for that website. We will talk about the following topics:

- Liferay Portal concepts
- Liferay architecture
- Pre-requisites for Liferay Portal installation
- Liferay Portal features

Let us get familiar with our chessboard first and then place the king, queen, rooks, and other pieces, before we start the game.

What is Liferay Portal?

Liferay Portal is a Java web application. In a web application, a user types in a Uniform Resource Locator (URL) string in a browser address box and fires it. The browser sends the URL as a request to a corresponding application server and waits. The application server receives the request and processes data according to parameter values in the received URL. It sends a Hypertext Markup Language (HTML) format file to the requesting browser as a response. The browser interprets the HTML file and renders a webpage to the user. All the typical characteristics of a web application apply to the Liferay Portal.

The following is a deployment diagram for a Liferay Portal instance:

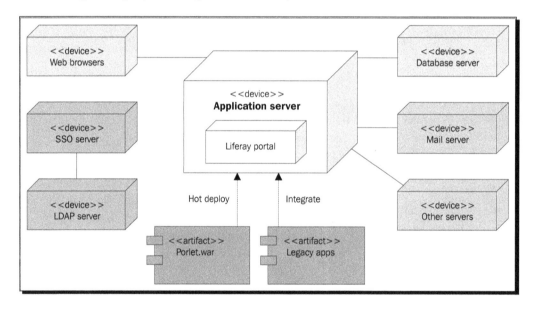

In this deployment diagram, a user accesses a Liferay Portal site with a web browser. Liferay receives the request and sends a request to the **Single Sign On (SSO)** server for authentication. The SSO server goes to the **Lightweight Directory Access Protocol (LDAP)** server to check the user's credentials. When that is successful, the SSO server tells Liferay Portal that the user is authenticated. Liferay Portal responds to the user request with a home landing page.

 Please note that not all Liferay Portal installations run with SSO. Some Liferay Portal installations are much simpler.

The Liferay Portal also runs portlet artifacts (please read on for an explanation of portlets). It relies on a **database server** to store data. It uses the **mail server** to send mails to the portal users. Optionally, Liferay Portal may also use other servers for additional functionalities.

Time for action – browsing sites based on Liferay Portal

The Liferay Inc. company site (`http://www.liferay.com/`) is based on Liferay Portal. Go to the Liferay company site and notice the Liferay logo, and the blue hue of the page, as shown in the following screenshot:

Now, go to the `http://www.sesamestreet.org/` site of Sesame Street. (Turn on your speakers to get the full experience of this site)

This is a very interesting site. I want to stay at the site for a while, even though I am no longer a child! Have you seen any traits of Liferay Portal there? You may not; the design of Liferay's look-and-feel is so flexible that it can be easily customized.

What just happened?

Liferay Portal adopts an architecture that is flexible. It divides a webpage into a theme, a layout template, and portlets. The look-and-feel of Liferay Portal can be completely customized.

Definition of a portal

In our context, a portal is a web portal. A **web portal** refers to a website that provides a broad array of resources and services, which typically include e-mail, forum, searching, and online shopping. Yahoo! was one of the first portals.

There are also web portals for enterprise use. These portals are called enterprise portals. An enterprise portal provides content and collaboration for the employees of an enterprise. It is set up as an intranet application. Liferay Portal is often customized into an enterprise portal.

Most content at a Liferay Portal site comes from its portlets. A Liferay Portal contains portlets, as a window contains panes. A portlet is different from a pane, in that it consists of text and images.

A portlet works like a servlet. A portal URL request to the application server will invoke one or more portlets. The portlets run and produce HTML markup. Liferay Portal assembles the HTML markup into an HTML file. It returns the HTML file to the requesting browser.

Horizontal vs. vertical portals

Liferay Portal was named a leader in the **Magic Quadrant for Horizontal Portals** report of Gartner in 2010 (http://www.gartner.com/technology/media-products/reprints/liferay/206214.html). What is a horizontal portal? A horizontal portal covers many areas. It can be used as a platform for multiple social and collaborative purposes. It can also be used by more than one company in the same industry. Liferay Portal is a horizontal portal, because it has a collaborative suite of blogs, wiki, mail, and calendar portlets. Its message board and chat portlets can be used for social activities.

A vertical portal focuses on one functional area. It is a specialized entry point to a specific market, industry, or subject area.

Time for action – comparing Yahoo! and YouTube

Do you have a **Yahoo** e-mail account? **Yahoo** was one of the earliest portals on the Internet. Many users are still using the e-mail service provided by **Yahoo**.

Go to the `http://www.yahoo.com/` site. You will find **Mail**, **Autos**, **Dating**, **Finance**, **Games**, **Health**, and **Jobs** links there. They cover various kinds of fields and industries, as is shown in the following screenshot:

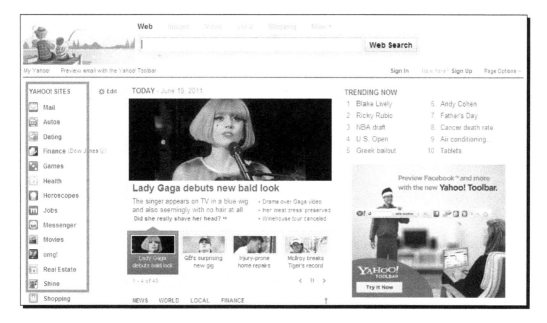

Sometimes, I like watching videos on **YouTube** for a break. **YouTube** is a well-known site for videos. Now, go to the site at `http://www.youtube.com/`. What do you find there? You may have found **Browse**, **Movies**, video **Upload** links, and advertisements. You can also create an account at the **YouTube** site, as shown in the following screenshot:

You can do a lot of things and get a lot of services at the **Yahoo** site, while do every video-related thing at the **YouTube** site.

What just happened?

The **Yahoo** site is a horizontal portal. It is a platform for multiple social and collaborative purposes. The **YouTube** site is a specialized entry point for video fans: it is a vertical portal.

Open source vs. commercial portals

A user uses an open source portal product, free of charge. He/she can modify and extend its source code. Liferay Portal is an open source portal. It is distributed under the GNU, Lesser General Public License (LGPL) (`http://www.gnu.org/copyleft/lesser.html`).

Liferay Portal is available in two versions: Community Edition (CE) and Enterprise Edition (EE). A client can use its community edition, free of charge. If a client wants support from Liferay, Inc., they can buy the Enterprise Edition.

You can study the source code of an open source portal to learn portal technologies (Refer to `https://github.com/liferay` for the source code of Liferay Portal). A commercial portal product is more expensive than the enterprise version of an open source portal. IBM WebSphere portal and Microsoft SharePoint portal are commercial portal products.

This book is based on Liferay Portal Version 6.0. We will use this CE version to illustrate the features of Liferay Portal and set up a sample website.

Time for action – finding the source code of Liferay Portal

Liferay, Inc. hosts its community edition source code at the **SourceForge** site (`http://sourceforge.net/projects/lportal/`).

It also hosts its latest version of source code at its own site at `http://www.liferay.com/downloads/liferay-portal/available-releases`.

Now, paste the previously-mentioned URL in your browser address box, click on the *Enter* key, and take a look at those packages.

What just happened?

Every release of Liferay Portal comes with the source code. You can compile and build the portal from the source code, if you choose to do so. You can study the source code to learn how Spring and Hibernate are used. You can modify the source code and re-build the portal if you like.

 Please note that Liferay Portal is also bundled in popular open source servlet containers or application servers in every release. It is easier to directly install with these bundles.

These are only some of the advantages of using an open source portal product.

Pop quiz – multiple choices

Which of the following statements are true about Liferay Portal?

     a.   Liferay Portal is a Java web application

     b.   Liferay Portal was first developed for a non-profit organization

     c.   Liferay Portal is an open source portal product

     d.   All of the above

Liferay Portal architecture

The popularity of Liferay Portal largely comes from its adaptable architecture. There are three aspects to it.

Web service provider

Liferay Portal adopts a Service Oriented Architecture (SOA). Its architectural diagram is as follows:

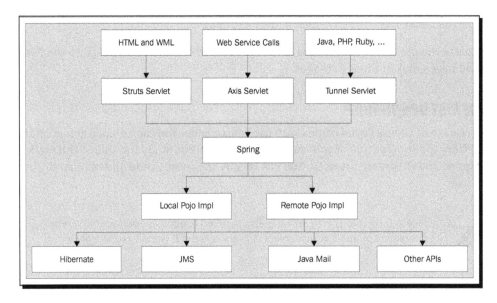

In this diagram, Liferay Portal handles Hypertext Transfer Protocol (HTTP) requests from a user. The request will first be received by the Struts servlet. This servlet runs and renders portlets. During the process, the code invokes singletons, configured with Spring Application Programming Interface (API) and plain Java objects. It uses the Hibernate API to get data from or enter data into the database. Optionally, it may use the Java Messaging Service (JMS) to send out messages.

On the other hand, Liferay Portal also provides web services for programs running on other servers. The portal uses Apache Axis specification to generate web services. The Axis configuration is specified in the `server-config.wsdd` file under the `portal/tunnel-web/docroot/WEB-INF/` folder. These are a list of Simple Object Access Protocol (SOAP) services. When an external program asks for a web service from the Liferay Portal, the Axis servlet in Liferay Portal will answer it. It will also call singletons initialized through Spring framework and call the plain Java objects. These plain Java objects will use Hibernate API to access the database.

Liferay is flexible

The architecture of Liferay Portal allows it to run on all major application servers and servlet containers, databases, and operating systems. It can be deployed on over 700 infrastructure combinations. For example, you can use MySQL or Oracle; you can run Liferay Portal in Tomcat or WebSphere.

You can plug in Solr for searching and Kaleo for workflow to Liferay Portal.

The portal administrator can apply different themes on different Liferay Portal pages. He can change the layout template of every portal page. By drag-and-drop, he can add portlets onto a portal page.

Liferay is standard compliant

Liferay Portal is compliant with Java and portlet standards. The following standards have been used in the development of Liferay Portal:

- Java Specification Request (JSR) 127 (JavaServer Faces Specification)
- JSR 168 (Portlet Specification)
- JSR 286 (Portlet 2.0 Specification)
- JSR 170 (Content Repository)
- JSR 208 (Java Business Integration)
- Asynchronous JavaScript and XML (AJAX)
- Web Services for Remote Portlets (WSRP)

Pop quiz – multiple choices

Choose the correct statements:

    a. Liferay Portal is a web service producer out-of-the-box

    b. Liferay Portal adheres to Portlet 2.0 Specification

    c. The development of Liferay Portal started in 2000

    d. All of the above

Main Liferay Portal features

Liferay Portal has award-winning features. It's hot-deployable themes, draggable-and-droppable portlets, and fine-grained permissions system, among others, make it an optimal choice among other portal products on the market.

Theme and layout

Liferay Portal themes take care of most of the look-and-feel of a Liferay Portal application. A theme usually contains a company logo, a navigation bar, footer, Cascading Style Sheet (CSS) code, and JavaScript code. A Liferay Portal site can have multiple themes. In this way, a user with proper permissions can dynamically apply a different theme to each portal page, if he/she chooses to do so.

Liferay Portal divides a page area into smaller sections with a layout template. Liferay Portal comes with 10 layout templates. A portal administrator will drag-and-drop one or more portlets into one such smaller section.

The theme and layout template makes a Liferay Portal site flexible. It is easy to change the look-and-feel of a Liferay site with the theme and layout template.

Communities and organizations

Liferay Portal provides communities and organizations for administering users and the sites. A user can belong to communities and/or organizations.

A community is a collection of users with similar characteristics and interests. The portal administrator can create a sub-site with each community.

An organization is a hierarchical collection of users. A user can be a member of multiple organizations.

Either a community or an organization can have public and private web pages. Any user at the Liferay Portal site can access the public pages, while only a member of a community or organization can browse the private pages of his/her community and/or organization.

Content Management System and Web Content Management

Liferay Portal has rich content management features.

The content displayed at a Liferay Portal site can be dynamic or static. The dynamic content can be updated by multiple users at any time. It usually comes from data saved in database tables and is presented with custom portlets. The static content is the files uploaded through the Document library portlet and web content created with the web content portlet.

The following portlets are part of the Content Management System (CMS) of Liferay Portal:

- ◆ Document library portlet
- ◆ Document library display portlet
- ◆ Image gallery portlet

The following portlets take care of Web Content Management (WCM) in Liferay Portal:

- ◆ Web content portlet
- ◆ Web content display portlet
- ◆ Web content list portlet
- ◆ Web content search portlet

The asset publisher portlet displays documents, images, blogs, wikis, message board entries, bookmarks, and web content.

Time for action – watching Liferay Portal portlets in action

The Liferay, Inc. company site is built on Liferay Portal. Now, go to `http://www.liferay.com/` and find a portal page similar to the following screenshot:

What are the parts in the rectangles made of? They are all made of the web content display portlet.

What just happened?

The static content at the Liferay, Inc. site is created with the web content portlet (or web content display portlet). It is displayed with the web content display portlet.

The Liferay forum site at `http://www.liferay.com/community/forums` is made of the messages board portlet, while the Liferay blogs site at `http://www.liferay.com/community/blogs` is set up with the blogs aggregator portlet and the blogs portlet.

Pop quiz

Which of the following statements are true?

    a. In a typical Liferay Portal page, a theme wraps a layout template, which in turn wraps portlets

    b. Liferay Portal has powerful web content management features

    c. Liferay Portal is pre-installed with more than 60 portlets

    d. All of the above

Preparation for Liferay Portal installation

Liferay Portal runs on all major application servers and servlet containers. It works with all the important database servers on the market. Its requirements are minimal on hardware and software.

In this section, we will talk about the running environment for Liferay Portal. We will also install Java Development Kit (JDK), which is the infrastructure for Liferay Portal to operate. We will install MySQL database for Liferay Portal to connect to. This is the preparation for the installation of a Liferay Portal site in *Chapter 2, Installing a Liferay Portal Instance*.

Hardware requirements

To install Liferay Portal, you need more than 300 MB of disk space and at least 1 GB of Random Access Memory (RAM). The application server or servlet container that houses Liferay Portal runs at a port. You should make sure that other applications on your computer are not using that port.

Liferay Portal is written in Java. It runs on any computer where you can install the Java Runtime Environment (JRE) and an application server or a servlet container. It runs on computers that support either 32-bit JVM or 64-bit JVM.

Some features of Liferay Portal also need a mail server for support.

Time for action – finding RAM information

Assuming that you are using a laptop computer that runs the Windows 7 operating system, carry out the following steps to get the information about RAM:

1. Click on the **Windows** icon at the bottom corner on the left-hand side.

2. Right-click on the **Computer** link and then click on the **Properties** link.

3. Find the RAM information, as shown in the following screenshot:

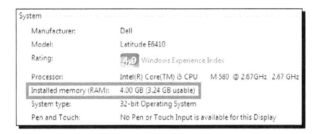

What just happened?

This machine has 4.00 gigabytes of RAM installed, of which 3.24 gigabytes are available. Because the available memory is larger than is required for running a Liferay Portal instance, we can install a Liferay Portal instance on this laptop computer.

Software requirements

Liferay Portal can be combined with multiple kinds of database servers and application servers.

As a web application, the running environment of Liferay Portal involves a browser, Java Virtual Machine (JVM), a database server, and a mail server.

 The Liferay Portal Tomcat bundle comes with a default database called **hypersonic**, which is an in-memory database. This database is good for non-production use. This means that a reader does not have to install a database server for Liferay Portal, if he/she is running Liferay Portal purely for study purposes.

Operating systems

Liferay Portal can be installed on multiple operating systems. In this book, we will install a Liferay Portal instance in a Windows operating system. The sample site is installed in a Linux operating system.

Java Development Kit

The **Java Development Kit** (**JDK**) includes code for the JVM in which Liferay Portal will run.

Let's say that your computer has the following specifications:

◆ Windows XP or Windows 7

◆ Processor: Intel(R) Core (TM) CPU

◆ Installed memory (RAM): 2.00 GB or more

◆ System type: 32-bit operating system

Time for action – installing JDK

Carry out the following procedure to install the latest version of JDK on your machine:

1. Go to `http://www.oracle.com/technetwork/java/javase/downloads/` `jdk-6u26-download-400750.html` and find a page with the content, as shown in the following screenshot:

Java SE Development Kit 6 Update 26		
Product / File Description	File Size	Download
Linux x86 - RPM Installer	76.93 MB	jdk-6u26-linux-i586-rpm.bin
Linux x86 - Self Extracting Installer	81.20 MB	jdk-6u26-linux-i586.bin
Linux Intel Itanium - RPM Installer	60.25 MB	jdk-6u26-linux-ia64-rpm.bin
Linux Intel Itanium - Self Extracting Installer	67.92 MB	jdk-6u26-linux-ia64.bin
Linux x64 - RPM Installer	77.15 MB	jdk-6u26-linux-x64-rpm.bin
Linux x64 - Self Extracting Installer	81.45 MB	jdk-6u26-linux-x64.bin
Solaris x86 - Self Extracting Binary	81.08 MB	jdk-6u26-solaris-i586.sh
Solaris x86 - Packages - tar.Z	136.89 MB	jdk-6u26-solaris-i586.tar.Z
Solaris SPARC - Self Extracting Binary	86.05 MB	jdk-6u26-solaris-sparc.sh
Solaris SPARC - Packages - tar.Z	141.37 MB	jdk-6u26-solaris-sparc.tar.Z
Solaris SPARC 64-bit - Self Extracting Binary	12.24 MB	jdk-6u26-solaris-sparcv9.sh
Solaris SPARC 64-bit - Packages - tar.Z	15.58 MB	jdk-6u26-solaris-sparcv9.tar.Z
Solaris x64 - Self Extracting Binary	8.50 MB	jdk-6u26-solaris-x64.sh
Solaris x64 - Packages - tar.Z	12.24 MB	jdk-6u26-solaris-x64.tar.Z
Windows x86	76.81 MB	jdk-6u26-windows-i586.exe
Windows Intel Itanium	63.32 MB	jdk-6u26-windows-ia64.exe
Windows x64	67.42 MB	jdk-6u26-windows-x64.exe

2. Click on the **jdk-6u26-windows-i586.exe** link. When a window pops up, click on **Run**.

3. Click on **Next** in the next pop-up window.

4. Accept the default installation folder and click on **Next**.

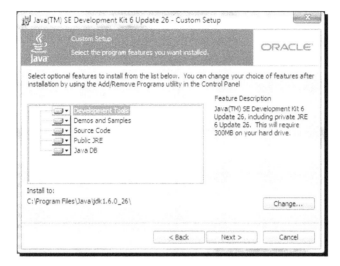

5. Accept the default installation directory for JRE and click on **Next**.

6. When the installation is done, click on **Finish**.

Now that the JDK is installed, we set the JAVA_HOME variable and put Java commands on the path. The following is the procedure:

7. Click on the Windows icon at the bottom corner on the left-hand side of the screen.

8. Right-click on **Computer**. Click on **Properties | Advanced system settings | Environment variables**.

9. Click on **New** in the System variables section. Define a JAVA_HOME variable and set its value to C:\Program Files\Java\jdk1.6.0_26:

10. Edit the Path variable in the System variables section. Add `%JAVA_HOME%\bin` as a value in the Path variable. It should be separated from other values by a semi-colon. A sample value for the `Path` variable is as follows:

```
%JAVA_HOME%\bin;%ANT_HOME%\bin;C:\Program Files\Common Files\
Microsoft Shared\Windows Live;%SystemRoot%\system32;%Syst
emRoot%;%SystemRoot%\System32\Wbem;%SYSTEMROOT%\System32\
WindowsPowerShell\v1.0\;c:\Program Files\Intel\DMIX;C:\
Program Files\Intel\WiFi\bin\;C:\Program Files\Common Files\
Intel\WirelessCommon\;c:\Program Files\WIDCOMM\Bluetooth
Software\;C:\Program Files\NTRU Cryptosystems\NTRU TCG
Software Stack\bin\;C:\Program Files\Wave Systems Corp\Gemalto\
Access Client\v5\;C:\Program Files\Common Files\Roxio Shared\
DLLShared\;C:\Program Files\Common Files\Roxio Shared\10.0\
DLLShared\;C:\Program Files\Windows Live\Shared;C:\Program
Files\TortoiseSVN\bin
```

11. Click on **OK** to save the settings.

12. Open a Disk Operating System (DOS) interface. On the command line, enter `java-version` and press *Enter*.

What just happened?

The previous screenshot confirms that the JDK has been successfully installed!

Application servers and servlet containers

You can download an application server or servlet container from its website and install the Liferay Portal Web Application Archive (WAR) file and dependency Java Archive (JAR) files in it. Alternatively, if Liferay has already bundled Liferay Portal with an application server or servlet container, you can download that bundle, unzip it, and install it.

Liferay Portal supports the following application servers:

- Apache Geronimo
- Borland ES
- JBoss
- JonAs
- Jrun
- OracleAS

- Orion
- Pramati
- RexIP
- Sun GlassFish
- Sun JSAS
- WebLogic
- WebSphere

Liferay Portal also runs in the following servlet containers:

- Jetty
- Resin
- Tomcat

For every release, Liferay, Inc. installs Liferay Portal in some open source servlet containers and application servers. The resulting packages are called Liferay Portal bundles, which are ZIP files. A user can download one such bundle, unzip it, and install it. The presently-available bundles are as follows:

- Tomcat bundle
- Resin bundle
- JonAs bundle
- Jetty bundle
- JBoss bundle
- Sun Glassfish bundle
- Apache Geronimo bundle

Database servers

We can connect Liferay Portal to the following database servers:

- Apache Derby
- IBM DB2
- Firebird
- Hypersonic
- Informix
- InterBase
- JdataStore

- MySQL
- Oracle
- PostgreSQL
- SAP
- SQL Server
- Sybase

In this book, and at the sample site, we will run Liferay Portal with MySQL database. MySQL is the world's most popular open source database. The current version of Liferay Portal requires MySQL version 5.0 or above.

Time for action – installing MySQL database server

If you have not already installed the MySQL database, follow these steps to install the latest version of MySQL Community Server on your computer:

1. Go to `http://dev.mysql.com/downloads/` to download the MySQL database installation package. You will find the page similar to the following screenshot:

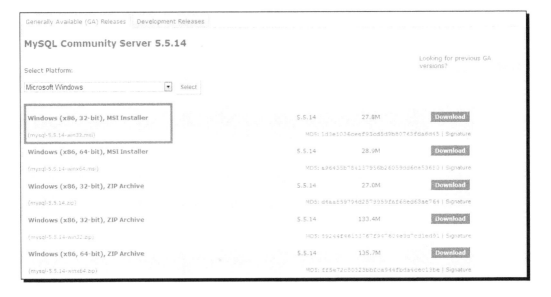

2. Download a **mysql-5.5.14-win32.msi** file to a local directory. That file is Microsoft Installer (MSI) for MySQL database server.

3. Double-click on the **mysql-5.5.14-win32.msi** file. A window pops up. Click on **Run**.

4. Click on **Next**. Check the **I accept the terms** in the **License Agreement** and click on **Next**.

5. For the setup type, choose **Custom** and click on **Next**.

6. For the installation folder, browse to **C:\mysql** and click on **Next**:

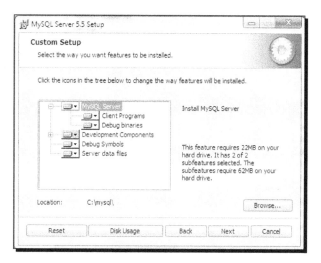

7. Click on **Next**. Click on **Install**.

8. When the installation is done, leave **Launch the MySQL Instance Configuration Wizard** checked and click on **Finish**.

9. Click on **Next** to configure the MySQL server.

10. Select **Standard Configuration** and click on **Next**.

11. Input the root password and click on **Next**.

12. Click on **Execute** to perform configuration.

13. When the configuration is done, click on **Finish**.

14. Add **C:\mysql\bin** as a value in the Path system variable, as we did for Java.

15. In a DOS window, type **mysql –uroot –p** on the command line. Press **Enter**.

What just happened?

The previous screenshot confirms that the MySQL database server has been installed successfully.

Web browser

You can use Firefox (3.0 and above), Internet Explorer (IE) (7.0 and above), Chrome, Safari, and Opera to browse a Liferay Portal site.

The ability of a web browser to access a website depends on the user interface (UI) technologies used in the development of that website. Because Liferay Portal is highly customizable, you may be able to interact with a customized Liferay Portal site with more varieties of browsers on the market.

A Liferay Portal theme decides most of the look-and-feel of a Liferay Portal site. In almost all situations, a client will develop a custom theme for their site. The user interface technologies that they use for their custom theme decide the accessibility of their site.

Liferay 6.0 CE uses Alloy user interface (Alloy UI). Alloy UI has combined the following technologies:

◆ Hyper Text Markup Language 5 (HTML5)

◆ Cascading Style Sheets Level 3 (CSS3)

◆ Yahoo! User Interface Version 3 (YUI3)

HTML 5 defines the HTML elements in a webpage. It is used for the structure of a portal page. CSS3 is used to add styles to document object models (DOM). YUI3, which includes JavaScript API, is used to make the HTML elements dynamic.

HTML 5 is the latest revision of the HTML standard. HTML 5 is still a work in progress. However, Safari, Chrome, Firefox, and Opera already support some of its features in their latest versions. IE 9 will also be available to support some HTML 5 features.

Liferay Portal has a feature to support browsing in iPad and smart phones in its 6.1 CE version. This is achieved by detecting the screen layout of the device with JavaScript code. When the computer screen layout is 960px wide, Liferay Portal knows that it is a desktop computer or iPad in landscape mode; when the screen layout is 320px wide, Liferay Portal knows it is a smart phone in portrait mode. Liferay Portal will apply a corresponding Cascading Style Sheet (CSS) class, and thus adjust the dimensions of an image and other content on the portal page.

Installing OpenOffice

Liferay Portal has a feature to convert web content, wiki articles, and message board content into PDF files and files of other formats. This feature relies on the integration of the **OpenOffice** application. OpenOffice is an open source office software that consists of a word processor, a spreadsheet program, a drawing tool, and a math program.

Time for action – installing OpenOffice

We install OpenOffice on our computer by carrying out the following steps:

1. Go to `http://www.openoffice.org/` and download the latest version of **OpenOffice.org** for Windows.

2. Save the **OOo_${VERSION}_Win_x86_install-wJRE_en-US.exe** file in a chosen folder.

3. Double-click on the **OOo_${VERSION}_Win_x86_install-wJRE_en-US.exe** filename; this triggers the installation process.

4. Click on **Next**, when you see the following pop-up window:

5. Accept the default folder for unpacking and click on **Unpack**.

6. Wait for the unpacking process to proceed.

7. Click on **Next** when a new installation window shows.

8. Input username and organization and click on **Next**.

9. Use the **Typical** setup type and click on **Next**.

10. Click on **Install**.

11. Click on **Finish**, when the installation wizard is completed.

What just happened?

Congratulations! You have successfully installed OpenOffice on your computer!

Liferay Portal depends on a service provided by OpenOffice to convert files.

Time for action – starting OpenOffice service

To start the OpenOffice service, do the following:

1. Enter DOS mode.

2. Go to the **C:\Program Files\OpenOffice.org 3\program** directory; this is where OpenOffice is installed by default.

3. Run the following command:
   ```
   soffice -headless -accept="socket,host=127.0.0.1,port=8100;urp;"
   -nofirststartwizard
   ```

A screenshot of the **DOS** window is as follows:

What just happened?

The previous command means that OpenOffice has started a service with the headless option. Now, this service will accept a request at port 8100. It is waiting for the request from a server, whose Internet Protocol (IP) address is 127.0.0.1, which means the local host.

We can check to see how the OpenOffice service is running.

Time for action – checking the OpenOffice service

To confirm that the OpenOffice service is running, perform the following steps:

1. Right-click the **Windows** task bar.

2. Click on **Start Task Manager**, and you will find a window similar to the following screenshot:

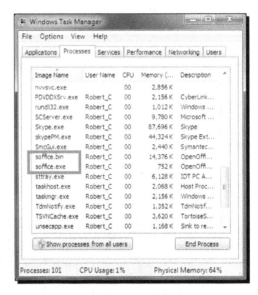

3. You can see that the OpenOffice service is shown in the list of running processes in Windows.

4. In the DOS window, run the `netstat -anptcp` command, which will show the network activities on the computer. The DOS window will show content similar to the following screenshot:

What just happened?

As you can see, a service is listening at port 8100 for a request from 127.0.0.1.

If you reboot your computer, this service will be stopped and gone, because you started it manually. So, a better choice is to set up this service as a Windows service, which will be started whenever your machine is rebooted.

Archive tools

You may install Liferay Portal in a bundle, such as `liferay-portal-tomcat-${version}.zip`, on your computer. If it is a Linux machine, you can run the `unzip liferay-portal-tomcat-${version}.zip` command to extract the files. On a Windows machine, an unzip tool may be already available, or you can download WinRAR at `http://download.cnet.com/WinRAR-32-bit/3000-2250_4-10007677.html` and install it to explode the ZIP file.

Pop quiz

Which of the following statements about the installation environment for Liferay Portal are true?

     a.   Liferay Portal can be installed on a laptop computer

     b.   Liferay Portal comes with a hypersonic in-memory database

     c.   Liferay Portal depends on **Java Virtual Machine**

     d.   All of the above

Summary

In this chapter, we have learned what Liferay Portal is. We now know the following facts about Liferay Portal:

- Liferay Portal is a Java web application
- Liferay Portal is a horizontal portal
- Liferay Portal has award-winning features

In addition, we have talked about the environment for Liferay Portal to run, including hardware and software. We have also installed JDK, MySQL database server, and the OpenOffice application.

Now that the infrastructure is set, we are ready to install a Liferay Portal instance on our computer, which is the topic of *Chapter 2,Installing a Liferay Portal Instance*.

2
Installing a Liferay Portal Instance

In the first chapter we learned what Liferay is all about and how it caters to various needs across domains. In this chapter we will see how to install Liferay in different servers.

With any web application, one of the major pain points is how to install the application in various servers. Many a time it happens that to just start-up the application, we spend lots of days' worth effort.

Luckily for us Liferay has provided bundles for various open source servlet containers and application servers and you would see how easy it is to start up Liferay on any of these servers.

By the end of this chapter, we will learn how to start up Liferay on the following servers:

- Apache Tomcat
- JBoss Application Server
- GlassFish
- Oracle WebLogic

We will see how to deploy Liferay in an existing Tomcat server.

Also, we will learn how to change the default database of Liferay from Hypersonic to MySQL.

Looking above it seems like an uphill task. So go grab a cup of coffee so that we can indulge!

Getting started

Before we start, please see that you already have the following:

- ◆ Download the latest JDK and create an environment variable named JAVA_HOME and set the path to the JDK (you should have done this in the previous chapter).

Liferay with Apache Tomcat

Apache Tomcat is an open source servlet container which is developed by the Apache Software Foundation. We will be using Tomcat server for the rest of our chapters.

Time for action – deploying on Tomcat

To start with, you will need to download the latest community version of the Liferay Tomcat bundle from the download page of Liferay (http://www.liferay.com/downloads/liferay-portal/available-releases). At the time of writing, the latest Liferay bundle that is available is Liferay 6.0.6. Next, follow these steps to configure Tomcat with Liferay:

1. Extract the zip file that you downloaded to the folder called bundles.

2. We will call the extracted folder LIFERAY_HOME.

3. There will be a tomcat folder inside LIFERAY_HOME which we will refer to as TOMCAT_HOME.

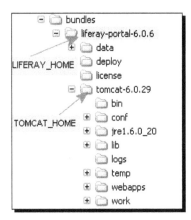

4. Navigate to TOMCAT_HOME/bin and double-click on startup.bat.

5. Your server should start up properly and you should see the console as shown in the following screenshot:

```
07:45:06.658 INFO  [ServiceComponentLocalServiceImpl:187] Running WSRP SQL scripts
07:45:07.096 INFO  [PortletHotDeployListener:220] Registering portlets for vsrp-portlet
07:45:07.267 INFO  [PortletHotDeployListener:374] 2 portlets for vsrp-portlet are available for use
Loading file:/C:/bundles/liferay-portal-6.0.6/tomcat-6.0.29/webapps/vsrp-portlet/WEB-INF/classes/service.properties
07:45:07.471 INFO  [DialectDetector:69] Determining dialect for HSQL Database Engine 1
07:45:07.471 WARN  [DialectDetector:84] Liferay is configured to use Hypersonic as its database. Do NOT use Hypersonic
07:45:07.471 INFO  [DialectDetector:49] Using dialect org.hibernate.dialect.HSQLDialect
Loading file:/C:/bundles/liferay-portal-6.0.6/tomcat-6.0.29/webapps/vsrp-portlet/WEB-INF/classes/service.properties
Mar 16, 2011 7:45:10 AM org.apache.coyote.http11.Http11Protocol start
INFO: Starting Coyote HTTP/1.1 on http-8080
Mar 16, 2011 7:45:10 AM org.apache.jk.common.ChannelSocket init
INFO: JK: ajp13 listening on /0.0.0.0:8009
Mar 16, 2011 7:45:10 AM org.apache.jk.server.JkMain start
INFO: Jk running ID=0 time=0/47  config=null
Mar 16, 2011 7:45:10 AM org.apache.catalina.startup.Catalina start
INFO: Server startup in 93417 ms
```

6. Open a browser and type `http://localhost:8080`; this will open the Liferay home page.

What just happened?

We have got Liferay up and running in Tomcat. We will be using this configuration for the rest of the chapters.

Now, we will see how to deploy Liferay on an Enterprise Application server, such as JBoss.

Liferay with JBoss Application Server

JBoss Application Server is a Java EE-based, free, and open source application server.

Time for action – deploying on JBoss AS

You can get the latest community version of the Liferay JBoss bundle from the download page of Liferay: (`http://sourceforge.net/projects/lportal/files/Liferay%20 Portal/6.0.6/liferay-portal-jboss-6.0.6-20110225.zip/download`).

Next follow these steps to start up JBoss Application server with Liferay:

1. Extract the zip file that you downloaded to the folder called `bundles` (which we created for the last exercise).

2. We will call the extracted folder `LIFERAY_HOME`.

3. There will be a `jboss` folder inside `LIFERAY_HOME`, which we will refer to as `JBOSS_HOME`:

4. Navigate to `JBOSS_HOME/bin` and double-click on `run.bat`.

5. Your server should start up properly and you should see the console as shown in the following screenshot:

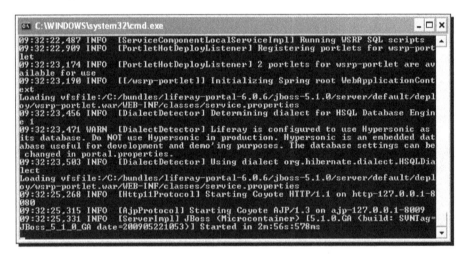

6. Open a browser and type `http://localhost:8080` and this will open the Liferay home page.

What just happened?

We have deployed Liferay with JBoss Application server.

Now we will install Liferay with GlassFish Application server.

Liferay with GlassFish

GlassFish is an open source application server for Java EE platform.

Time for action – deploying in GlassFish

You can get the latest community version Liferay GlassFish bundle from the download page of Liferay (`http://sourceforge.net/projects/lportal/files/Liferay%20 Portal/6.0.6/liferay-portal-glassfish-6.0.6-20110225.zip/download`).

Next follow these steps to deploy Liferay with Glassfish:

1. Extract the zip file that you downloaded to the `bundles` folder (created earlier).

2. We will call the extracted folder `LIFERAY_HOME`.

3. There will be a `tomcat` folder inside `LIFERAY_HOME`, which we will refer to as `GLASSFISH_HOME`:

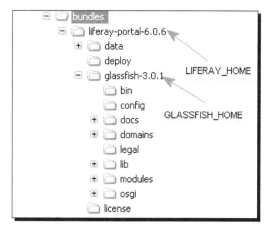

4. By default, when we install GlassFish, a default domain named `domain1` is created. Our Liferay is inside this domain.

5. So to start Liferay, navigate to `GLASSFISH_HOME/bin` from a command prompt.

6. Issue the command `asadmin start-domain domain1`.

7. Wait for the domain to start. After the domain is started, it takes some time to deploy the application for the first time.

```
C:\bundles\liferay-portal-6.0.6\glassfish-3.0.1\bin>asadmin start-domain domain1

Waiting for DAS to start ........
Started domain: domain1
Domain location: C:\bundles\liferay-portal-6.0.6\glassfish-3.0.1\domains\domain1

Log file: C:\bundles\liferay-portal-6.0.6\glassfish-3.0.1\domains\domain1\logs\s
erver.log
Admin port for the domain: 4848
Command start-domain executed successfully.
```

8. You can check the log at
`GLASSFISH_HOME/domains/domain1/logs/server.log`.

9. You can also navigate to the admin console to see all the web applications that are deployed on the server.

10. To access the admin console open a browser and type `http://localhost:4848`.

11. You can see all the web applications which are deployed by clicking on **Applications** on the left navigation tree. Wait till you see Liferay-portal in the available application from admin console.

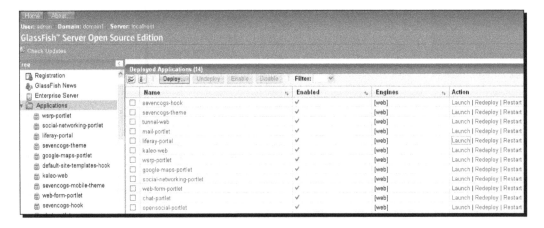

12. Open a browser and type `http://localhost:8080`; this will open the Liferay home page.

13. You can stop the server typing the command `asadmin stop-domain domain1`.

What just happened?

We have deployed Liferay in GlassFish Application Server and seen how to start and stop the GlassFish server using Liferay.

Now we will deploy Liferay in Oracle WebLogic, which is a well-known proprietary application server.

Liferay with Oracle WebLogic

Oracle WebLogic is a proprietary application server for building and deploying enterprise Java EE applications.

Time for action – configuring Weblogic

You can get the latest version of Oracle WebLogic from their download section: `http://www.oracle.com/technetwork/middleware/weblogic/downloads/index.html`.

We are going to use WebLogic 10.3.4 for Windows in this particular exercise. Besides that, since we don't have any bundle for Oracle WebLogic, we would need to download the standalone Liferay Portal war and the dependencies jar that are required for starting up Liferay. You can download the standalone war and dependencies from the following locations:

`http://sourceforge.net/projects/lportal/files/Liferay%20Portal/6.0.6/liferay-portal-6.0.6-20110225.war/download`.

`http://sourceforge.net/projects/lportal/files/Liferay%20Portal/6.0.6/liferay-portal-dependencies-6.0.6-20110225.zip/download`.

Since here we don't have a bundle, we will see how to install Liferay from scratch in a plain vanilla Weblogic server. So the configuration steps can be divided into two as follows:

- Configuring Oracle WebLogic
- Deploying Liferay in WebLogic

Configuring Oracle WebLogic

Follow these steps to configure Oracle WebLogic:

1. Double-click the executable file you downloaded for Oracle WebLogic. You will be presented with the following screen:

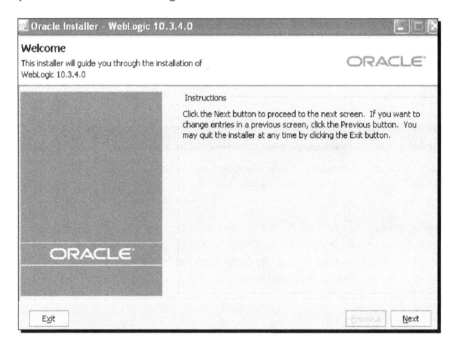

2. Click on **Next** and when it asks you for a path, select the option **Create a new Middleware home** and then provide the location where you want to install the server. We will refer to this as WEBLOGIC_HOME.

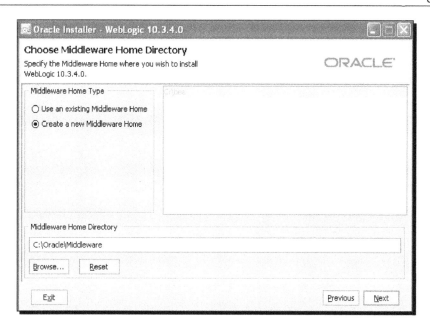

3. Click on **Next** until it shows you the screen where you see the installation progress as follows:

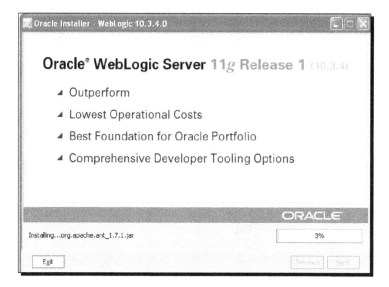

4. Once Weblogic is done with the installation it will show the following screen, with the option checked to **Run Quickstart**. Quickstart is a one stop point for creating new domains and upgrading domains from the previous version. It also provides online documentation to get started with.

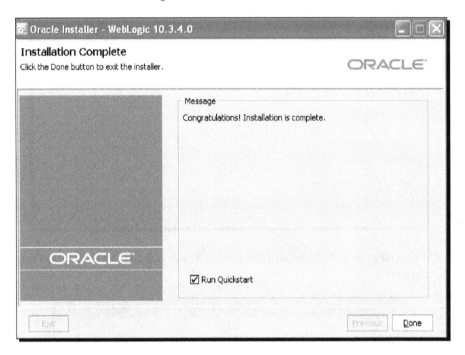

What just happened?

We have installed WebLogic. Now we will see how to deploy Liferay on WebLogic.

Deploying Liferay on WebLogic

In this section, we will go through the steps needed to deploy Liferay on WebLogic:

1. Continuing from where we left off, when we click on the **Done** button, we are presented with the **QUICKSTART** screen as I mentioned earlier.

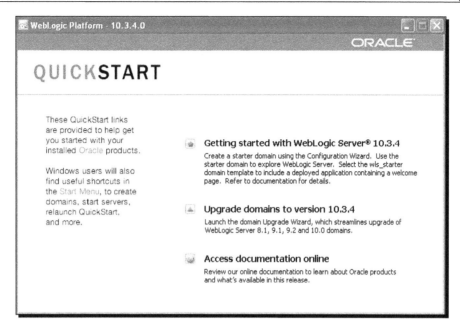

2. Let us create a domain for Liferay. Click on **Getting started with WebLogic server**. This will bring up a screen with two options for creating a new WebLogic domain or extending an existing WebLogic domain. Select the option to create a new WebLogic domain and click on **Next**:

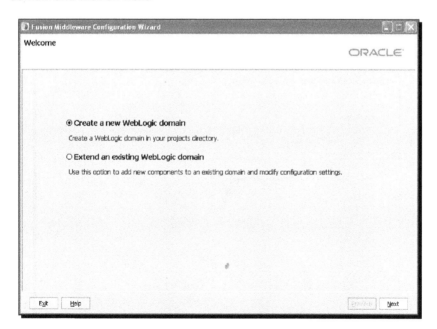

3. Provide the name of the domain. It would be good if we name it Liferay. Also, you will have to provide the location of the domain. This is where our Liferay would go. So we would call this DOMAINS_HOME for future reference.

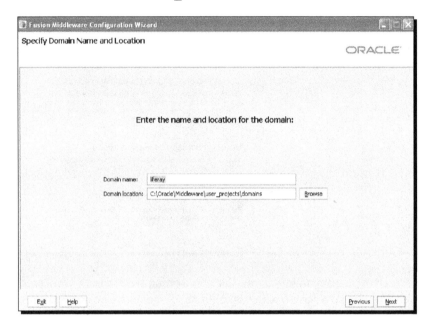

4. When you click **Next** it will give you an option to set the name and password for the administrator user. Provide the credentials you would like to have and click on the **Next** button:

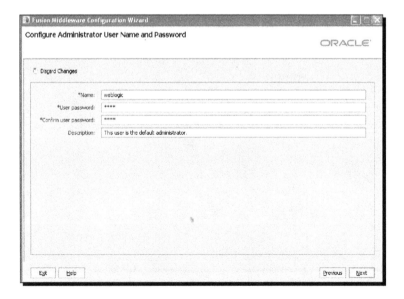

5. This will bring you a screen from which you can select the mode as well as JDK. We will use Sun JDK and keep the mode as **Development** for now.

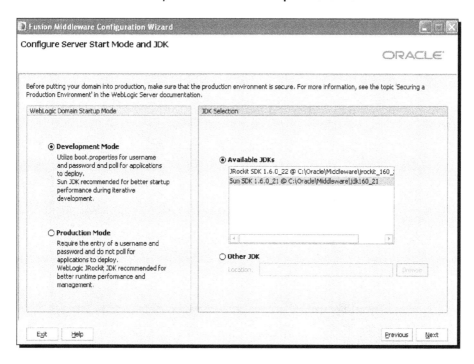

6. The next screen will ask you for the components that you want to install. Right now just check **Administration Server** and move on.

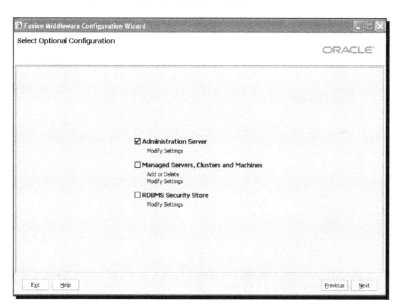

7. Finally, you are given the option to configure your server, where you can specify the server name and the port it listens to. Keep the defaults and move on to the next screen.

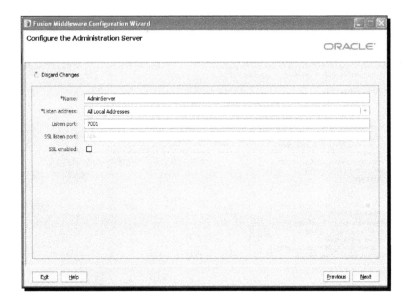

8. You can check your configuration summary and finish off your installation.

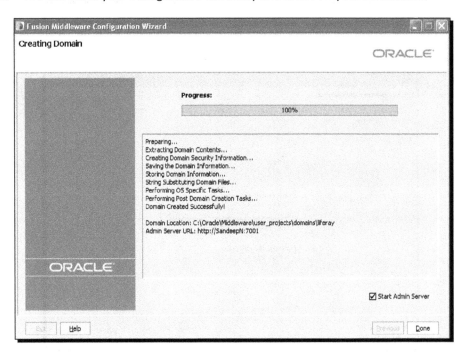

9. While finishing the installation, we made sure to start the server. So the server should startup in a few minutes. When the server is started up, you can open a browser and type this URL: `http://localhost:7001/console`. This should bring up the admin console as follows:

10. Now that we have set up a domain for Liferay, let us actually deploy Liferay in it. Stop the server. You can start or stop the server using the shortcut that the configuration wizard has created for you in the **Start** menu. In our case to stop, it will be **Start | Oracle Weblogic(BEA 1) | User Projects | Liferay | Stop Admin Server**. Copy the dependencies jar that you downloaded earlier to `DOMAINS_HOME/Liferay/lib`.

11. Next go to `DOMAINS_HOME/Liferay/bin`. Open the file called `setDomainEnv.cmd` and change `XX:MaxPermSize` from 48m to 128m to increase the PermGen Space memory. After restarting the server, navigate to the admin console URL that we accessed earlier and log in with your credentials.

12. You will be presented with the dashboard of the WebLogic server on successful login. Click on the link called **Deployments**, which can be found in the dashboard, and will lead to a screen from where you can deploy your web application. Click on **Install** and navigate to the location where you have standalone Liferay war downloaded. Select the radio button next to the war and click on **Next**. Select the option to install the deployment as a web application and wait for the server to deploy. We are installing Liferay on Admin server instance for testing purposes only and this is not meant for production environments.

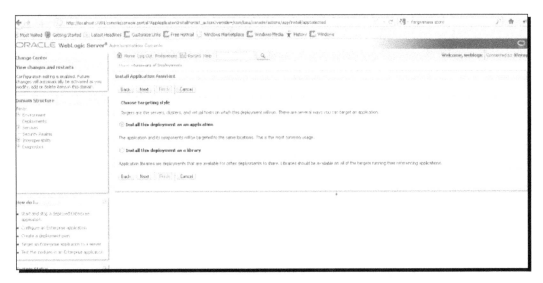

13. Check the console to see if Liferay has deployed. Once deployed successfully, open the browser and type `http://localhost:7001` and it should bring up the Liferay home page. Voila! You have successfully configured Liferay in WebLogic.

What just happened?

We have configured Liferay with Oracle WebLogic which is one of most widely used proprietary Java EE Application Server.

Now we will see how to configure Liferay in an existing Tomcat server.

Liferay on existing Tomcat

In the beginning of this chapter, we saw how easy it was to run Liferay with Liferay Tomcat Bundle. However, most of the production environments will need to have Liferay in existing Tomcat. Before moving on, please download the following files that are required for our exercise:

Tomcat 6: `http://apache.mirrors.timporter.net/tomcat/tomcat-6/v6.0.33/bin/apache-tomcat-6.0.33.exe`.

Liferay Portal WAR: `http://sourceforge.net/projects/lportal/files/Liferay%20Portal/6.0.6/liferay-portal-6.0.6-20110225.war/download`.

Liferay Portal Dependencies: `http://sourceforge.net/projects/lportal/files/Liferay%20Portal/6.0.6/liferay-portal-dependencies-6.0.6-20110225.zip/download`.

Time for action – deploying Liferay

Next, follow these steps to configure Liferay with Tomcat:

1. Create a folder called `Liferay`, which we will refer to as `LIFERAY_HOME` from now on.

2. Extract the Tomcat zip file you have downloaded earlier to `LIFERAY_HOME`. You should see a folder named `apache-tomcat-6.0.33` inside `LIFERAY_HOME`. From now on this folder will be referred to as `TOMCAT_HOME`.

3. Create a folder called `ext` inside `TOMCAT_HOME/lib`. Extract the Portal Dependencies jars zip that you downloaded earlier to this `ext` folder.

4. Copy the jars like `mysql.jar`, `jta.jar`, and `mail.jar` inside the `TOMCAT_HOME/lib` folder, which has been provided to you in the code folder of this chapter.

5. Create a file called `ROOT.xml` inside `TOMCAT_HOME/conf/Catalina/localhost`. Add the following content inside `ROOT.xml`:

   ```
   <Context path="">
   </Context>
   ```

6. Open the file `TOMCAT_HOME/conf/catalina.properties` and find a property called `common.loader`. Append `${catalina.home}/lib/ext/*.jar` at the end as follows:

   ```
   common.loader=${catalina.base}/lib,${catalina.base}/lib/*.
   jar,${catalina.home}/lib,${catalina.home}/lib/*.jar,${catalina.
   home}/lib/ext/*.jar
   ```

7. Delete the contents inside `TOMCAT_HOME/webapps/ROOT` folder and extract the contents of Liferay Portal war that you downloaded before.

8. Open `catalina.bat` from `TOMCAT_HOME/bin` using a text editor. Find a line which starts with `rem ----- Execute`.

9. Below that line add the following to increase heap space and save the file:

   ```
   set JAVA_OPTS=%JAVA_OPTS% -Xms128m -Xmx512m -XX:MaxPermSize=128m
   -Dfile.encoding=UTF8 -Duser.timezone=GMT
   ```

10. Start the server by double-clicking `startup.bat` inside `TOMCAT_HOME/bin`.

11. The server will start up and the default Liferay home page will be opened automatically in the browser.

What just happened?

You have just seen how to deploy Liferay in an existing Tomcat server.

Next let's see how we can configure a production database with Liferay.

Database configuration

Liferay ships with Hypersonic database, by default. Now this is fine, as long as you are using it for a demo. However, for the production environment, it is not advisable to use Hypersonic. In this section, we will see how to configure Liferay to use the MySQL database. MySQL is an open source RDBMS which is used widely in production environments.

Time for action – creating the database

You can download MySQL from the following URL:
`http://dev.mysql.com/downloads/mysql/5.1.html`. Let us first install MySQL:

1. Double-click on the installable file that you just downloaded, which will show the following screen:

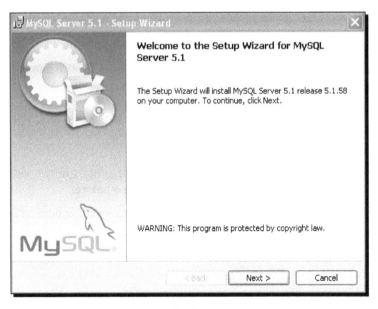

2. Click on the **Next** button and accept the terms of use and again click **Next**, which will bring up a screen as shown in the following screenshot to select the type of setup:

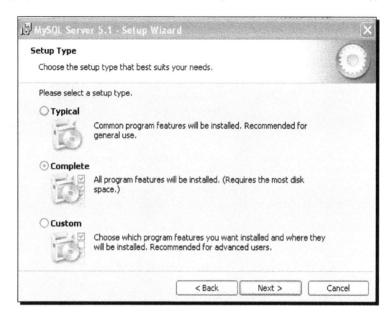

3. Select the radio button next to **Complete**, again click on **Next**, and then click on **Install**, as shown in the following screenshot:

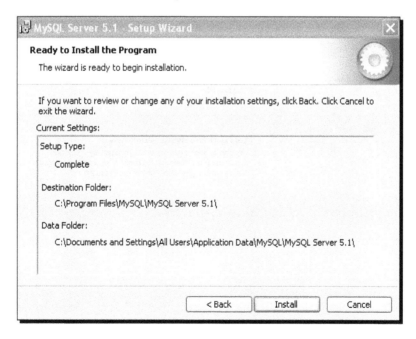

4. This will start the installation of MySQL and after it is done it will show a couple of screens on which you have to click **Next** again:

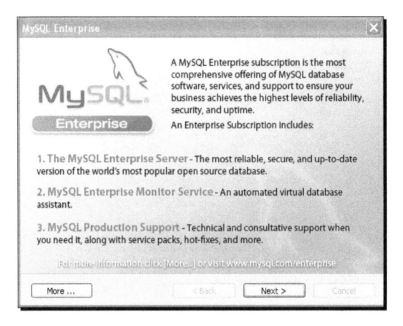

5. Once installed, it will bring up the following screen, which will ask for configuring MySQL server:

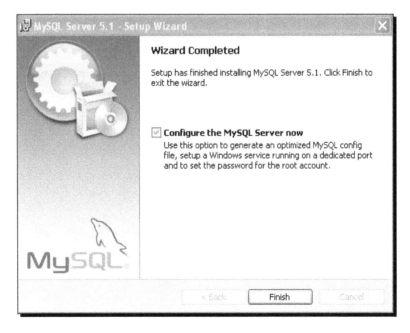

6. Make sure you have ticked the checkbox against **Configure the MySQL Server Now** and then click on **Finish**, which will show up the starting screen. Click on the **Next** button to reach the following screen:

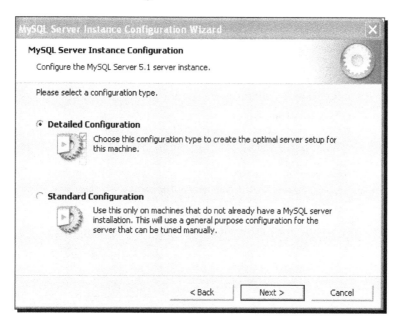

7. Select **Detailed Configuration** as shown in the preceding screenshot and click on **Next**, which would show you a screen to select a server type as shown in the following screenshot:

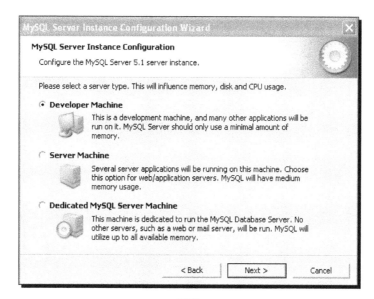

8. The memory, CPU usage, and disk usage would be decided based on the server type. For the moment, select **Developer Machine** and click on the **Next** option, which will show you the following screen:

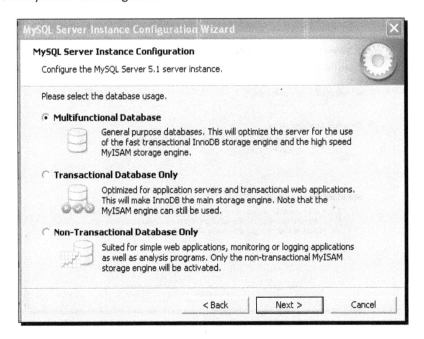

9. Keep the default selection, **Multifunctional Database**, and click on the **Next** button, which will ask you to select path for the data file. Keep the default settings and click on **Next**, which will bring up the following screen:

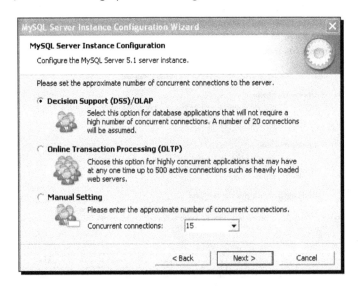

10. Select the default option, which is for **DSS/OLAP** to have 20 concurrent connections to the server, and click on **Next**. This will open up a screen showing the default port on which MySQL server will be running. Leave the default and click on **Next**, which will show the following screen:

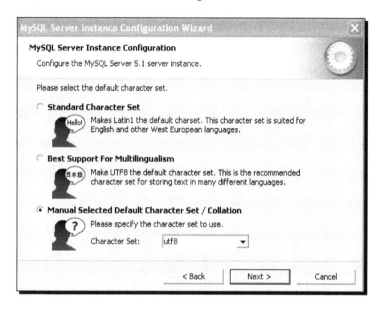

11. Select the option **Manual Selected Default Character Set/Collation** and from the **Character Set** drop-down select **utf8** and then click **Next** to show up the following screen:

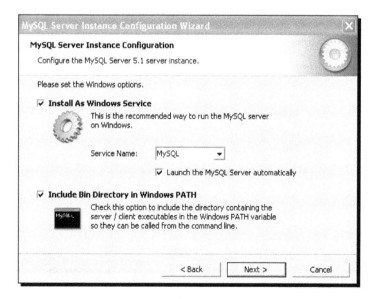

12. Leave the option to install MySQL as window service and enable the checkbox to include bin directory of MySQL to Windows PATH variable so that we can run MySQL from command prompt. Click on **Next** to show the following screen:

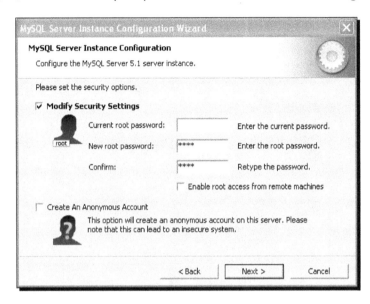

13. Give the root password to root as of now and then click on **Next** which will bring up the final screen as shown in the following screenshot and click on **Next**, which will show the following screen:

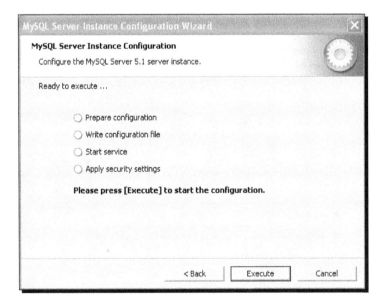

14. Click on the **Execute** button to configure the server. To make sure MySQL has been properly installed open up your command prompt and type `mysql -u root - p` and press *Enter*. This will ask for a password. Give the password as `root` and press *Enter* again and it should show the following screen:

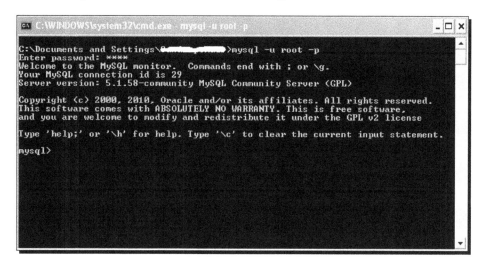

15. Now, to create the database issue the following command:

`CREATE DATABASE neighbourhood_portal CHARACTER SET utf8;`

16. This will create a database as shown in the following screen:

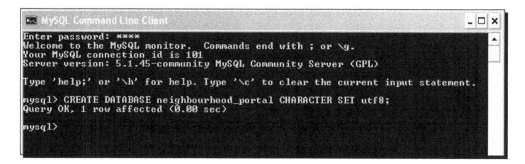

17. Next, we will create a user and grant him admin rights on our table so that he is just able to work with our database. Type the following in the command prompt and press *Enter*:

`GRANT ALL PRIVILEGES ON neighbourhood_portal.* to admin@localhost IDENTIFIED AS 'root';`

What just happened?

Your database has just been created and you have created a user called admin whose password would be root and he has been given all the privileges on our `neighbourhood_portal` database.

Configuring Liferay to use MySQL

In Liferay, most of the configuration-related settings are done in a property file called `portal.properties`. Our database-related property is specified in this file too. This property is packaged in a jar called `portal-impl.jar`, which can be found in `WEB-INF/lib` of the Liferay web application. More on this property file will be discussed in later chapters. But for now, just assume that any modifications required for changing the settings of Liferay should not be made by directly editing this. Then how do we go about doing this?

The answer is that `portal-ext.properties`. `portal-ext.properties` can be saved at two places. The first is inside `WEB-INF/classes` of your Liferay Portal web application. This can usually be used for any property addition that developers want to control and add. The second place is in `LIFERAY_HOME` for more accessible changes by system admins, so that they can add database or mail server-related settings or any system-related properties.

Time for action – changing the file

So first create a property file called `portal-ext.properties`, within the `LIFERAY_HOME` directory and add the following properties into it:

```
jdbc.default.driverClassName=com.mysql.jdbc.Driver

jdbc.default.url=jdbc:mysql://localhost/neighbourhood_portal?useUnicod
e=true&characterEncoding=UTF8&useFastDateParsing=false

jdbc.default.username={your_username}

jdbc.default.password={your_password}
```

Replace `{your_username}` and `{your_password}` with your actual credentials for MySQL.

Downloading the example code for this book

You can download the example code files for all Packt books you have purchased from your account at http://www.PacktPub.com. If you purchased this book elsewhere, you can visit http://www.PacktPub.com/support and register to have the files e-mailed directly to you.

What just happened?

Restart your server and Liferay will now be using MySQL instead of Hypersonic database.

```
m [file:/D:/Liferay/portal-ext.properties, jar:file:/D:/Liferay/apache-tomcat-6.
0.33/webapps/ROOT/WEB-INF/lib/portal-impl.jar!/portal.properties]
Loading jar:file:/D:/Liferay/apache-tomcat-6.0.33/webapps/ROOT/WEB-INF/lib/porta
l-impl.jar!/portal.properties
Loading file:/D:/Liferay/portal-ext.properties
19:06:25,421 INFO  [DialectDetector:69] Determining dialect for MySQL 5
19:06:25,531 INFO  [DialectDetector:49] Using dialect org.hibernate.dialect.MySQ
LDialect
19:06:31,171 INFO  [PortalImpl:278] Global lib directory /D:/Liferay/apache-tomc
at-6.0.33/lib/ext/
19:06:31,171 INFO  [PortalImpl:298] Portal lib directory /D:/Liferay/apache-tomc
at-6.0.33/webapps/ROOT/WEB-INF/lib/
```

For Oracle WebLogic, place the `portal-ext.properties` in `WEBLOGIC_HOME\user_ projects\domains`. Besides that you also need to copy `mysql.jar` in the `DOMAINS_ HOME\Liferay\lib` along with the other dependencies. Restart the server and you should be able to see that now Liferay is using MySQL.

Summary

In this chapter, we have seen how Liferay Portal can be installed on various servers:

◆ Liferay comes pre-bundled with many open source application servers and servlet containers such as Tomcat, JBoss, and GlassFish

◆ Liferay can also be installed on a proprietary server like Oracle Weblogic

◆ We also saw how to deploy Liferay on an existing Tomcat server

◆ The default Liferay bundle ships with a Hypersonic database, which is not recommended for production use

◆ Liferay is database agnostic and can support many databases such as Oracle, SQL Server, MySQL, and so on

Though we have seen how to install Liferay in most of the application servers and servlet containers, we will be using Tomcat as our web server for the rest of the exercise.

So you're all set with Liferay up and running on your Tomcat, and it's time to get started with some Portal Basics and changing the whole look and feel of your portal with themes in Liferay.

3
Understanding Portal Basics and Theming

In the previous chapter, you saw how to install Liferay Portal on various application servers including the default bundle with Tomcat, Glassfish, JBoss, WebSphere, and so on. If you have followed the instructions mentioned in the previous chapter, you should have the Liferay instance ready by now.

In this chapter, you will understand the basic concepts of the portal. Once the portal is installed, you may want to configure the portal to fit in your environment and satisfy your requirements. This can be performed using Liferay's UI, which may include page-level settings or admin panel settings.

You will learn the following aspects in this chapter:

- Liferay user interface—Using the dock bar to navigate around Liferay.
- Liferay basic administration—How to do basic admin using the Control Panel, which serves as an admin dashboard.
- Theme basics—Get an overview of a theme and understanding the importance of themes in a portal. You will also install a new theme to the portal.

At the end of this chapter, you should be able to understand Liferay core concepts, Liferay navigation, and basic settings using the Control Panel.

Now, it is time to get familiar with Liferay Portal first and then visit all the components we have mentioned above. So fasten your seat belts and get ready for the Liferay drive!!!!

Understanding a portal

By now, you have probably heard that "Liferay is a Portal Server"! Now the question is, "What do we really mean when we use the term Portal Server?"

Well, to get the answer we should first understand what a portal is. A portal is a web-based application or gateway which hosts and runs different applications required by the user. All these applications are integrated to achieve different benefits, such as availability of information at a central location, collaboration, reducing costs, and streamlining your business processes.

To make sure all of the above-mentioned benefits are achieved, Liferay Portal adds one or more applications on a portal page. This application is known as a **portlet**.

A portlet is a web application which runs in a fragment of a page. These portlets are used by portals as pluggable user-interface components which provide a presentation layer to the Information System. One or more portlets get combined and generate a complete web page or document, which is displayed to a user. This is known as **aggregation**. Liferay *Portlet Container* plays a vital role in achieving this. In the following screenshot, three portlets have been aggregated by the Portlet Container to form the welcome page:

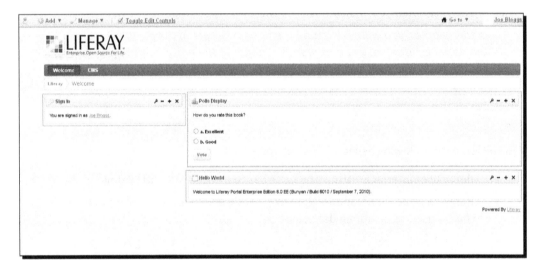

The Portlet Container is a logical component in Liferay (and in any standard Portal Server) which runs the portlets and provides them with the required runtime environment. It is also responsible for managing the lifecycle of a portlet. To understand the role of the portlet container, let's look at what happens when you request to access a page in a portal:

1. You send an HTTP request via a web browser to the portal.
2. The portal receives the request.

3. The portal determines if your request contains any action targeted to any of the portlets which are associated with the page.

4. If there is any action involved, the portal requests Portlet Container to invoke that particular portlet to process the action. Rest of the portlet will only get re-rendered once the action phase of the portlet is completed.

5. The Portlet Container provides the fragment of the individual portlet back to the portal. The fragment can be any markup (HTML/XHTML/WML).

6. The portal aggregates the output of the portlets on the portal page and sends it back to the browser for you to access.

The lifecycle is explained in the following diagram:

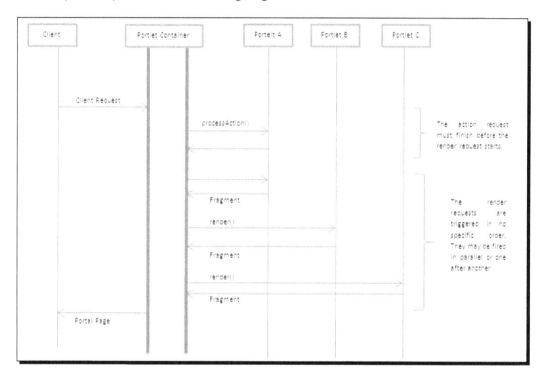

Liferay Portal supports portlet standards JSR-168 and JSR-286, which are also known as Portlet 1.0 and Portlet 2.0 specifications, respectively.

Navigating Liferay

As we now have some basic information about a portal, let's learn how to navigate Liferay Portal. Start your server, if it is not started already.

You will see the Tomcat console and different processes running on the console when starting the server. Notice the messages on the console and try to find out the database used by the Liferay default bundle. When the server is started, you will get a message on your console that **Server has started in XXXX ms**. Open a browser and type in `http://localhost:8080/web/guest/home`.

As you will notice, you can still access the page with a very simple interface even though you are not logged in. This is because you are accessing a public page of Liferay. A public page can be accessed by anyone, including non-logged in (guest) users.

You will see a link—**Sign In**—on the top-right corner of the page. Click on this link to log in to Liferay. When you click on the link it will display a **Sign In** portlet as displayed in the following screenshot. You can use this portlet to provide you with the credentials to log in to Liferay Portal. You can also create a new user account or request a new password, if you have forgotten your password. Liferay also supports logging in using an OpenID account, if you already have one. The next chapter explains how to configure the OpenID.

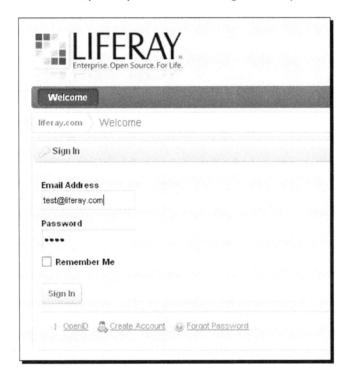

If you create a new account using this portlet, that account will have very limited access to the portal. This means you cannot access Liferay admin functions using this account. We will not create a new account at this moment. We will use Liferay's default admin credentials.

Time for action – signing in to Liferay Portal

So far, you have started the server and understood the Liferay **Sign In** portlet. Now, let's log in to Liferay Portal for the first time. Follow these steps to sign in to Liferay with default admin credentials:

1. Use the following credentials to log in to Liferay and then click on the **Sign In** button:
   - ❑ **User Name**: test@liferay.com
   - ❑ **Password**: test

2. The first page you will see is the **Terms of Use** page. This is a page which mentions all the terms and conditions of your portal. A user has to agree to these terms before accessing the portal. Go ahead and agree to the terms of use by clicking **I Agree**.

3. The next page that you will see is the **Password Reminder Query** page. You can set the password reminder query and the answer to recover the password, in case you forget it. Choose your question and provide an answer; click on **Save** to set your reply.

4. You will now be able to see the home page of Liferay.

What just happened?

You have started Liferay Portal and logged in with default user credentials—**User Name**: **test@liferay.com** and **Password**: **test**.

Before accessing the home page, you agreed to the **Terms of Use** of the portal. This page will be displayed to the user when he or she logs in for the first time. This page can be modified to display organization-specific terms of use. A portal admin can turn this feature off, if it is not required by the portal.

You also agreed to the password reminder query, which is used to recover your password if you forget it. This feature can also be turned off by the portal administrator.

Getting familiar with the Dockbar

Once you agree to the **Terms of Use** and provide the password reminder query, you will see the home page. This page is also called the default landing page. The default landing page is the page that is displayed first after logging in. This can be configured through the portal configuration. We will discuss this in a later chapter. You will also notice that now you can see the horizontal Dockbar, which appears across the top of the page as displayed in the following screenshot:

The Dockbar is key to navigating in Liferay. A user can use this Dockbar to navigate and access the admin functions. The Dockbar is available on all the pages, so a user can navigate from anywhere in the site. The access to Dockbar is modular, which means that, based on the role that a user has, one can access all of its options or just a few. Currently, you have logged in as an admin user, so you will be able to access all the options of the Dockbar.

We will now discuss all the options of the Dockbar in detail.

The Add option

The first icon that you will see in the Dockbar is a pin-like icon which is displayed in the previous screenshot, first from the left before the **Add** option. This pin is used to decide if you want to see the Dockbar when you scroll down your page. If you click on this pin, it will always display the Dockbar on the top of the page even if you scroll down. If the pin is not pressed, the Dockbar will not appear if you scroll down your page.

The second option you will see in the Dockbar is **Add**. Just scroll your mouse over the **Add** button. On doing so, you will find a list of items which you can add as displayed in the next screenshot. The options are divided into two broad areas—**Page** and **Applications**. When you click on **Page**, it will add a new page to the same level as you are. You can also see the newly added page in the page navigation.

The second area is **Applications**, which is a portlet in the portal world. By default, it displays four commonly-used portlets—Web Content Display, Asset Publisher, Document Library Display, and Navigation portlets. You can directly click on the portlet to add it to the page. Alternatively, you can drag the portlet and drop it to the page. You can also change the list of the default portlets by modifying the `dockbar.add.portlets` property in the `portal-ext.properties` file. You need to specify the portlet ID in a comma-separated list.

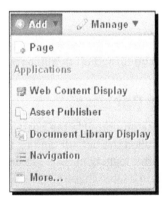

We have discussed how to add the most common portlets to the page. There will never be a case when you will only need these four portlets in your portal. You normally need a lot more portlets to be added to the page to achieve your required functionalities. If you want to add any other portlet apart from the four common portlets, you can click on the **More** option. When you click on it, a pop-up will be opened with the list of all the portlets available in Liferay. It is displayed in the next screenshot:

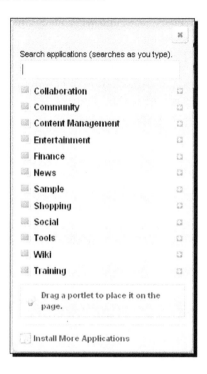

You will see a list of categories in the pop-up. Liferay comes with more than 60 portlets pre-bundled. All the portlets are divided into different categories, for example, Web Content. The Display portlet is part of the **Content Management** category and the Blogs portlet is a part of the **Collaboration** category. You can see a list of portlets by clicking on the plus sign next to each category. As mentioned earlier, you can directly click on the **Add** button next to the portlet to add the portlet to the page or drag it and drop it to the page.

This pop-up also provides the functionality to search for portlets. If you know the name of the portlet which you want to add to the page but are not sure about the category it falls in, then you can simply write the name of the portlet in the search box which appears below the text **Search applications (Searches as you type)** in the pop-up, and it will display the category and the portlet as a result as you type in.

Have you noticed any difference between the portlet icons when you click on different categories? Not yet! Try clicking on the **Content Management** category. You will notice that there are some portlets such as **Asset Publisher** and **Breadcrumb** which have green icons; while other portlets such as **Document Library** and **Image Gallery** have purple icons. What is the significance of these colors?

Well, all the portlets with a green icon are instanceable portlets. This means you can have multiple instances of this portlet on a page and within a community or organization and each of the instances can hold different data.

Portlets with a purple icon are non-instanceable portlets, meaning you can only have one instance of this portlet across an organization or community. You cannot add this portlet more than once to the page. Also, they share the same or common data within the organization or community that they are in.

We will discuss organization and community later in this chapter.

As discussed, Liferay comes with more than 60 portlets pre-bundles. If you want to install more portlets/applications, it can also be done from the **Install More Applications** link provided on the **Add Application** pop-up. When you click on this link, it will take you to the **Control Panel | Plugin Installation** interface. You can add new applications (portlet, theme, layout, hooks, and so on) from this screen. It is displayed in the following screenshot:

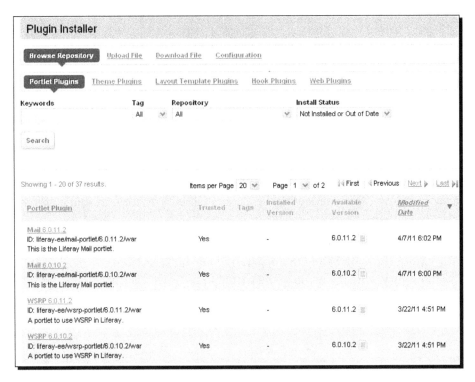

This interface is divided into different tabs as follows:

Tabs displayed in the top:

- **Browse Repository**—This will browse through all the different types of plugins from the repository configured under the **Configuration** tab. This tab has the following options:
    - **Portlet Plugins**—Displays a list of the portlets available in the repository
    - **Theme Plugins**—Displays a list of the theme plugins available in the repository
    - **Layout Template Plugins**—Displays a list of the different layouts available in the repository
    - **Hook Plugins**—Displays a list of the different hook plugins available in the repository
    - **Web Plugins**—Displays a list of web modules available in the repository
- **Upload File**—Allows you to upload a WAR file for a new theme, layout, or portlet.
- **Download File**—Allows you to specify the URL from which a new portlet, theme, or layout can be downloaded.
- **Configuration**—This has a different configuration option for the Liferay Portal Server.

Time for action – creating a new page and adding a portlet

You have gone through the **Add** option of the Dockbar. Let's now use this knowledge to create a new page and load the page with a couple of portlets:

1. Click on the **Add** option in the Dockbar. Select the **Page** option from the drop-down.

2. It will display a textbox with the yellow background in the page navigation.

3. Add the name of the page here, **Collaboration**, and click on the tick mark next to the textbox. You should now see the page added to the page navigation.

4. Click on the **Add** option from the Dockbar and select **More** from the drop-down.

5. Search for the Blogs portlet and Polls Display portlet. Add these portlets to the page.

6. Try adding the same portlets a second time and see what happens.

You would be able to add another polls display portlet to the page but not another blogs portlet. Can you tell why this happened? If you cannot, revisit the last section. It is related to the portlet instance.

What just happened?

You got familiar with the **Add** option of the Dockbar.

You have created a new page and added one instanceable and one non-instanceable portlet to the page.

You are now familiar with the difference between an instanceable and a non-instanceable portlet.

You should now have a **Collaboration** page added to your portal. You should also have Blogs and Polls Display portlets added to the **Collaboration** page.

Have a go hero – installing a new portlet

We have seen how to add a new portlet to the page. Now, get ready to install a new portlet to your portal. We will use the **Install More Applications** link available in the **More** application's pop-up. You must be connected to the Internet to perform this exercise.

1. Click on the **More** option under **Add** in the Dockbar.
2. You will see a pop-up to add a new portlet on the page.
3. Now, click on the **Install More Applications** link.
4. You will see an interface displayed in the previous screenshot.
5. You can see the **Configuration** tab on the top. Click on this tab.
6. This tab contains different configurations, for the server including **Deploy Directory**, **Destination Directory**, **Interval**, **Blacklist Threshold**, and so on.

> **Blacklist threshold**: The Portal Server extracts the `.war` file of the plugins (portlet, theme, and so on) from the `deploy` directory and installs it on the portal. The blacklist threshold is the number of times the portal server tries to extract the `.war` file. If the `.war` file cannot be extracted by the number mentioned in the blacklist threshold, then the server will blacklist the `.war` file and will not try to extract it again. To remove the application from the blacklist, you need to remove the `.war` file and restart your application server.

7. You will find two textboxes, named **Trusted Plugin Repositories** and **Untrusted Plugin Repositories**.

8. **Trusted Plugin Repository** contains the URL of Liferay's official plugins repository. **Untrusted Plugin Repository** contains the URL of Liferay's community plugin repository. You can configure more than one repository here and your Liferay server will pull plugins from the repositories and display them to install on your local installation. To configure multiple repositories, you have to give each repository URL in new line.

9. You should see the **Untrusted Plugin Repository** box with the following URL. If it is not present, add the URL `http://plugins.liferay.com/community` and click on **Save**.

10. Once you have saved it, click on the **Browse Repository** link at the top. The **Portlet Plugins** tab will be selected by default and you will see a list of portlets under it. If the repository was not configured earlier, you will see more portlets in the list than earlier.

11. Click on any of the portlet names. This will take you to the interface to install the portlet. Click on **Install**.

12. The portlet will be installed to your local environment. You can watch the Tomcat console. Once you get a message **One Portlet for xxx-portlet is available for use**, the portlet is deployed on your application server and ready to be added to the page.

13. Go to your home page and add the newly added portlet to your page.

This way you can add more portlets, themes, hooks, or web modules using this feature. Hooks or web modules are again other types of plugins.

Pop quiz – true or false

Please state whether the following statements are true or false:

1. Every user will get the same view of the Dockbar.

2. It is possible to add the portlet more than once to the page if it is an instanceable portlet.

3. All the portals must have the **Terms of use** page.

4. Non-instanceable portlets can display different data if added on different pages of the same organization or community.

Using the Manage option

We have discussed how to add a new application to your portal in the previous section. Now, let's go back and discuss other options available in the Dockbar. Click on the **Back to Liferay** link from the **Control Panel** to go back to the page.

The third option you see in the Dockbar is **Manage**. This option is useful to manage the current page and various other settings. When you roll your mouse over the **Manage** option, you can see different options—**Page**, **Page Layout**, **Sitemap**, **Settings**, and **Control Panel**. This is displayed in the following screenshot:

When you click on the **Page** option, it will allow you to do various settings for the current page. You can change the name of the page, provide the HTML title of the page, change the friendly URL (partially), and also provide Meta tags to the page to make it SEO-friendly. If you want to add a sub-page or child page, you can click on **Children** and add a child page under the current page. You can also change the look and feel of the page by clicking the **look & feel** tab. We will discuss these options in detail later in this book.

The next option under **Manage** is **Page Layout**. Layout is a grid-like structure which works as a portlet place holder. It is used to arrange the portlets in a certain fashion on the page. The default layout is **2 columns** (30/70). When you click on the **Page Layout** option, it will open a pop-up with all the default layouts available as displayed in the following screenshot:

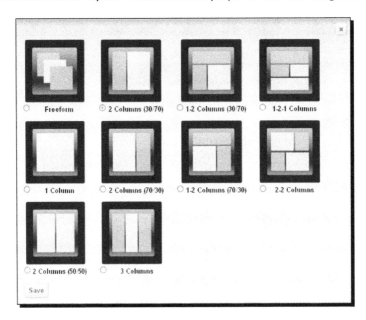

You can change the layout of the page by selecting the layout and clicking on the **Save** button.

Another option under **Manage** is **Sitemap**. This option will allow you to see the sitemap of the pages you are accessing. You can see the names of pages, add a new page under the same site, change the look and feel, and change the display order of the pages. We will discuss this option in detail, when we discuss **Manage Pages**.

You will also see an option called **Settings** under **Manage**. The **Settings** option will allow you to do different community or organization page-level settings. The options available are **Virtual Host**, **Logo**, **Sitemap**, **Robots**, **Monitoring**, and **Staging**. A brief introduction of each section is as follows:

- ◆ **Virtual Host**—This option will allow you to provide a domain name for your community or organization, for example, `www.mydomainname.com`. This feature is also helpful when you want to host multiple websites as separate communities in Liferay. You can provide a virtual host to each community and each of them will behave as a separate website.

- ◆ **Logo**—This option will be used to upload a logo for your organization or community pages. This logo will be displayed instead of the default Liferay logo. If you have more than one community hosted as a separate website and you want to have different logos for each website, you can use this feature.

- ◆ **Sitemap**—This option publishes your site to Google and Yahoo search engines using the sitemap protocol. Once it is published, the Google and Yahoo search indexes will use the site map to index your site. It also allows you to view your sitemap before publishing.

- ◆ **Robots**—This option will allow you to set the `robots.txt` file for your public and private pages of the portal. You have to set the virtual host for the public and private pages before setting the `robot.txt` file. This file will be used for SEO (Search Engine Optimization) purposes and notifies the indexes whether to index any page or follow the links on the page. This option will appear if you are using an enterprise edition of Liferay.

- ◆ **Monitoring**—This option will allow you to integrate your portal pages with Google Analytics to do the traffic analysis using the Google Analytics tool. You need to have a Google Analytics ID and provide it in the text field given on this option.

- ◆ **Staging**—This tab will allow you to set up staging for your site. This will be helpful to view/check your work before publishing to a live site. This will be explained in detail in *Chapter 10, Liferay Server Administration*.

The preceding options will be used in the next few chapters of this book.

When you click on the next option called **Control Panel** under **Manage**, it will take you to the Admin Interface of Liferay known as **Control Panel**. This is a centralized admin space. It consists of all the admin portlets which you can use to manage different aspects of your portal. We will discuss **Control Panel** in detail in another section of this chapter.

The next thing you will see in the Dockbar is an option called **Toggle Edit Control**. This option will allow you to turn on or off the edit controls that you can see on top of every portlet window. The portlet window has **Configuration**, **Minimize**, **Maximize**, and **Remove** options. If you turn off the control by disabling the **Toggle Edit Control** option, those options will disappear. This feature will be helpful to the admin to see how the page will be displayed to a normal user who does not have all these edit permissions.

Now, the next option you can see in the Dockbar is **Go To**. If you bring your mouse pointer to this option, it will expand. This section will display all the places of the portal which you have access to. The place which you are currently on will be highlighted. As you can see, currently you are in **liferay.com** community. This is a default community of Liferay which has a public page. Everyone is able to access the public page of the guest community. It is displayed in the following screenshot:

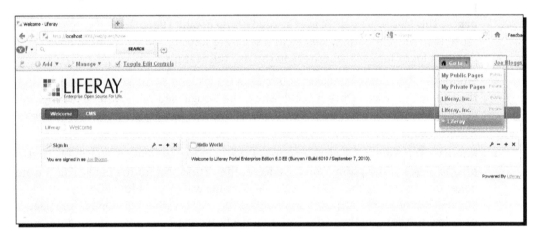

Another thing you will notice in the same drop-down is **My Public Pages** and **My Private Pages**. By default in Liferay, each user has his/her set of private and public pages. A user can manage the public and private pages and will behave as an admin of these pages even if the user does not have an Admin role at portal level. Anyone can access a user's public pages by the URL, whereas private pages can be accessible to the user only. This feature is very helpful in an intranet-fashioned portal where users need their own space to play on the portal. For the internet fashioned portals, this feature can be turned off by an admin.

You can also see the user's first name and the last name in the Dockbar and a sign out link. On clicking the username, it will take you to the user's profile. A user can edit his/her profile by clicking this option.

The **Sign out** link will log you off from the portal.

Time for action – accessing a portal with a normal user account

Now you are familiar with the Dockbar. We have also discussed how a Dockbar would be displayed to the admin user. However, what if you are accessing the portal as a normal user? What happens in this case? Would you be able to see all the options as an admin user can? Let's check it out:

1. Sign out from the portal by clicking on the **Sign Out** link in the Dockbar.

2. You will see a **Sign In** link on the top-right corner of the page. When you click on the link, it will display the **Sign In** portlet. Click on the **Create Account** link in this portlet. You will see the form displayed to create your account, as shown in the following screenshot:

3. Fill the form to create your account and click on the **Save** button. When you click on the button, it will submit the form and display a message with the temporary password. It will also directly display the **Sign In** portlet for you to log in. Use the password to log in to the portal.

4. Observe the Tomcat console at this moment. You should see a message **Failed to connect to a valid mail server. Please make sure one is configured**. This is because Liferay will send the temporary password to the e-mail address you provide during account creation. Since we have not configured the mail server, it will fail to connect to the server and will not send the password.

5. Accept the terms of use and provide a password reminder query. Observe the Dockbar. Can you see all the options that were displayed when you logged in as an admin user? Also, try accessing the control panel. You will not be able to see most of the options that were appearing to the admin user—**test@liferay.com**.

6. This happened because you have logged in as a normal user. Liferay has a very fine-grained permission system and access can be provided or restricted based on the role a user has. When you logged in with the default admin account, you had a Portal Admin role which enabled all the access in Liferay Portal. We will discuss about the roles in another section of this chapter.

7. Take your mouse over to the **Go To** section. You will see **My Public Pages** and **My Private Pages** options but cannot see the **liferay.com** community. This happens because you are not yet a member of the **liferay.com** community.

8. Click on the private or public pages link under the **Go To** section and observe the Dockbar. Can you see any difference from the previous view of the Dockbar? Also, try accessing the control panel from this page and you should see all the options. Sit back, relax, and think why this has happened!

> Your private and public pages belong only to you. You are the owner of those pages, so you have all the options available on those pages as an owner. Also, when you go to the control panel from your public or private pages, you can add or modify content of your community. So it displays all the links under **My Community** section.

Now, once you understand why this happened, click on your name, which appears in the top-right corner. It will take you to your profile page as displayed in the following screenshot:

Go through the different links in your profile. At this moment, you may not be able to get much out of these links, but don't worry. We will cover these links in detail in the following chapters.

Click on the link **Password**. It will allow you to change your password. Change your password and click on **Save**.

What just happened?

You have created a new user account. This is a normal user and not an admin. Liferay provided you a temporary password for this user account. When you logged in as the user, you had very limited access to the Dockbar because you do not have permissions to access all the options. When you went into **My Public Pages** and **My Private Pages**, you had full access to the Dockbar, because every user will behave as an admin of his/her public and private pages.

You have also modified your account by changing the password. As a normal user, you would be able to edit your account only. If you are a Portal Admin, you can edit any user's account.

You are now aware of the following concepts:

- Portal basics
- Different options available under Dockbar
- Difference between accessing the portal as an admin and as a normal user
- User's private and public pages

Pop quiz – select the correct answer

1. Which of the following is true?
    a. Every user must have public and private pages in a portal
    b. Every user must have public pages in a portal
    c. Every user must have private pages in a portal
    d. A user can have public and private pages by default

2. When would you prefer to provide public and private pages to the user?
    a. A public facing website where a user can open his/her account freely
    b. An intranet-fashioned website where you have a limited set of users
    c. In all of the website

3. Toggle Edit Control Functionality is used to:
    a. Keep the Dockbar always on the top
    b. Disable edit control options on the top of the portlets
    c. Add new controls for editing a portlet

4. A user's private pages are visible:
    a. To the user only
    b. To the members of the same organization or community only
    c. To the user's friends only
    d. Everyone
    e. To user and portal admin only.

5. Sitemap option under the **Manage** section of the Dockbar is used to:
    a. Display the sitemap of the portal
    b. Publish your site indexes to Google and Yahoo search engines for indexing

Getting an overview of Liferay Portal Architecture

You are now aware of the Portal basics and Liferay Portal's Dockbar. Before we go ahead with the rest of the chapters of this book, it is important to understand the Portal Architecture of Liferay. When we use the term *Portal Architecture*, it includes the basic building blocks of the Liferay Portal and relationship between each block.

In this section, we will get an overview of the Liferay Portal Architecture. We will get familiar with different components and understand their role in Liferay. We will, however, discuss these components in detail in *Chapter 5, Building Your First Liferay Site*.

Understanding the Liferay building blocks

Let's start discussing this topic with a question! We have been talking about Portal since the beginning of this chapter. Whom do we build/develop a portal for? The answer can be content creators, bloggers, content approvers, certain type of admins, visitors, and so on. If we want to use only one word, collectively for all these people, then the word would be users. This means we develop the portal for the user. The user can be anyone from just a visitor to portal admin.

Now, when we say all of the above mentioned people are just the users of the portal, there is a significant difference between each of the users in terms of what they can do in the portal. For example, a visitor would not be able to add any content, content creator would not be able to approve the content, and content approver may not be able to create/edit any users. So each of the users is distinguished by the function he/she can do in the portal. These functions in the portal are associated with the user's role in the portal. There is a certain set of permissions associated with each role. When you assign a user to the role, the user will get all the permissions/privileges associated to the role.

Now, think of a site such as http://www.cnn.com, where you have to deal with a huge amount of content. What happens if you have only one person who creates the content called content creator and only one person who approves the content called content approver for this site? There would be a bottleneck. Also, one user may not be able to create all the content which is required for your site. In that case, you would need more than one person who can perform a similar function, for example creating content or approving content. Yes, you guessed it! Here, we are talking about the User Groups. Users who do the same function or have something in common, can be collected into user groups. To make user management easier, an entire user group can be assigned to a role as well, so all the users who are part of the user group will get the privileges or permission associated with that role.

By keeping the preceding discussion in mind, we can make the following statements:

- Portals are developed for the users and accessed by the users.
- Users having common characteristics can be collected into a user group, for example content creator.
- Users can be assigned to a role, which will give them all the permissions/privileges associated with the role.
- User group can also be assigned to a Role. This will give all the users, members of the user group, all the permissions/privileges associated with the role.

In addition to the preceding components—User, User Group, and Role—Liferay consists of a few more building blocks—Organization, Community, Page, and Team.

The community is a group of people who have common interest. It is very similar to the concept of the community in the social networking world, where people with common interests get connected. In Liferay, you can create different communities and assign users to the communities.

Users can be collected into an Organization, which is a hierarchical collection of users. Organization in Liferay can represent an Organization in real life.

You can create multiple Organizations and Communities in Liferay Portal.

User, User group, and Organization can be members of a community who have common interests.

To understand these concepts, let's have a look at the following diagram. This diagram shows all the components of Liferay Portal and their relationships with one another. The arrows in the diagram mean "can be assigned to" or "can be a member of".

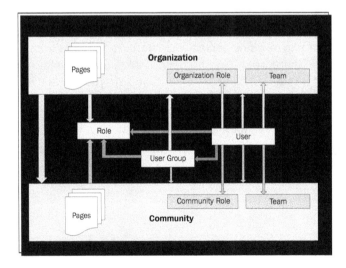

This diagram is a pictorial representation of the Liferay Portal Architecture. The outer square box represents a portal which is a physical Portal Instance. We can extract the following facts from the diagram:

- ◆ User is in the heart of the portal, which means all the activities are performed by keeping user in the centre.

- ◆ An Organization, a Community, a User, User Group, and Roles are created at a portal level.

- ◆ You can create multiple Organizations, Community, Users, User Groups, and Roles within a Portal.

- ◆ A user can be assigned to more than one Role, User Group, Organization or a Community.

- ◆ A User Group can be assigned to a Role.

- ◆ An Organization or a Community can also be assigned to a Role. On doing so, all the members of the Organization or Community will get permissions associated with that role.

- ◆ Organization and Community have their own resources—Organization/Community Roles, Pages, and Teams.

- ◆ When a User is assigned to an Organization or a Community, the user becomes a member of the Organization or Community. A member can access resources of an Organization or Community.

- ◆ A User has to be a member of an Organization or a Community before assigning to an Organization or Community-level role or team created within an Organization or a Community.

- ◆ A page in Liferay Portal, is not a separate entity and cannot be created at a Portal level. A page has to be created within an Organization or a Community.

- ◆ We can also create a role at an Organization or Community level.

- ◆ A team can be created within an Organization or a Community.

Now, as we have taken an overview of the Liferay Portal Architecture, let's talk about each component.

User

User is a physical entity in Liferay Portal. It represents a real-world user in the portal. Each user except the Guest user has his/her account in Liferay and uses the account to access the portal. A user is always created at a portal level can then can be assigned to an Organization or a Community. Remember, a user is never created within an Organization or a Community.

As displayed in the pictorial representation of the Liferay Portal Architecture, a user can be collected in the following ways:

- User can be assigned to a Role which has specific permissions associated with
- A user can be assigned to a specific user group like content creators
- A user can be a member of one or more Organization which represents an organization in real life
- A user can be a member of one or more Community which is created for the users having some common interest like stamp-collector's community

User group

A user group is a simple, arbitrary collection of users. A user group is created at a portal level and can be created by a Portal Admin only. Users can be assigned to the user group and then the user group can be assigned to a role. On doing so, all the users who are a part of the user group will get the permissions defined for that role. It is not possible to directly assign any permission to the user group. You can also assign the user group to a Community or an Organization. When we do that, all the users in the User Group will become members of the Community or Organization respectively.

User groups make user management simpler and easier.

Role

Role is used to define a permission to do a certain task in the portal. As we have seen earlier, permissions cannot be given to an individual user or a user group. In order to give some permissions to the user, we have to follow a three-step process as follows:

1. Create a Role.
2. Define permissions for the Role.
3. Assign the Role to a User or User Group.

Liferay has a very fine-grained permission system and a Role plays an important part in the permission system. We can create three types of Roles in Liferay:

- Portal Role
- Community Role
- Organization Role

These types are based on the scope of the role. When we create a role at a portal scope with some pre-defined permissions to perform certain actions, a user having this role can perform those actions in the entire portal—including all the organizations or communities of the portal. If the same role has been created with a community scope, then a user having this role in a community can perform those actions within that community only. Same thing applies to the organization scope as well.

Let's understand this with an example. Let's consider that we have a portal instance and we have created two Communities—C1 and C2—and two Organizations—O1 and O2—in the portal. As mentioned earlier, it is possible to create multiple organizations and communities in one portal instance. We will do this in *Chapter 5, Building Your First Liferay Site*. We have created a user, John, in the portal.

Now, if the user John has an Admin role at a portal level, then he can perform admin activities in all the communities and organizations across the portal, which includes C1, C2, O1, and O2.

If John has an Admin role in C1 (Community Admin), then he can perform all the admin activities in C1 only and not in C2, O1, and O2.

Similarly, if the user John has Admin role in O2 (Organization Admin), then he can perform all the admin activities only in O2 and not in C1, C2, and O1.

We can assign an individual user, user group, organization or community to the role.

We will do all these activities practically in *Chapter 4, Knowing Tips and Tricks—Advanced Configuration*, and *Chapter 6, Managing Pages, Users, and Permissions*.

Community

Community in Liferay is created to group the users having a common interest. These communities are very similar to the communities we are familiar with in the social networking world, where users having a common interest can join or leave at their will. The connection between the user and the community is ad-hoc.

You can create three types of communities in Liferay:

- Open
- Restricted
- Private

A user can join or leave an open community by will. This can be done using the Liferay control panel or the My Communities portlet of Liferay.

A user needs an approval of the community administrator to join a restricted community. A user has to request for membership of the Restricted community.

A private community is very similar to a restricted community but a user cannot see the private community under the list of communities in the My Communities portlet. The community admin has to add users to the private community. The private community is also sometimes called the hidden community.

In Liferay, a community can behave as a separate site. You can create pages, roles, and teams within a community.

It is also possible to create more than one community in the portal. Each of the community can be assigned a virtual host to behave as a separate site.

Organization

An Organization in Liferay can represent an organization in real life. Organizations are hierarchical collections of users. You can create an entire real-world organization structure using Liferay's organization feature. An Organization can have sub-organizations and each sub-organization can have numerous sub-organizations. This can go up to *n* level.

A user can be a member of more than one organization.

You can create pages, organization roles, or teams within an organization.

Organizations are of two types:

- Regular organization—You can create a sub-organization under a regular organization by default.
- Location—This is a special type of organization. It behaves as a leaf node. It is not possible to create a sub-organization (sub-location) under a location, by default.

It is also possible to define custom-type organizations. This has to be done by extending the `portal.properties` file, which is a default configuration file for the portal. You can find it in the `portal-impl.jar` file under the `WEB-INF/lib` folder of your Tomcat server.

The sub-organization is the same as a normal organization but it has some other organization as a parent organization.

When a user becomes a member of a child organization, he/she automatically becomes the member of the parent organization by default. This can be turned-off if required.

An individual user or a user group can be a member of the organization.

An entire organization can be assigned to a role or a community.

Similar to community, an organization can also behave as a separate site in the portal. It is also possible to create multiple organizations within a portal. We can provide a virtual URL to an Organization to make it behave like a website. We will add multiple organizations in *Chapter 5, Building Your First Liferay Site*.

The `Portal.properties` file contains all the properties related to Liferay Portal. The properties are set in Key-Value pair. We can add or modify the properties by creating a `portal-ext.properties` file in the portal.

To add new Organization types in the portal you need to copy the following property in the `portal-ext.properties` file and add new types to the property.

```
organizations.children.types[regular-
organization]=regular-organization,location
```

To restrict a user from becoming a member of the parent organization by default, set the following property to `true`. The default value of the property is `false`.

```
organizations.membership.strict=false
```

Teams

Team is a new concept added in Liferay 6. A team belongs to the organization or community which it was created in. A team can be created by an Organization or Community admin and is a collection of organization or community members. A team is created to assign special tasks to certain members of the organization or community only. For example, we can have a stamp-collector's community which requires a blogger team to update other members by writing new blogs about this hobby.

You may think that the preceding requirement can also be fulfilled by a community role. You're absolutely right! But, when you create a community-scoped role for stamp-collector's community, it also appears in other communities even though it is not required. However, when you create a team, it is visible only within the organization or community it has been created in.

Teams are very useful because they can be created by a community admin or an organization admin. Admins can delegate their work to certain team by creating team and assigning certain permissions to the team.

To become the member of a team, a user first has to be the member of an organization or community. It's pretty obvious! You cannot be a manager of any company without being an employee of the company!

We are yet to discuss when to create an organization versus when to create a community. We also need to discuss when to create user groups in real projects. Well, don't worry about all these questions for the moment. We will discuss them in detail in *Chapter 5, Building Your First Liferay Site*.

Pop quiz

1. Which of the following are true?

    a. A user can be created within an Organization or Community

    b. A user can be created at Portal level only

    c. A Page can be created at a Portal level

    d. A page can be created within Organization or Community only

2. Which of the following can be a member/part of the Organization?

    a. User

    b. User Group

    c. Role

    d. Community

3. If a team is created in one organization, it also appears in other organizations created in the same Portal.

    a. True

    b. False

4. Which of the following are types of community?

    a. Open

    b. General

    c. Restricted

    d. Private

5. Which of the following are types of Organization?

    a. Location

    b. Special Organization

    c. Regular Organization

    d. Static Organization

6. If a user has a community admin role of one community, he/she will become admin of all the communities in the portal.

    a. True

    b. False

7. If a community-scope role is created for one community, the same role will also appear in other communities in the same portal.

    a. True

    b. False

Before going to the next topic, Control Panel, let's summarize what we have done so far.

In the last topic, we have discussed Liferay Portal Architecture and the basic components of the architecture. You know that a Portal consists of different building blocks like User, Role, User Group, Organization, Community, Page, and Team. We are also aware of what can be created at a Portal level and what can be created at Organization or Community level. We have gone through the portlet concept in Liferay and added a few portlets to the page as well.

We have also discussed different scopes of role, different types of communities, and different types of organizations. You should now be aware of the difference between an organization or community scope role and a team.

Before going through the next topic, go back to the Portal Architecture diagram and look at all the relations between each of the components. The diagram should now make more sense than when you looked at the same for the first time.

Basics of the Control Panel

In the previous section of the book, we have seen that the Control Panel is the admin interface of Liferay. You can create different components and manage several aspects of Liferay using it. In this section, you will get familiar with the Control Panel interface and know that all the components can be created or managed using the Control Panel.

We will also discuss basic configuration, which can be done through the Control Panel. You will learn about detailed configuration in the next chapter, *Chapter 4, Knowing Tips and Tricks—Advanced Configuration*.

Visiting the Control Panel

Access to the Control Panel is modular. Let's visit the Control Panel and look at its different.

Log in with default admin credentials—**test@liferay.com** and password: **test**.

Move the mouse over to the **Manage** option in the Dockbar and click on **Control Panel**. This will take you to the Control Panel. You will see the interface displayed as shown in the following screenshot:

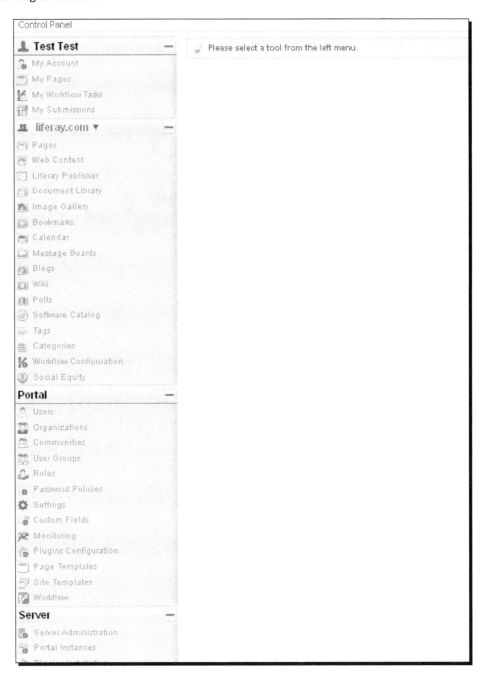

It is very easy to navigate through the **Control Panel**. It is divided into four main sections—
Personal, **Content**, **Portal**, and **Server**. Each of the sections contains different links to the
portlets. Let's get to know more about each section:

♦ **Personal**: The **Personal** section displays personal information of the logged in
user. This is the place where you can view your profile and change your profile
information. You can click on different links in this section to get information about
your profile.

Every user, whether or not an admin user, will have access to this section.

♦ **Content**: The **Content** section contains links related to Liferay's content
management portlets or functions. You will see name of the organization or category
in this section with an arrow. When you click on the arrow it will display all the
Organizations or Communities created in your portal instance. The content in Liferay
has a scope of Organization or Community. It means, if you create content in one
community, it will not be visible or accessible in another community or organization.

You can create or manage page, web content, document, image, bookmark,
message board, poll, wiki, and so on using this section. Normal user does not have
access to this section. A user will need special roles or permission to access this
section.

♦ **Portal**: The **Portal** section is normally used by the Portal Admin to create
and manage user, user group, organization, communities, roles, and so on.
A portal admin can also use this section to configure password policies and
do portal-specific settings.

This section cannot be accessed by a normal user. In the majority of cases, only the
portal admin has access to this section.

♦ **Server**: The **Server** section is also used by the portal admin to do various
configurations related to the server. The admin can do server administration,
create virtual portal instances, and install new plugins from this section.

This section is not accessible to a normal user.

To recap our discussion, let's go over the following:

♦ Control Panel is an admin interface of Liferay.

♦ It is divided into four main sections. Access to control panel is modular.

♦ Control Panel can be used to create and/or manage a user, user group, role,
organization, community, password policies, authentication options, default
user association, server administration, file upload types, and so on.

♦ Control Panel contains admin portlets. A developer can create new portlets
and those portlets can also be added into control panel. This has to be done
programmatically and not through configuration.

Now, we will look at the use of some of the most commonly used links in the control panel. We will discuss detailed configuration using the control panel in the next chapter.

The following table describes links and their use:

Section	Links	Use	Accessible by
Personal	**My Account**	Displays information about the logged in user account. A user can edit his/her account information from this link.	Any user except guest
	My Pages	Displays a user's public and private pages of a user's **My Community**	Any user except guest
Content	**Page**	Displays manage page interface for the organization or community	Role-based access
	Web Content	Displays an interface to create and manage web content, structure, template	Role-based access
	Document Library	Displays document library portlet to manage documents	Role-based access
	Image Gallery	Displays Image Gallery portlet to manage images	Role-based access
	Bookmarks, Calendar, Blogs, wiki	Displays respective portlets to manage bookmarks, calendar events, blogs, and wiki	Role-based access
	Polls	User can configure a Poll using this link	Role-based access
Portal	**User**	Displays an interface to create and manage users	Role-based access, mainly Portal Admin
	User Group	To create and manage User groups	Role-based access, mainly Portal Admin
	Organizations, Communities	To create and manage organizations and communities respectively	Role-based access, mainly Portal Admin
	Roles	To create and manage Roles, define permissions to those roles	Role-based access, mainly Portal Admin
	Password Policies	To configure portal-specific password policy	Role-based access, mainly Portal Admin
	Settings	To do various portal settings like authentication, user-related settings, mail hostnames, e-mail notifications, display settings, and so on	Role-based access, mainly Portal Admin

Section	Links	Use	Accessible by
	Custom Fields	To add custom fields to out-of-the-box portlets	Role-based access, mainly Portal Admin
Server	**Server Administration**	Used for general server administration	Role-based access, mainly Portal Admin
	Portal Instances	To create and maintain virtual portal instance	Role-based access, mainly Portal Admin
	Plugin Installation	To install more plugins from the repository, configure various parameters of the server for installation, and plugin deployment	Role-based access, mainly Portal Admin

The list of the links mentioned in the preceding table is only the links which are used very commonly. We will be using these links to create and manage various components of the portal in further chapters of the book.

Time for action – creating a new user

We have gone through the basics of the control panel. Let's apply our knowledge and create a new user:

1. Log in to Liferay using default admin credentials.

2. Go to **Control Panel** from the Dockbar.

3. You will see different sections in the **Control Panel**. Click on the **Users** link under the Portal heading. You will see an interface on the right panel. Click on the **Add** button. You will see an interface displayed as shown in the following screenshot.

4. Provide your details in the fields and click on **Save** under the **User Information** panel to create your account.

5. When you save the user, it sends an e-mail to the e-mail address you provided along with a temporary password. Currently, we have not configured the mail server for our portal, so it will not send an e-mail. You can see the failure message on your Tomcat console.

6. Once a user is saved, you will see that a few more links have appeared on the right **User Information** section. These links can be used to edit user information. Since we don't have a temporary password, let's change the password from here.

7. Click on the **Password** link and provide a new password for your account and click **Save**:

Now, you have created your account. Click on the links under **User Information** to see this user's associations. You can edit any user from this screen if you have Portal Admin role. Click on the **Roles** link and observe the default role provided to you.

What just happened?

We have gone through the basic information of the **Control Panel** and looked at the links available in **Control Panel**.

You have created a user from the **Control Panel** and changed the password of the user.

Changing Portal's look and feel with themes

Till now we have discussed the basic concepts of the portal and building blocks of Liferay Portal, which are important for portal design. Now, whenever any company wants a portal to be developed, the bare minimum requirement is that the portal should represent the company. This can be achieved by providing the company or organization specific look and feel. The company may have its own logo, its own colour scheme, and specific styling which it wants to be represented in its portal. Liferay Portal achieves this requirement by using themes.

Themes in Liferay can be created as hot deployable plugins and they can transform the look and feel of the entire portal. When you start the Liferay out-of-the-box server, it starts with the default look and feel. Liferay's Classic theme is responsible for this look and feel.

Liferay introduced the concept of theme in version 3.5. The motive behind theme was to provide developers a way to change the look and feel of the portal. The theme in Liferay is a CSS-based environment. We can change the following aspects of portal with the use of theme:

- All the images used in the portal
- All the images used by the default theme
- Liferay portlet's internal images
- HTML code of the page
- The position and behavior of the navigation

Liferay theme uses the following technologies:

- CSS
- HTML/XHTML
- Velocity or FreeMarker
- JavaScript

Whenever we create a theme in Liferay, it will always be based on the differences of one master theme. The final theme will be a result of combination of the master theme and the differences.

It is possible to install a new theme from the Plugin Installer, which we have discussed earlier in the chapter. In most of the cases, Liferay theme developer develops a new theme based on the differences of the parent theme, which is also known as the base theme which consists of basic styling and placeholders for the theme. The theme is created in plugins-SDK, which is a development environment provided by Liferay. Once the theme is developed, any target can be used to deploy the theme on the application server. The theme gets converted into the `.war` file and the file goes into the `deploy` folder of the Liferay Portal server. Once the `.war` file is extracted by the Liferay, it becomes available and can be used to change the look and feel of the portal.

Since we are not covering any development aspect of Liferay in this book, we have created a theme and provided a `.war` file to you. The theme is called **CIGNEX Neighbourhood theme**. We will be creating CIGNEX Neighbourhood portlet in the further chapters of the book. We can change as many aspects of the theme as we want, but for the simplicity we have only changed the logo of the portal. Instead of displaying Liferay Company logo on the top-left corner of the page, it will display a logo of the CIGNEX Neighbourhood community. We can change the theme using the **Manage Page** option available in the Dockbar.

Time for action – installing a new theme and applying it to the portal

Now, you will install a new theme in Tomcat. Follow these steps to install the theme:

1. Start your Liferay Portal server.

2. Copy `7003OS-chapter-03\code\Cignex Neighbourhood-theme-6.0.11.1.war` from the downloaded code and place it in the `/deploy` directory of Tomcat. You can find the deploy directory at the same level as your `/TOMCAT_HOME` directory.

3. After placing the file, observe your Tomcat console. You will see the theme is being extracted. Once the theme is extracted and deploy on the server, you will see a message that **1 theme for Cignex Neighbourhood-theme is available for use**.

4. Once you get the message, go to your browser and log in with Liferay default admin credentials. Move the mouse over to the **Manage** option and click on **Page**. You will see the **Manage Page** screen.

5. By default, the **Pages** tab will be selected; click on the **Look and Feel** tab next to **Pages**. You will see the interface displayed as shown in the following screenshot using which you can change the look and feel of the page:

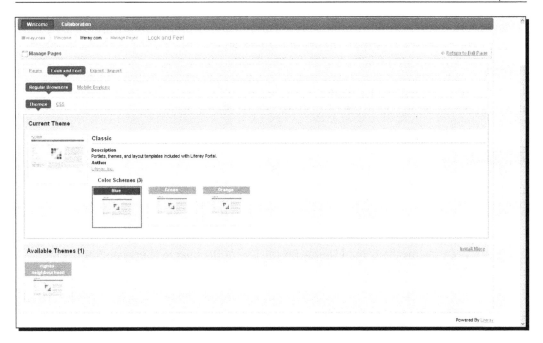

6. You will see the Cignex Neighbourhood Theme under the **Available Themes** option.

7. Click on the theme to apply the theme on the portal.

8. Once you click, you will see a success message on the page. Click on **Return to Full Page** link.

9. You will notice that the portal logo on the top-left corner has changed from Liferay to CIGNEX Neighbourhood as displayed in the following screenshot:

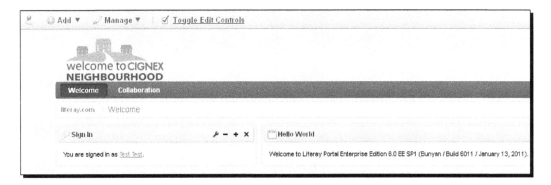

What just happened?

In this theme, we have kept the majority of the look and feel similar to the Liferay Classic theme only. You can install and apply any theme by the above mentioned way.

Currently, we have applied the theme to all the pages of Liferay Community. However, it is also possible to apply the theme to an individual page as well.

Summary

In this chapter, we have covered the basic concepts of Liferay Portal. You are now aware of following aspects:

- ◆ Portal basics.
- ◆ Navigation mechanism of Liferay Portal. Use of Dockbar in Liferay and different options available in Dockbar.
- ◆ Different building blocks of the portal—user, user group, role, organization, community, page, and team.
- ◆ Basics of Control Panel. Links used very commonly in the Control Panel.
- ◆ Theme basics and applying a new theme to the portal.

We have used most basic configurations of Liferay in this chapter. Now it is a time to learn about advanced configuration options available in Liferay. So get ready to look at *Tips and tricks of Portal Configuration*—which is the subject for the next chapter.

4
Tips and Tricks-Advanced Configuration

In the last chapter, you saw the basics of the portal. You learned about how to navigate around in Liferay, and the basic concepts: what a community and an organization are, the portal architecture, and theming.

In this chapter, we will explore more, see how we can tweak Liferay a bit, and learn about some advanced configuration.

By the end of this chapter, we will understand how to do the following:

- Rename our portal
- Enable OpenID SSO
- Enable Terms of Use
- Enable Email Notification
- Add custom attribute
- Integrate OpenOffice
- Change the hostname
- Configure the Mail server

Renaming our portal

All the public pages that you see when you start Liferay and visit the website are created in a default community called Guest. We will see in the following section, how to change the name of our portal to what we want.

Time for action – changing our portal name

To change the name of our website, please follow the steps mentioned below:

1. Log in to Liferay, if you have not already done so.

2. Navigate to **Control Panel** by clicking on **Manage | Control Panel** from the dock bar.

3. Click on **Portal Settings**, available in the **Portal** section on the left-hand side, which will take you to the following screen:

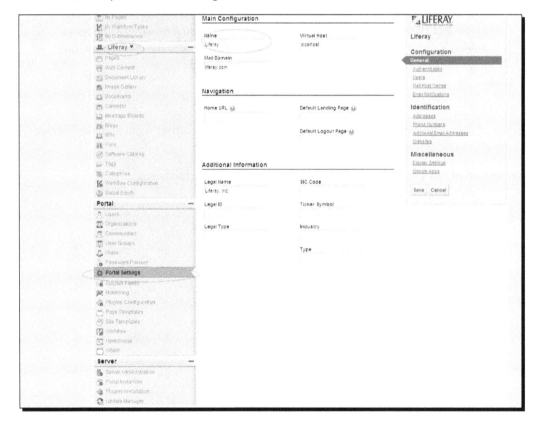

4. Note that the name of the default community is given as **Liferay**.

5. Change the name to **Cignex Neighborhood** and click on the **Save** button.

6. Notice that the name of our portal website has changed from **Liferay** to **Cignex Neighborhood**:

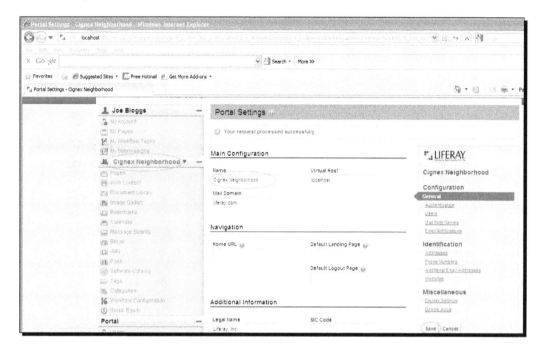

What just happened?

We have seen that Liferay by default ships with Guest Community, in which all the default public-facing pages are there. The name of the portal by default is given as **Liferay**. We have changed the name of our portal from **Liferay** to **Cignex Neighborhood**.

SSO with OpenID

OpenID is a **Single Sign On** (**SSO**) system, allowing you to use same account name for logging into different websites. In simple words, the user does not have to register in your website to access the website, he or she can just use his or her OpenID credentials to log in to your website. There are many OpenID providers, the popular ones being **Yahoo!** and Gmail. So, you can use your **Yahoo!** or Gmail credentials to get into the Liferay website.

Time for action – using OpenID for authentication

Let us see how we can enable OpenID in Liferay, and how we can log in using our **Yahoo!** credentials:

1. Log in to Liferay as an administrator, that is, using **test@liferay.com** as the username and **test** as password.

2. Navigate to the **Control Panel** by clicking on **Manage | Control Panel** from the dock bar.

3. Click on **Portal Settings** available in the **Portal** section, and click on **Authentication** from the right side. Then click on the **OpenID** tab, as shown in the following screenshot:

4. Check the **Enabled** checkbox, if it is not already checked. This would enable OpenID. To confirm whether OpenID is enabled, log out from the portal. You should see the **OpenID** option available in the **Sign In** portlet, as shown in the following screenshot:

5. Click on the **OpenID** link available, which would bring up the following screen:

6. Type in **yahoo.com** in the text box provided, as we will be using **Yahoo!** as OpenID service provider, so make sure you have a Yahoo! account created, and click on **Sign In**, which will take you to the Yahoo! login screen.

7. Once logged in, you will see a screen like the following one:

8. Fill in the details that you need to submit just once. Sign out again and follow the same step.

9. This time you would be only authenticated and would be redirected to the home page of Liferay.

What just happened?

You have just enabled SSO in Liferay using OpenID, and you have used the Yahoo! credentials to authenticate yourself in Liferay. Enabling this allows people to use their existing account, such as their Gmail or Yahoo! account for instance, to log in to multiple websites, without having to create any new password.

Ask users to accept terms before accessing Liferay

Now, since this is a portal that is allowed to be accessed by anyone, we need to make sure that we have some standard terms of use, and the user accepts those before accessing the site. This section will show you how to achieve that. Also, we will see how to change the default terms of using messages.

Time for action – enabling Terms of Use

To enable the terms of use in our website, please follow the steps mentioned below:

1. Log in to Liferay using admin credentials.

2. Navigate to the **Control Panel** by clicking on **Manage | Control Panel** from the dock bar.

3. Click on **Portal Settings**, available in the Portal section on the left-hand side, and click on the **Users** option from the right, as shown in the following screenshot:

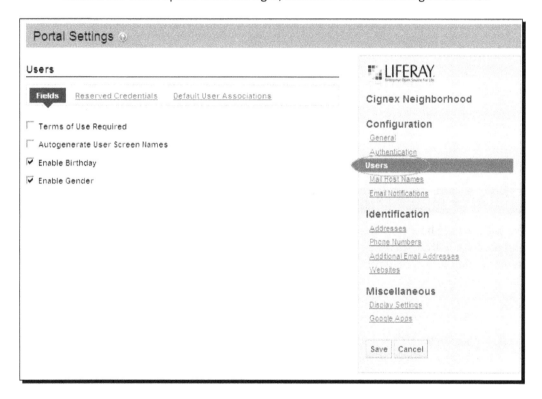

4. Select the checkbox against **Terms of Use Required**. Note that this will not be checked by default, if you have used Liferay bundle, whereas if you have deployed Liferay in your existing server, this is activated by default.

5. Well that's pretty much about it. Now, any user after creating an account will be provided with the **Terms of Use** page, which he has to accept before accessing the site, as shown in the following screenshot:

Terms of Use

Welcome to our site. We maintain this web site as a service to our members. By using our site, you are agreeing to comply with and be bound by the following terms of use. Please review the following terms carefully. If y terms, you should not use this site.

1. **Acceptance of Agreement.**
    You agree to the terms and conditions outlined in this Terms of Use Agreement ("Agreement") with respect to our site (the "Site"). This Agreement constitutes the entire and only agreement between us and you, and su contemporaneous agreements, representations, warranties and understandings with respect to the Site, the content, products or services provided by or through the Site, and the subject matter of this Agreement. Th amended at any time by us from time to time without specific notice to you. The latest Agreement will be posted on the Site, and you should review this Agreement prior to using the Site.

2. **Copyright.**
    The content, organization, graphics, design, compilation, magnetic translation, digital conversion and other matters related to the Site are protected under applicable copyrights, trademarks and other proprietary (includi intellectual property) rights. The copying, redistribution, use or publication by you of any such matters or any part of the Site, except as allowed by Section 4, is strictly prohibited. You do not acquire ownership rights t document or other materials viewed through the Site. The posting of information or materials on the Site does not constitute a waiver of any right in such information and materials.

3. **Service Marks.**
    Products and names mentioned on the Site may be trademarks of their respective owners.

4. **Limited Right to Use.**
    The viewing, printing or downloading of any content, graphic, form or document from the Site grants you only a limited, nonexclusive license for use solely by you for your own personal use and not for republication, assignment, sublicense, sale, preparation of derivative works or other use. No part of any content, form or document may be reproduced in any form or incorporated into any information retrieval system, electronic or for your personal use (but not for resale or redistribution).

5. **Editing, Deleting and Modification.**
    We reserve the right in our sole discretion to edit or delete any documents, information or other content appearing on the Site.

Time for action – changing Terms of Use

We will now see how to change the default Terms of Use message that is shown to an end user. We will create a web content and use that for our custom Terms of Use. Two items needed for configuration are the article ID of our web content and group ID of our community. The steps for this are given below:

1. Log in to the portal as administrator and navigate to **Control Panel**.

2. Click on **Web Content**, and then click **Add Web Content**. This would bring up a screen as shown in the following screenshot:

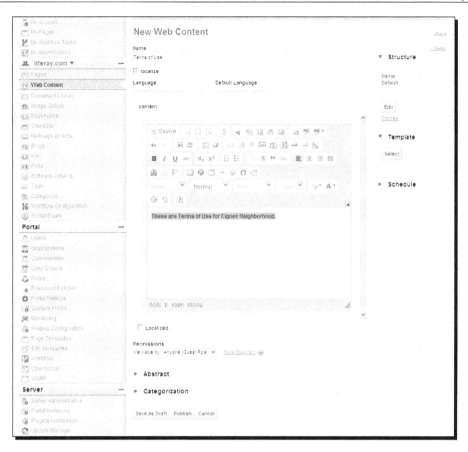

3. Enter the name and fill in the body with the content that you want to show in your custom Terms of Use. Click on **Save**, which will take you to the listing page, as shown in the following screenshot. Just copy the article ID of the web content somewhere for the steps ahead, as shown in the following screenshot:

4. Next, we need the group ID of the community in which we have created the web content. In the **Control Panel**, click on **Communities** from the left side, and click on the **Actions | Edit** button against the **Cignex Neighborhood** community. This will show the following screenshot:

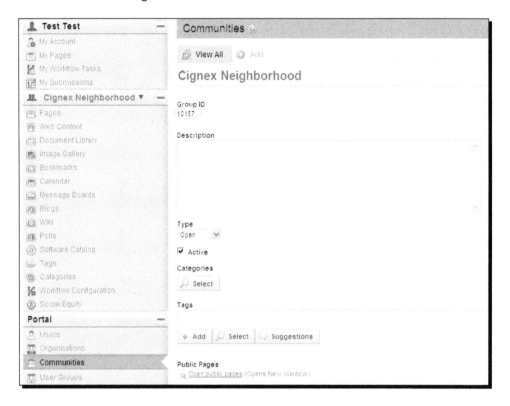

5. Copy the group ID that you see marked in the previous screenshot too.

6. Now, open `portal-ext.properties` that we created earlier inside the `LIFERAY_HOME` directory, and add the following properties:

```
#
# Specify the group id and the article id of the Journal article
that will
# be displayed as the terms of use. The default text will be used
if no
# Journal article is specified.
#
terms.of.use.journal.article.group.id=10157
terms.of.use.journal.article.id=12303
```

7. Any newly created user who now tries to log in to our portal will see our custom Terms of Use page.

What just happened?

We have enabled the feature, which asks users to accept Terms of Use before accessing the website for the first time. Also, we have seen how we can have our custom Terms of Use set, using the web content.

E-mail notifications

Whenever a user account is created by admin, we need a mechanism to send an e-mail to the user, notifying him of the created account with auto-generated passwords. Liferay provides an easy way to actually do this, and to change the message body without touching a piece of code!

We will see how this can be achieved in this section.

Time for action – enable notification for account creation

1. Log in to Liferay using admin credentials.

2. Navigate to the **Control Panel** by clicking on **Manage | Control Panel** from the dock bar.

3. Click on **Portal Settings**, available in the Portal section on the left-hand side, and click on **Email Notifications** on the right-hand side, which would bring up the following screenshot:

4. You will see that the first tab **Sender** is selected by default. This screen is meant for specifying the name and e-mail address of the sender. Change the name to **Cignex Neighborhood Admin** and the e-mail address to **neighbourhood_admin@cignex. com**, and click on **Save**.

5. Click on the **Account Created Notification** tab, which will bring up the following screenshot:

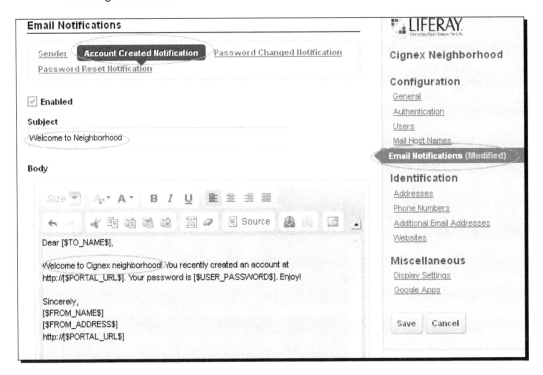

6. Make sure that the checkbox **Enabled** is selected, and change the subject and body to whatever you want. This is the mail template that will be sent to users, when they create an account. There are some predefined variables (definitions of which are given below), that you can make use of while creating the template.

7. Click on **Save**.

What just happened?

We just configured Liferay to change the following e-mail notification settings:

- ◆ We have changed the name and e-mail address of the sender, which means whenever someone receives an e-mail from Liferay, the from address and name will be the one that we just set. We have changed the mail template that is used, while sending mails to the user whose accounts are newly created.

Adding custom attributes for User

Often there is a requirement that we need to have additional information to be associated to User or Organization about what Liferay provides. Normally, in any other application, this has to be done with lots of coding effort. But in Liferay, we can make use of custom attributes to have any extra attributes to be associated with any entity.

Time for action – giving the option to add a user's favorite sport

Our Cignex neighbourhood members are fanatic sport fans, and they want an option to add their favorite sport. Let us see how we can do this:

1. Log in as portal admin, and navigate to **Control Panel**.

2. Click on the **Custom Fields** option from the left-hand side, which will bring up the following screenshot:

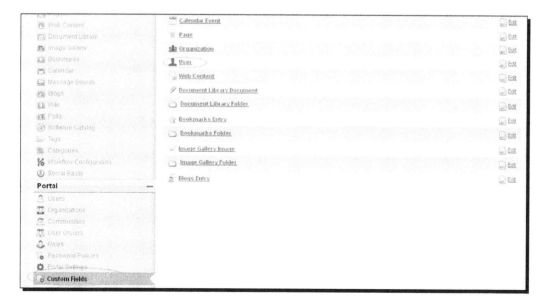

3. Click on the **User** link, which will bring you to the screenshot shown as follows:

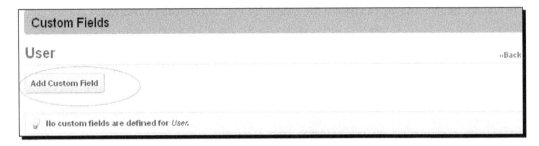

4. Click on the **Add Custom Field** button, which will give you a screen to add your custom field attribute, as shown in the following screenshot:

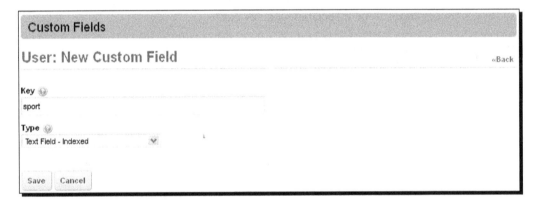

5. Give the value of **Key** as **sport**. Next, there is a **Type**, wherein you can select whether you want text, selection box, or text box. Leave the selection of **Type** as **Text Field – Indexed**. Click on **Save**, which will result in the following screenshot, notifying that the custom field sport is added for **User**, as follows:

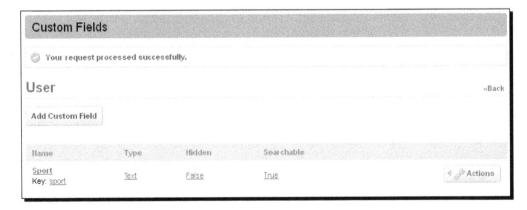

6. Now, let us see how a user can enter the value for the newly created custom attribute. Click on the **My Account** option from the **Control Panel** on the top left-hand side:

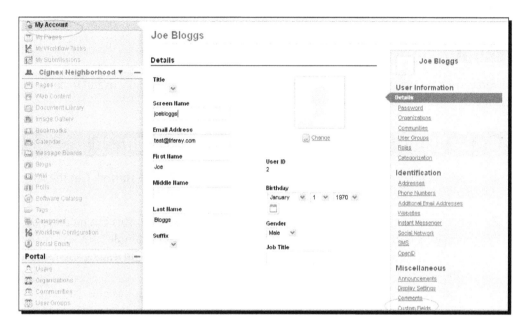

7. Click on the **Custom Fields** link available at the bottom-right, which shows you the option to type in your favorite sport. Enter the name of your favorite sport and just hit **Save**, as follows:

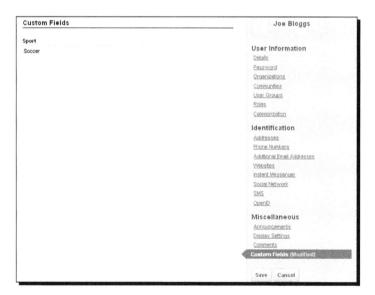

Have a go hero – add more custom attributes

Since we have learnt how to add custom attributes, go add some additional custom attributes for **User** that you would like to have in the website.

OpenOffice integration

In Liferay, we have an option of integrating Open Office. This is especially useful to convert documents from one format to another.

Time for action – enabling OpenOffice integration

1. For doing this, we need OpenOffice installed, and the service started. Get the latest version of OpenOffice and install it.

2. After installing, we may need to start the OpenOffice service. This can be done by navigating to the folder where OpenOffice is installed (for example, `C:\Program Files\OpenOffice.org 3\program`) from the console, and issuing the following command:

    ```
    soffice -headless -accept="socket,host=127.0.0.1,port=8100;urp;"
    -nofirststartwizard
    ```

3. This should start up OpenOffice as the service running on port 8100.

4. Log in to Liferay using admin credentials.

5. Navigate to **Control Panel** by clicking on **Manage | Control Panel** from the dock bar.

6. Click on the **Server Administration** from the bottom-left, and then click on OpenOffice, as shown in the following screenshot:

7. Check **Enabled** and click on **Save**.

What just happened?

We have integrated OpenOffice, which will be used later for file conversion.

Changing the hostname

Since we are going to develop a cool website on Neighborhood, we need to get the name right when users are accessing the portal. So, let us give a hostname to our website.

Time for action – changing our portal name

We will be using Apache, which is most widely used as a web server to act as a proxy server to redirect all the requests it receives to the Liferay server behind it. The steps for this are as follows:

1. Download and install the latest version of Apache. This would start Apache as a service.

2. Navigate to `conf` folder inside Apache, which has a file called `httpd.conf`.

3. Open the file and uncomment the following line:

   ```
   LoadModule proxy_module modules/mod_proxy.so
   ```

4. Add the following lines at the end of the file, and then save the same:

```
ProxyRequests On

ProxyPass / http://localhost:8080/
ProxyPassReverse / http://localhost:8080/
```

5. Restart the server.

6. We need to add a DNS entry for setting up a virtual host, so for the moment we will just add the host entry. Open the hosts file in `C:\WINDOWS\system32\drivers\etc` and add an entry as follows:

```
127.0.0.1 neighborhood.cignex.com
```

What just happened?

Open your browser and hit `http://neighborhood.cignex.com`. You should be able to access the website. We have enabled `mod_proxy`, so that all the requests that are made to `neighborhood.cignex.com` are sent to `http://localhost:8080`.

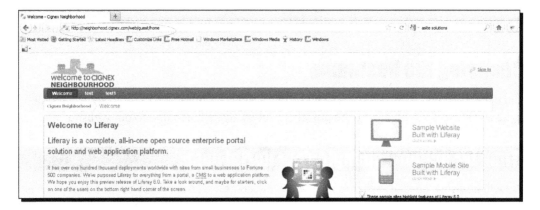

Mail server

In this section, we will see how to configure the mail server for our application.

Time for action – enabling the mail server

1. Log in to Liferay using admin credentials.

2. Navigate to the **Control Panel** by clicking on **Manage | Control Panel** from the dock bar.

3. Click on **Server Administration**, and then click on the **Mail** tab, which will bring up the screenshot as follows:

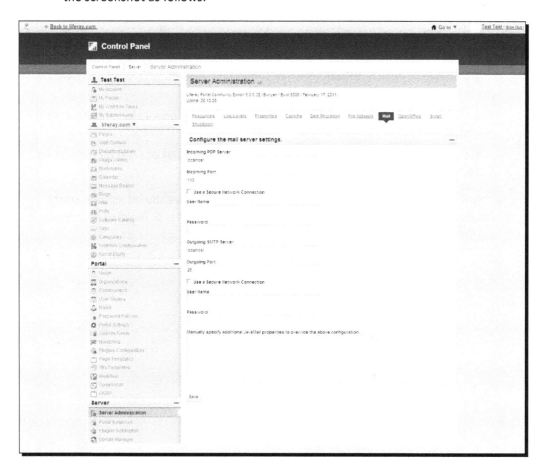

4. We will use Gmail as our mail server. For Outgoing SMTP Server, type the value as **smtp.gmail.com**. For Outgoing Port, put the value as 465. Select the checkbox, which says **Use a Secure Network Connection**. For **User Name** give your full Gmail address, and for the **Password**, give your Gmail password.

5. Click on **Save**.

Summary

Phew! That was some exercise, wasn't it? We learned to tweak Liferay a bit.

Specifically, we have covered the following points:

- We have renamed our portal as Cignex Neighborhood, configured the mail server, and changed the hostname to neighborhood.cignex.com.

- We have enabled SSO using OpenID, so users can log in with any of their OpenID accounts.

- We made it mandatory for users to accept terms before actually accessing the website.

- We enabled e-mail notifications when someone's account is created, tweaked the mail template, and mail sender details.

- We added a custom attribute to User, so that users can now enter their favorite sport from the My Account screen.

- We integrated Liferay with OpenOffice, which will be used later on for converting documents.

- Now that we are done with all the configuration stuff, we should actually start building our site, which is the discussion topic for *Chapter 5, Building Your First Liferay Site*.

5
Building your First Liferay Site

In the previous chapter, you saw the advanced configuration of Liferay. You now know how to rename the portal, enable **OpenID SSO**, *enable* **Terms of Use** *for your portal, change the hostname, configure the mail server, and so on. After successfully completing all the exercises mentioned in the previous chapter, you should have the above mentioned topics configured in your portal instance. Also, you can access your portal using* `http://neighbourhood.cignex.com` *instead of* `http://localhost:8080`.

Now, we have done all the groundwork to build a Liferay website. In this chapter, you will start building your Liferay site. In the rest of the book, we will keep building our CIGNEX Neighborhood portal. This chapter will serve as a foundation to the rest of the chapters of this book. You will go through the following concepts in this chapter:

♦ Components of the site

♦ Community and organization—the most basic need of any Liferay Portal

♦ Knowing the user group

♦ Knowing page templates

At the end of this chapter, you will be aware of how to design the site, how to create an organization and a community, the difference between an organization and a community, the concept of the user group in Liferay, and the association between the user group and the page template.

Before starting the actual site implementation, we will first learn the approach we should take to design the site. We will also learn about the components of the Liferay Portal.

Designing the site – painting the full picture

Whenever we get the requirements of the portal, we should first ask ourselves, how would the portal look when it goes live? This one small question will open a door to a lot of other questions and a lot of information which will be required to implement the portal.

You should always think of the end state of the portal and then start painting the complete picture of the portal. This approach is known as beginning with the end!

Now, as we have just discussed the approach we should take while starting the site design, let's understand the information we can retrieve or get when we ask ourselves this question. We will discuss four main components of the Liferay Portal design.

Users

No matter what the size of the portal is—small, medium, or large—it will always be designed for the users. Users are at the centre of any portal application.

Let's think of a very common portal, `http://www.cnn.com`. Just imagine that you have to implement this portal. You are sitting in your nice comfy rocking chair and thinking of the users of this portal. What questions would you ask yourself (or the client, if he/she is with you) about the users of this portal?

1. Who will be using this portal?
2. Will all the users of this portal have the same privileges? Or will some of the users have more privileges than others?
3. Can we collect the users into any specific group?
4. Are these users organized in any kind of hierarchy?
5. Can the users leave or join this portal at will? And so on.

Now, try thinking of the answers of the preceding questions and any other question, if you have thought of any more. Can you co-relate these questions with the topic *Knowing Liferay Building Blocks* discussed in *Chapter 3, Understanding Portal Basics and Theming*?

Let's discuss the answers to the preceding questions and the information we can retrieve from them:

◆ If we want to provide an answer to the first question in only one word, then it can be—Users. It is quite obvious that the portal will be used by the users. However, if we go into the detail of this question we can get an answer like—all the employees of CNN, users from all over the world, John Walter who will be responsible for administration of the entire portal, and so on. So the answer to this question will give us the information about all the players associated with the portal.

- If all the users of the portal have the same privileges, then it's pretty obvious that every user will be able to perform the same function in the portal. However, this may not be the case with our portal, `http://www.cnn.com`. Here, we have end users who will come to the portal and will access the information; we can also have a group of internal users who can create the content. Similarly, there can be a group who can approve the content and another group can publish the content; there can also be users who are responsible for user management and one or more users who are responsible for portal management.

- So this kind of question will give us the information about different roles and permissions associated with each role in our portal. It will also give us the information for which user should be associated with what kind of role. This information is very useful when we are working on the security piece of the portal.

- If the answer of the third question is Yes then we can either create a user group in our portal or group the users into a specific role. This question will give us the information about user grouping in the portal.

- Now, the answer to the last two questions will be discussed in more detail in this chapter. However, these questions will help us to determine if we should use an organization or community or mix of both in our portal. Every Liferay Portal must have at least one organization or community.

Once we get the information about the users in our portal, we should think of the content next.

Content

No portal can exist without any kind of content. The content can be a static HTML, a static article, a video, an audio, podcast, document, image, and so on. To make the portal more effective, we have to manage the content properly.

We will continue with our example of `http://www.cnn.com`:

1. What kind of questions can we ask to ourselves or to the client about the content?
2. What are the types of content we will use in the portal?
3. Where are we going to store the content? To Liferay database or some other external database?
4. Do we have to create the content from scratch?
5. Do we need to migrate existing content to Liferay?

And a few more...

I am sure you must be visiting many portals every day. Can you think of the possible answers to the preceding questions? Also, think of the information which can be retrieved from those answers:

◆ The answer to the first question can be—document, images, web content, video, podcast, and so on. This answer will give us an idea about the content types which need to be implemented in the portal. Some of the contents like web content and documents can be available out of the box in Liferay, while other content types like video and podcast may not be available out of the box. This information will enable us to determine the types of content and effort required to create the new content.

◆ The second question is a bit tricky. By default, Liferay stores the content in a database. However, if the client wants we can store the content in a shared location as well. For example, storing documents in the file system. Also, it requires high availability. You can refer to wiki about this on `http://goo.gl.dmM1Y`. An answer to this question will give us information like if we need to add any additional hardware or not, if we should do any specific configuration to meet the requirements, and so on.

◆ Answers to the third and fourth questions will be mainly used for effort estimation. If a portal like `http://www.cnn.com` is using a huge amount of content and all of the content has to be built from scratch, then it may take a good amount of time. If the content is already available, we need to consider the effort of migrating and organizing the content.

◆ We can also think of other questions like the requirement of workflow, the type of the flow, if staging is required for the content or not, and so on.

All of the preceding questions will give us a good picture about the content to be created or used in our portal. Once we are thorough with this section, it becomes easy to appoint someone to do content management design for your portal.

Applications

We have discussed the user and the content of the portal. However, what about the applications which will be hosted on the portal? We cannot imagine a portal without any application nowadays. A portal can contain different applications like a forum, wiki, blog, document viewer, video player, and so on. Let's get a list of questions which you should ask yourself while designing the portal:

1. What are the different applications required for this portal?

2. Do we have any application available out of the box in Liferay?

3. Do we need to modify/extend any existing application available in Liferay?

4. Do we have to create any new application for the portal? If yes, what is the complexity of this application?

Liferay ships with more than 60 applications pre-bundled, known as portlets. These applications are very commonly used in many of the portals.

When we ask the preceding questions to ourselves, we get the following information:

- Number of applications required in the portal.
- How many applications are available out of the box? If we have more applications available OOTB (out of the box) then it can reduce the development time.
- Scope of the project. Do we need any integration with external system or not?
- Kinds of applications we have to develop from scratch.

Once we go through the preceding set of questions, it becomes very easy to get a picture of the applications required in our portal. It will also provide us information about the efforts required to implement the portal. So, if you are managing a portal development project, you should definitely have this information ready before starting the project.

Security

Security is one of the most important aspects of any portal. When we think about security of any portal, we must consider access to the content and the applications on the portal.

You must have come across many of the portals so far. Some of the portals allow you to create your account freely; some of the portals require an authorization before creating the account while some other portals don't allow creating an account at all. Also, there are some portals which display the same information to all the users while other portals display certain information to members only.

To put this in a nutshell, each of the portals has its own security policy and operates based on that policy only. Once we have thought about users, content, and application in portal design, we should consider the security aspect of the portal.

Now, let's think of some of the questions which we should normally ask ourselves/client while considering security aspect of the portal:

1. Can everyone freely create an account with the portal?
2. Do we need to migrate the users from an existing user base like LDAP?
3. Can everyone access the same information or do we need to display certain information to portal members only?
4. Can all the members of the portal access all the applications with the same privileges or do certain users have more privileges over other members?

And so on....

When we get answers to the preceding questions, we get the following information about the portal security:

♦ If everyone can create an account with the portal, then in that case we need to provide the create account functionality to the users. Also, we don't need to do any authorization on account creation. If the answer to the first question is NO, then we need to either provide some kind of authorization on account creation or we need to remove the account creation facility completely.

♦ If we have to migrate the users from an existing user base, then we have to think about the migration and integration. Liferay provides integration with LDAP. If the user base is not present, then we will end up creating all the accounts manually or provide users an ability to create their accounts.

♦ If all the users (including non-logged in users) can access the same information then we will keep all the information on public pages but if we want certain information to be accessed by members only, then we might consider putting that information on the pages which can be accessed only after logging in.

♦ If all the members of the portal can access the same information with the same privileges then we will not need any special role in the portal. However, if a certain group or set of users have more privileges over another—like only content creators can create content—then we will have to create a role and provide the required permission to the role.

When we think of the security of the portal, we are thinking about users and their access, applications and access to those applications, and other security-related aspects of the portal. It is very important to think about security before implementing the portal, to prevent unauthorized and unauthenticated access to the portal and applications within the portal.

Have a go hero – finding out information for an intranet portal

We have discussed the portal components and their importance in portal design. We have also discussed the approach we should take in portal implementation. Now, it is your turn to implement the knowledge you have gathered so far.

Let's assume that you are implementing an intranet portal for a business school. The portal will be used by the students, lecturers, and external users. The portal will be used to provide information about the school to external users and keep internal users (students and lecturers) updated with day-to-day activities.

Now, implement the beginning with the end approach discussed so far. Come up with a set of questions and possible answers and put the design of the portal on paper.

Discuss and review the design with someone who you know is working in the portal world.

Knowing the portal requirements

You are now aware of the portal components and the way to get information related to each component. Now, we will discuss the requirements of the portal (CIGNEX Neighborhood) which we are going to implement in this book.

CIGNEX Neighborhood portal

We need to implement a portal for CIGNEX Neighborhood—`http://neighbourhood.cignex.com`. The portal will be used by the CIGNEX Neighborhood members. We want to replicate the existing structure of CIGNEX Neighborhood to this portal. All the members are organized as shown in the following diagram:

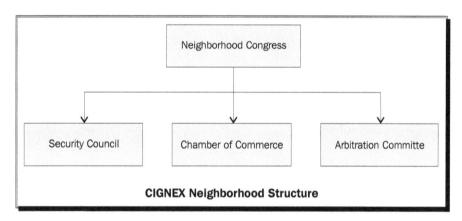

CIGNEX Neighborhood Structure

In the preceding structure, the Neighborhood Congress is the top-level entity and Security Council, Chamber of Commerce, and Arbitration Committee are the sub-level entities. The permissions flow from top to bottom. We want our users to be structured in this format. We need to provide different applications in each group for the members to be productive and collaborative.

Along with the applications mentioned in each group, the group members are also interested in other activities like General Sports and Games, Cricket, Gardening, Collaboration, and Shopping. We want these group members to have some place in our portal where they can connect to one another based on their common interest. There is no restriction for any member to join these activities; for example two members from the Neighborhood Congress, one member from Security Council, and three members from the Chamber of Commerce can be interested in the Gardening activity. All of these members should be able to collaborate at one place in any activity which is related to gardening. This is very similar to the communities in social networking websites where members from different groups can join based on their common interest.

See the following diagram, which explains this scenario:

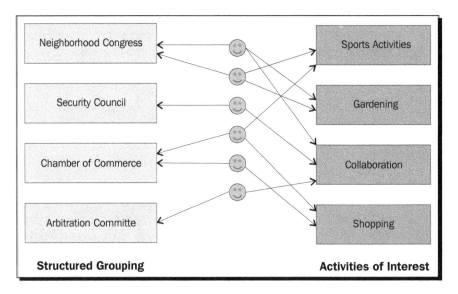

The preceding diagram mentions that users are associated with their respective group based on their function, but the area of interest cuts across the structural grouping. For example, a user who is a member of the Neighborhood Congress and another user who is a member of the Security Council will not have anything in common as long as their structured grouping is concerned, but both of them can be interested in Gardening activities.

It is also possible that one user can be a member of more than one structured group, like the Security Council and Chamber of Commerce.

Each of the structured groups like the Chamber of Commerce and the activities space in the portal will contain applications which will be used by the members of the respective group or space on their pages. See the following table to find out the pages and applications associated with each of the groups and activity spaces:

Name	Page	Application
Neighborhood Congress	wiki	wiki
	Your Opinion	Forum
Security Council	Security	Panorama
Chamber of Commerce	Neighborhood Prosperity	Blogs
Arbitration Committee	Arbitration Result Page	Result Display
Sports and Game	Online Game	Game Application
Cricket Players	Latest Matches	Match Information Display
Gardening DIY	Schedule	Application to display when you can plant which vegetable
Neighborhood Exchange	Gossip	Chat
	Video	Video Player
	Breaking News	News
	Photo Sharing	Photo Display
Around the Corner	Shopping	Shopping Cart

All of the pages mentioned in the preceding table should be accessible only to members. A non-logged in user cannot access any of the application or the page mentioned previously.

On top of the previously mentioned structured groups and communities, the portal should allow an external user to create his/her own account. Once the account is created, a user can be assigned to the structured group by the portal admin. Once a user becomes a member of the portal, he/she can join any of the activities based on their interests.

Now, we have the requirements of the portal. We will start building our portal based on these requirements. First of all, we have to understand how the structure will be implemented for CIGNEX Neighborhood Portal. In order to do so, first we have to understand the concept of organization and community in Liferay. We had discussed organization and communities in brief in *Chapter 3, Understanding Portal Basics and Theming*. But we will discuss these components in detail in the next section.

Organizing users in an organization and a community

We have all the requirements for the CIGNEX Neighborhood portal. If you remember the section we discussed in the beginning of this chapter, *Designing the site—Painting the full picture*, we mentioned that we should always start with the information about the users. As per our requirements, the portal users are organized in a structured grouping. They are also interested in other activities and want to collaborate with one another using the portal.

Let's see how Liferay can help us to meet these requirements.

Organization—structured grouping of users

An organization in Liferay represents an organization in real life. The organization can be a very small organization like a sports club in our neighborhood or it can be as large as a Fortune 500 company. Liferay Organization can be used to replicate any organization in the real world.

The organization is a hierarchical collection of the users. It is also possible to create a sub-organization under any organization. You can create sub-organizations up to nth level.

The organization can be used to represent a fully functional portal. It means you can create pages within an organization and load them up with required applications. You can also assign users to the organization and provide them access to certain pages or applications within an organization.

Once the user is created or added to the portal, you can assign the user to as many organizations as you want. You can also create a user group in the portal and assign the entire user group to the organization. On doing so, all the users of the user group will become members of the organization. We will perform all these exercises in this chapter.

Liferay provides a facility to add the organization in the Portal. Let's explore more on it.

Adding the organization

If you look at the user structure of the CIGNEX Neighborhood Portal in the earlier section, you will notice that it is hierarchical. We have users associated with the Neighborhood Congress, which is at the top level in the hierarchy and other users are associated with Security Council, Chamber of Commerce, and Arbitration Committee, which are one level below the Neighborhood Congress.

We have to create this hierarchical structure in Liferay. Let's see how we can use Liferay to replicate the hierarchical structure.

Time for action – creating organization for CIGNEX Neighborhood

1. Start your server. Once your server is started type in `http://neighbourhood.cignex.com`.

2. Log in to the CIGNEX Neighborhood Portal with Liferay default admin credentials: Username: **test@liferay.com** and Password: **test**.

3. Select **Control Panel** from the **Manage** option in the Dockbar. On the left-hand panel, you will see four sections: **Personal**, **Content**, **Portal**, and **Server**.

4. Click on the **Organizations** link under the **Portal** section as displayed in the following screenshot:

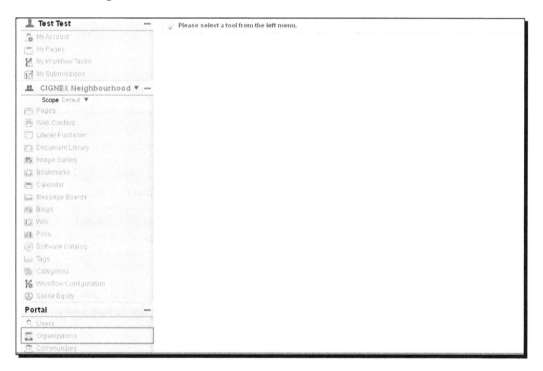

5. On clicking the link, it will open an interface which displays a list of all the organizations created in the portal. Currently, we have not created any organization, so the list will be empty. It is displayed in the following screenshot:

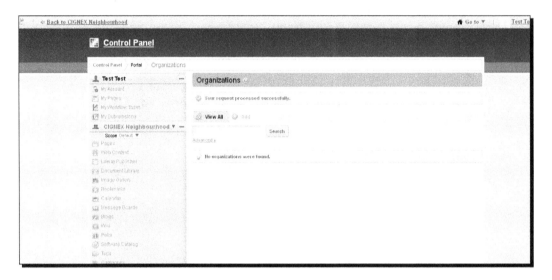

 Sometimes when you start Liferay with a default hypersonic database, it may give you an empty list of organization. However, if you search for the organization, they may be displayed. This happens due to an indexing issue. To resolve the issue click on the **Server Administration** link under the **Server** section in the **Control Panel**. You will see a list of options under **Actions** in the right panel. Click on the **Execute** button opposite to **Reindex All Search Indexes** option. This will reindex all search indexes of the portal. Wait for a while, you will be able to see all the organizations in the list.

6. Currently, you see an empty list under **Organizations** because we are connected to MySQL database and have not created an organization so far. To add a new organization, click on the **Add** option. This will open an interface to add a new organization to the portal. It is displayed in the following screenshot:

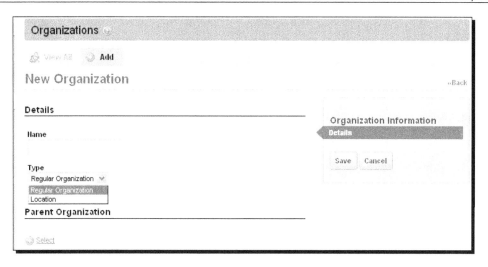

7. In the preceding interface, the **Name** field indicates the name of the organization. Currently, we want to create a top-level organization—Neighborhood Congress. Provide this name in the **Name** field.

8. The next option is the **Type**. This is a drop-down field. It contains two values— **Regular Organization** and **Location**. As discussed in *Chapter 3, Understanding Portal Basics and Theming*, **Regular Organization** is a normal organization or sub-organization, while a **Location** is a special type of organization. If you select the **Organization** type as a **Location** then that organization becomes the leaf node and you cannot create any sub-organization below it. Here, we want to keep our organization as a **Regular Organization** so select this value from the drop down.

9. The option in this interface is **Parent Organization**. If you want to select any other organization as a parent organization of our organization, you can click on the **Select** link and it will open a list of organizations. You can choose from the list and provide that organization as a parent organization of the one we are creating. As we know the Neighborhood Congress is the top-level organization, so we will not select any organization as the parent.

10. Once you have provided all these values, click on the **Save** button from the right panel under Organization Information.

Once you save it, the organization will be added to our portal. You will also notice that the **Organization Information** panel has expanded and now you will see many links under it. It is displayed in the following screenshot:

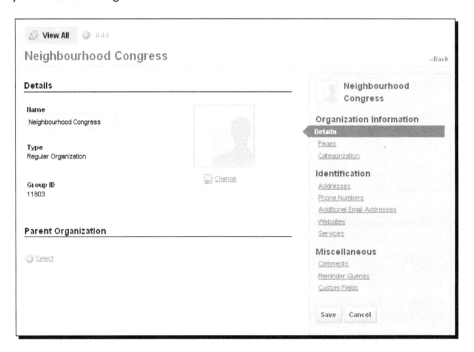

You can add an image for the organization you have created. You can also select each of the links and provide information for the organization. The links and descriptions of the links are given in the following table:

Section	Link	Use
Organization Information	**Details**	Contains details of the organization.
Organization Information	**Pages**	Provides information of Public and Private pages of the organization.
Organization Information	**Categorization**	This link is used to add categories and tags to the organization.
Identification	**Address**	It is used to provide address details of the organization.
Identification	**Phone Numbers**	Used to provide phone numbers of the organization.

Section	Link	Use
Identification	**Alternate Email Address**	It is used to add e-mail addresses of the organization. You can add multiple e-mail addresses and make one of them primary.
Identification	**Website**	It is used to provide a URL of the organization.
Identification	**Services**	You can add services details and operating hours for each service. These services can be Administrative, Contracts, Donation, Retail, or Training. They can be related to the organization and you can add operating hours for each of the services related to the organization.
Miscellaneous	**Comments**	Any comments can be added to the organization.
Miscellaneous	**Reminder Queries**	It is used to specify custom reminder queries for the users of the organization.
Miscellaneous	**Custom Fields**	It will display the custom fields added to the organization.

Now we have added the organization, let's get familiar with all the actions associated with an organization.

Time for action – understanding actions associated with the organization

Once you have created the top-level organization and saved it, you will see it is added in your portal. Click on the **View All** option next to the **Add** option in the organization interface. It will display a list of all the organizations in the portal. Let's look at the different actions associated with the organization:

1. Click on the **Actions** button displayed with the Neighborhood Congress Organization.

2. It will open a list of actions which you can perform with the Neighborhood Congress Organization.

3. The options and their uses are as follows:

- **Edit**—It will take you to the edit screen of the Organization, which we have discussed in the previous section.

- **Manage Pages**—It will take the user to the **Manage** page interface of the organization. You can add and/or manage pages for the organization.

- **Manage Teams**—You can add and/or manage teams for an organization.

- **Assign User Roles**—You can assign organization roles to the users within an organization.

- **Assign Members**—You can add existing users and/or user groups to the organization.

- **Add Users**—You can add a new user to the organization. This will take you to the **Add User** screen with this organization already assigned in the user's organization list.

- **View Users**—You can view a list of the users who are members of the organization.

- **Add Regular Organization**—You can add a new sub-organization under the organization.

- **Add Location**—You can add a location under the organization.

- **View Suborganizations**—You can view all the sub-organizations of the organizations.

- **Delete**—You can delete an organization.

> You cannot delete an organization if the organization has any members—users or user groups—associated with it or any sub-organizations created under it. To delete an organization you must remove all the associations first.

What just happened?

You have created a top-level organization—Neighborhood Congress. You got familiar with all the options available in the **Edit organization** option.

We have also discussed all the actions associated with an organization. You are now aware of two ways of adding a sub-organization to the organization:

- You can select **Parent Organization** while creating an organization

- You can click on the **Action** button associated with the organization and select the **Add Regular Organization** option

Currently, we have not added any pages to our organizations. We will discuss page management and adding pages to our organizations in the next chapter.

Have a go hero – adding a sub-organization to Neighborhood Congress

Now, you are aware of how to add an organization. We have also discussed how to add a sub-organization under an organization. Do you feel confident about the topics we have discussed so far? Do you feel that you can now create sub-organizations independently? Well, let's check it out.

As per our requirements, we need three more sub-organizations under Neighborhood Congress—Security Council, Chamber of Commerce, and Arbitration Committee. Log in as a default admin (**test@liferay.com** / **test**) and create three sub-organizations under Neighborhood Congress Organization:

- To create the Security Council sub-organization, select the top organization while creating the organization. We have discussed this option when creating the Neighborhood Congress Organization.

- To create the Chamber of Commerce sub-organization, use the **Actions** button next to Neighborhood Congress organization and add sub-organization using the **Add Regular Organization** option.

- Add the third organization, Arbitration Committee, with any of the preceding methods that you are most comfortable with.

> In the preceding section, we have mentioned that a **Location** is a leaf node and we cannot create a sub-organization under a **Location**. However, this is a default behavior and there is one property in `portal.properties` responsible for it—`organizations.rootable[location]=false`. You can set this property in the `portal-ext.properties` file to `true` to add sub-organizations under a location. `organizations.rootable[location]=true`

Understanding the difference between a Location and Regular Organization

So far, we have discussed how to create the organization. We created a top-level organization and then created sub-organizations as well. While creating the organization, we had an option to choose from **Regular Organization** or a **Location**. A simple question which may arise, is what is the difference between a regular organization and a location? When do we create a regular organization and when do we use a location?

Well, we know that if you declare an organization as a **Location**, then you will not be able to create a sub-organization under it, by default. However, that can also be changed by changing the property in `portal-ext.properties`. So, again we are back to the same question—when should we use an organization and when should we use a location?

As we know, the organization in Liferay represents an organization in real life. Similarly, the location in Liferay represents a location in real life. We can have an organization structure which contains a location as well and we want to implement the same structure in Liferay. For example, we can have a top-level organization as a `MyBigCompany` which may have sub-organizations like Finance, Sales, and IT. Now, being a multi-national organization, we may have a Sales department in New York and in London as well. So here, we will implement Sales as a regular sub-organization and New York and London as locations in Liferay. Normally, Sales in New York does not need to be sub-divided so locations are created as a leaf node.

So to put this in a nutshell, we will define the organization as a **Location**, if we want to represent a real-life location in our structure.

Pop quiz – true or false?

Please state if following statements are true or false:

1. Organizations can have only users as members.
2. Every organization must have at least one parent organization.
3. Default Organization types are—Regular Organization and Location.
4. It is not possible to create a sub-organization under location by any means.
5. An organization can have more than one parent organizations.
6. An organization can behave as a fully-functional website.

Community—a collection of users having common interests

Community in Liferay is a collection of users having common interests. There are some similarities between an organization and a community. For example:

- Community is also a collection of user
- Community can also have a set of pages
- Community can also be represented as a fully-functional website

However, there is one fundamental difference between the organization and the community. The communities in Liferay are not hierarchical. They are designed in Liferay in such a way that anyone from any organization can join them based on the interest. So, we can use a community in the portal in a case where the interest is cutting across the Organizational structure. Also, a user does not have to be a member of any organization to join the community. The user can be created in the portal and assigned to the community.

Let's go back to our requirements to understand the statement mentioned in the previous paragraph. We have created four organizations because we had a requirement to organize the users in a structured and hierarchical manner. Now, the requirements also mention that the members of the CIGNEX Neighborhood Portal are also interested in other activities like gardening, sports and games, cricket, collaboration, and shopping. These users may be associated with any of the four organizations we have created earlier but are also interested in one of these activities regardless of their association in the organization hierarchy. Go back and visit the image, which displays the user's association with the organizations and activities in CIGNEX Neighborhood portal to make this clearer.

In this scenario, the interest of the activity—gardening, sports, cricket, and so on—is cutting across the organization. So, we can create one community for each of the activities and users can join these communities. Now, in future if the user loses interest in the activity, he/she can leave the community at his/her will. A user's association with the community is not so tight as with the organization. Also, one user can be interested in more than one activity and hence can become a member of more than one community.

When you log in to Liferay for the first time, the default page you see is a part of Liferay Portal's default community—`liferay.com`. We have renamed this community to CIGNEX Neighborhood in our last chapter. There may be a scenario where you don't even need an organization in your portal; in that case you can only create a community and publish it as a website.

We have discussed enough about the community. Now, let's see how we can add the community in Liferay Portal.

Adding the community

As discussed, as per the structure of the CIGNEX Neighborhood Portal, we will require four organizations and five communities. We have created four organizations. Now, we will create five communities—Gardening DIY, Sports and Games, Cricket Players, Neighborhood Exchange, and Around the Corner—in this section. Let's use Liferay's out-of-the-box features to create these communities in the CIGNEX Neighborhood portal.

Time for action – creating a community for CIGNEX Neighborhood

1. Start your server. Once your server is started type in
   `http://neighbourhood.cignex.com`.

2. Log in to CIGNEX Neighborhood Portal with Liferay default admin credentials:
   Username: **test@liferay.com** and **Password**: **test**.

3. Select **Control Panel** from the **Manage** option in the Dockbar. Click on the
   Communities link under the **Portal** section as displayed in the following screenshot:

4. On clicking the link, it will open an interface which displays a list of all the
   communities created in the portal. Currently, we have only one community—
   CIGNEX Neighborhood (`liferay.com`) in our portal. Click on the **Add** option to
   add a new community. You will see the following interface, when you click on the
   Add button:

5. In the preceding interface, the **Name** field indicates the name of the community we are creating. Give the name as **Gardening DIY** community. The **Description** field allows you to add the description of the community. Just type in—**this is a Gardening Do It Yourself Community**.

6. Next, you will see a drop-down having **Open** as a default value. This drop-down is used to define the **Type** of the community. The community can be **Open**, **Restricted**, or **Private**. We have already discussed the community types in *Chapter 3, Understanding Portal Basics and Theming*.

    Here, we want everyone to join the Gardening DIY community freely. So keep the community type as **Open**.

7. You can use the next checkbox to define, if your community is active or inactive. Keep the **Active** box checked at this moment.

8. The next option in the interface is **Categories**. Currently, we do not have any category created. So keep it blank.

9. The last option you will see is **Tags**. It is very similar to category. You can attach tags to your community as well. To do so, you can either select from the existing tags or type in a new tag name or click on the **Add** button. We don't want to provide any tag to this community, so leave this field blank and click on **Save**.

10. Once you click on **Save**, you will see a success message and the community will be added to the portal. You will now be able to see two communities—**CIGNEX Neighborhood** and **Gardening DIY community**.

What just happened?

You became familiar with the community concept in Liferay. You are now aware of the difference between an organization and a community and the following about the community in particular:

- We have discussed two ways to add the community to the portal—from the **Control Panel** and using the **My Communities** portlet.

- You have added a new community—**Gardening DIY**—from the **Control Panel**. We have also discussed different actions associated with the community.

Time for action – understanding actions associated with the community

Once you have created the community and saved it, you will see it is added in your portal. Click on the **View All** option next to the **Add** option in the **Communities** interface. It will display a list of all the communities in the portal. Let's understand different actions associated with the community.

1. Click on the **Actions** button displayed next to the **Gardening DIY** community.

2. It will open a list of actions which you can perform with the **Gardening DIY** community. It is displayed in the following screenshot:

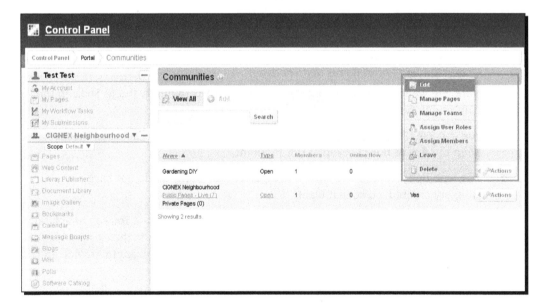

The options and their uses are as follows:

- **Edit**—It will take you to the edit screen of the community and you will be allowed to edit the community.

- **Manage Pages**—It will take the user to the **Manage** page interface of the community. You can add and/or manage pages for the community.

- **Manage Teams**—You can add and/or manage teams for the community.

- **Assign User Roles**—You can assign **Community Roles** to the users within the community.

- **Assign Members**—You can add existing users, user groups, or organizations to the community.

- **Leave**—You can leave the community, if you are already a member of the community.

- **Delete**—You can delete the community from the portal.

You can also create a community using Liferay's My Communities Portlet. You can select **My Private Pages** from the **Go To** section in the **Dockbar**. Once you go to your private pages, you will find My Communities Portlet. It has three tabs—**Communities | Own, Communities | Have Joined**, and **Available Communities**. Under the **Communities | Own** tab, you will see a button **Add Community**. You can click on this button to add a new community. It will show you the same interface to add a community which you just used to add the **Gardening DIY** community.

Have a go hero – adding more communities to the CIGNEX Neighborhood

We have just discussed about the communities and ways to add communities in Liferay Portal. Are you confident enough to add a new community to the portal on your own? Well, let's check it out.

As per our requirements, we still need to add four more communities to the portal—Games and Sports, Cricket Player, Neighborhood Exchange, and Around the Corner. Log in to Liferay as a default admin (**test@liferay.com / test**) and create the following four communities:

- To create Games and Sports, go to **Control Panel** and create this community selecting the **Communities** option. Keep this community as an open community.

- To create Cricket Players, use the My Communities Portlet. Keep this community as an Open community.

- Use one of the two preceding methods to create Neighborhood Exchange and Around the Corner communities. Keep both of these communities as open communities as well.

Once you are done, you should have five communities added to the portal.

Pop quiz – true or false?

State whether the following statements are true or false:

1. Every portal must have at least one community.
2. It is possible to create a child community under any community.
3. All types of communities are visible in My Communities portlet.
4. Communities can be Open, Restricted and Private.
5. You can assign an entire organization to the community.
6. It is possible to categorize a community while creating it.

What suits your portal—organization or community?

We are now aware of the organization and community concepts in Liferay. We discussed the similarities between organizations and communities when we started discussing the topic of community.

Now, the question is: how do you determine what suits your needs? In other words, when should you use the community and when should you use the organization in your portal?

Using organizations

You should consider the following points when you want to use the organization in your portal:

- The users of the portal fit in some sort of hierarchy like the Company-Department-Team
- When a user and the group has very tight coupling, for example, the user cannot join or leave the group at his/her will very easily
- When you have some kind of delegation chain in the hierarchy
- When you want the admin of the group to manage the member's profile

Using communities

You should consider the following points when you want to use the community in your portal:

♦ The users of the portal do not fit in any hierarchy. They are like an ad-hoc group of people and join or leave the group at any point of time.

♦ There is some function or area of interest which cuts across the entire structure of the portal.

We have used organization and community both in the implementation of our CIGNEX Neighborhood Portal.

Now, take a break from reading and think of the scenarios when you would consider using only organizations or only communities in a portal implementation.

User groups—arbitrary collection of users

We have discussed two ways of collecting users—organizations and communities. Both of them have their own set of pages and the users who are member of the organization or community can access those pages.

Now, think about a situation where you have a portal for the intranet and we have a few members who like to blog in that portal. So we have a small group of bloggers inside a community. How do we handle this situation? We know that to organize users, we create an organization or a community. However, when it comes to organizing a group which does not fit in the organization or community definition, we can use the user group functionality of Liferay.

User groups are arbitrary collections of users and are created by the portal admin. We create user groups when the users don't have any obvious organization- or community-based attribute which can bring them together. Once the user group is created, we can assign users to the user group. User groups can be assigned to a role, organization, or a community as well. On doing so, all the members of the user group will get permissions associated with the role or become member of the organization or the community respectively.

Time for action – adding a user group to CIGNEX Neighborhood

Since we have discussed user groups, let's add one the portal:

1. Start your server, if not already started. Once your server is started type in
   `http://neighbourhood.cignex.com`.

2. Log in to CIGNEX neighborhood portal with Liferay default admin credentials:
   Username: **test@liferay.com** and **Password**: **test**.

3. Select **Control Panel** from the **Manage** option in the Dockbar. On the left-hand
   panel, you will see four sections: **Personal**, **Content**, **Portal**, and **Server**.

4. Click on the **User Groups** link under the **Portal** section as displayed in the
   following screenshot:

5. On clicking the link, it will open an interface which displays a list of all the user
   groups created in the portal. Currently, we do not have any user groups created in
   CIGNEX Neighborhood. Click on the **Add** option to add a new user group. You will
   see the following interface, when you click on the **Add** button:

6.   In the preceding interface, the **Name** field indicates the name of the user group we are creating. Give the name as **Bowlers**. The **Description** field allows you to add the description of the user group. Just type in **This is a Bowlers user group created for the Cricket Player Community**.

7.   Once you are done, click on **Save** to add the group to the portal.

This group has been created within the portal for the Cricket Player community. So you have to assign the group to the community. Follow these steps to assign the user group to the community:

1.   Click on the **Communities** link under the **Portal** section in the control panel.

2.   Click on the **Action** button associated with the Cricket Players community and select the **Assign Members** option.

3.   You will see an interface to assign members to the community.

4.   Click on the **User Group** tab from the three options—**Users**, **Organizations** and **User Groups**.

5.   You will see the **Current** and **Available** tabs under it on selecting the user groups.

6.   Click on the **Available** tab. You will see **Bowlers** user group. Check the box associated with the user group and click on the **Update Associated** button.

7.   Once you click on that, you will see a message that **Your request has processed successfully**. This will associate the user group to the community.

8. You can assign a user or organization to the community in the same way you assigned the user group.

Remember, the user group is always created at the portal level and never within an organization or a community. However, you can assign the user group to the organization or the community.

Time for action – understanding the actions associated with the group

Once you have created the user group and saved it, you will see it is added in your portal. Click on the **View All** option next to the **Add** option in the user group interface. It will display a list of all the user groups in the portal. Let's look at the different actions associated with the user group:

1. Click on the **Actions** button displayed against the **Bowlers** user group.

2. It will open a list of actions which you can perform with the **Bowlers** user group. It is displayed in the following screenshot:

3. The options and their uses are as follows:

- **Edit**—It will take you to the edit screen of the user group and you will be able to edit name and description of the user group.

- **Permissions**—It defines which role can perform what actions on this user group.

- ❑ **Manage Pages**—User groups cannot have their own set of pages. However, you can create page template for the user group. When a user is assigned to the user group having the page template, the page template will automatically be copied to that user's personal pages.

- ❑ **Assign Members**—This option will allow you to search for and add the users to the user group from the portal.

- ❑ **View Users**—You can view the users who are added to this user group.

- ❑ **Delete**—You can delete the user group from the portal.

What just happened?

You have created a user group and understood all the actions associated with the user group. You have also associated the user group with the community.

We have also seen that a user group is always created at a portal level and then assigned to an organization or a community.

User group and page templates

In the previous section, we mentioned that we can assign a page template to the user group. This feature of Liferay can be useful when we want to provide a different page configuration to each user depending on the user's profile. For example, we can have a portal of a company and we want to have certain applications to be on the user's page, if the user is in HR group or other applications, if the user is in Finance group. We can do that by creating HR and Finance user groups and associating page templates with those groups. Once the page template is created, we can add portlets to the page template.

Let's see how we can create a page template, add applications to the page template, and how they will affect the user's personal pages.

Time for action – creating a page template for the Bowlers user group

1. Log in to CIGNEX Neighborhood portal using default admin credentials.

2. Go to **Control Panel** and click on **User Groups** under the **Portal** section.

3. Click on the **Action** button next to the **Bowlers** user group and select the **Manage Pages** option. You will see the following screen:

4. You will notice that the **Public Pages** tab has been selected for the Bowlers user group. The **Name** field allows you to add the name of the page. Add the name as **Bowler's Page**, keep type as **Portlet**, and click on the **Add** page.

5. We will discuss all the options of the **Manage** page in detail in the next chapter.

6. This will add a new public page template called **Bowler's Page** in the Bowlers user group. You will notice that the page has been added under the Bowlers public page as displayed in the following screenshot. Select the **Bowler's Page** and click on **View Pages**. It will open the page in a new tab.

7. When the **Bowler's Page** is opened in a new tab, click on the **Add** application and add a **Message Board** portlet to the page. Drag the portlet to the right column of the layout. Once done, close the page.

8. Now, click on the user group again and select the **Assign Members** option from the **Action** button of the Bowlers user group.

9. Currently, you will not have any user associated with the group. So you will not be able to see any user under the **Current** tab. Click on the **Available** tab. You will see the **Test** user (Liferay default admin) under this tab. Check the box associated with the **Test** user and click on **Update Association**. This will add the **Test** user to the **Bowlers** user group.

10. Now, click on the **Back** button to go back to **Control Panel**. Once done, click on **My Public Pages** under the **Go To** section from the Dockbar.

11. You will see that the **Bowler's Page** has been added to your public page. Click on the page. You will see that the page has the **Message Boards** portlet on it as displayed in the following screenshot:

This is how you can associate page templates to the user group. You can add as many portlets to the page template as you like. The page will be available to a user's personal pages once the user is associated with that user group.

What just happened?

We have seen the relationship between the user group and the page template. You are now aware of how to associate a page template to the user group. You also know when you should use a page template in the portal.

Pop quiz – multiple choice

1. Users groups in Liferay are created under:
    a. Community
    b. Organization
    c. Portal
    d. All of the above

2. User groups in Liferay can be assigned to?
    a. User only
    b. Role only
    c. Organization
    d. Community

3. A page template in Liferay is assigned to?

    a. An individual user

    b. Organization

    c. User group

    d. None of the above

Summary

We have understood site designing concepts in this chapter. You should now be aware of the following topics:

◆ Basics of the portal design. Components involved in portal design.

◆ CIGNEX Neighborhood portal requirements.

◆ The Beginning with the End approach of portal design.

◆ Organization and community concept of Liferay. We also discussed when to use the organization and the community in portal design.

◆ User groups in Liferay Portal. We have discussed the importance of page templates and the way to associate page templates with the user groups.

Now, as we have the groundwork ready for the portal implementation, we will start building our portal by adding pages to the organization and communities, adding users, and creating roles in the organizations and communities. So get ready for managing users, pages, and permissions, which are discussed in the next chapter.

6
Managing Pages, Users, and Permissions

Pages, users, and permission are critical aspects of any site. Pages define any site structure. Users are the backbone and consumers of a site. Permissions and roles act as a security guard to a site. This chapter will focus on creating and managing them.

In the previous chapters, we have learned how to configure a neighborhood site to have a domain name. We have renamed the guest community to CIGNEX Neighborhood and have started building a Liferay site by adding communities, organizations, and user groups.

In this chapter, we continue site building by adding pages, users, and permissions. We will start learning about page management, which includes adding pages, understanding page-level attributes, and other features provided by Liferay for page management. After that we will learn about user management, which will include adding users, modifying their profile, and associating them with the community. In the last section, we will explore permission management in Liferay, which will include creation of roles, assigning community/organization roles to users, defining resources, and portlet-level permission.

In this chapter, we shall learn how to:

- ◆ Add pages to communities/organizations using Manage Pages Interface
- ◆ Define page-level attributes to provide page metadata
- ◆ A create administrator user to manage a neighborhood site

- Modify a user profile to change personal details of user
- Add neighborhood members
- Add users to communities and organizations
- Disable self registration to a site for guest users
- Create a portal role and define page-level permission to restrict access
- Create community/organization-specific roles
- Define permission for entry-level resources

So let's dive into it.

Checklist

This chapter is a continuation of the Neighborhood site example we started in the previous chapters. Before we begin with this chapter, the following should be already done:

- Configuration of Neighborhood domain name as discussed in *Chapter 4, Tips and Tricks-Advanced Configuration*
- Renaming of Guest community to CIGNEX Neighborhood as discussed in *Chapter 4, Tips and Tricks-Advanced Configuration*
- Creation of Neighborhood communities and organizations as discussed in *Chapter 5, Building Your First Liferay Site*

Creating pages for the Neighborhood site

In the last chapter, you created various neighborhood communities and organizations. Now let's define their structure by adding pages to them. Pages are the building block of any website. Liferay pages belong to communities and organizations or a user's personal community. Liferay has divided pages into two categories—public and private.

Public pages are by default accessible to all the users including guest users, that is non-registered users. They generally used to define most of the public facing websites with unrestricted access. However, Liferay permission system allows you to restrict access to public pages by modifying page-level permission.

Private pages are accessible only to members, that is private pages of a specific community will be available to only that community's members. It will not be available to guest users and other site users. The same holds true for private pages of the organizations and user's personal community, that is My Community.

Liferay provides the Manage Pages Portlet to manage pages. Let's explore more of it.

Creating pages for Neighborhood communities

In this section, you will create pages for communities of a Neighborhood site.

Time for action – creating pages for Neighborhood communities

1. Log in to the Neighborhood site as default Administrator (**test@liferay.com** / **test**).

2. In Top menu items, under the **Manage** menu click on **Control Panel**. It will open Control Panel for you. As you have learned in *Chapter 3, Understanding Portal Basics and Theming*, **Control Panel** consists of four sections, **Personal**, **Content**, **Portal**, and **Server**. The **Content** section allows you to mange various assets (pages, blogs, wiki, and so on) for communities and organizations.

3. In the **Content** section, by default **CIGNEX Neighbourhood** (Guest) community will be selected. This indicates that any content added using links of this section will be a part of this community.

4. Now when you click on the **Pages** link under the **Content** section, it will open the Manage Pages interface as shown in the following screenshot. As you know, the Manage Pages interface has a top-level menu and sub-level menu. The top-level menu contains three links, **Public Pages**, **Private Pages**, and **Settings**. By default, **Public Pages** link is selected and the sub menu of the **Public Pages** is visible, which contains menu items **Pages**, **Look and Feel**, **Export/Import**. Out of these, **Pages** is by default selected. It contains a tree view of pages and an interface to add new pages as shown in the following screenshot. Notice the **Welcome** page in the page tree. By default, this page gets created during installation under the Guest community and it's landing page to a site.

5. Under the **New Page** section, enter the page name **User Registration** in the **Name** field. In the **Template** field drop-down, leave the default value **(None)**. This drop-down contains other options as well like **Blogs**, **Content**, and **Wiki**. Page templates in Liferay allow you to create pages with predefined portlets. Blogs, content, and wiki are three out-of-box page templates created by Liferay during installation. You can create more page templates using the **Page Templates** link under the **Portal** section.

6. Next is the **Type** field, which defines the type of content the page will contain. As the User Registration page will contain a set of portlets, select **Portlet** in this field. Other options of this drop-down will be explained in a later section of this chapter. Leave the **Hidden** checkbox unselected as this page needs to be visible on the site. After that, click on the **Add Page** button. You will be staying on the same screen with the **User Registration** page being added to the CIGNEX Neighborhood community under the **Welcome** page.

The hidden checkbox allows you to make any page hidden from users. If you select this checkbox, then the page will not be visible in the page navigation menu of the site.

7. Now add one more top-level page **About Us** to the **CIGNEX Neighbourhood** community. Enter **About Us** in the **Name** field and leave other fields with their default values. Now click on the **Add Page** button. This will add **About Us** top-level page under the **CIGNEX Neighbourhood** community.

8. Let's now add a child page to the **About Us** page. By default pages are added to top level, so first you need to select the page under which you want to add the child page. Select **About Us** from left hand-side page tree by clicking on it.

9. You will then be brought to a screen as shown in the following screenshot. It has three top-level menu **Page**, **Children**, and **Look and Feel**. By default, the **Children** menu item will be selected. Now enter the page name as **History** in the **Name** field and leave other fields as they are and click on the **Add Page** button.

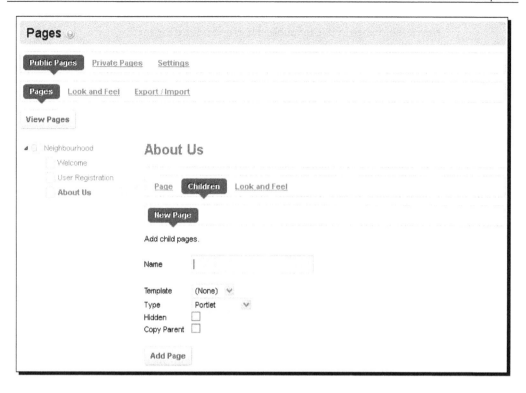

10. In order to view the newly added page, expand the **About Us** page. You will see the **History** page under the **About Us** page. Similarly, add the **Area Map** children page under the **About Us** page.

11. Now to create private pages select **Private Pages** from the top menu.

12. Private pages are created just like public pages. Enter page name as **Gossip** in the **Name** field and leave the other fields as it is and click on **Add Page**. It will create the **Gossip** page.

13. Now let's see how pages appear for the **CIGNEX Neighbourhood** community. Click back on **Public Pages** from the top menu. After that, click on the **View Pages** button. A new browser window/tab will open to show public pages of the community in a new tab. You can see all three public pages appearing in the top-level menu. Mouse over to the **About Us** page and notice that **History** page appears in second-level menu. Similarly, click on **Private Pages** from the top menu and click on the **View Pages** button to see the private pages of the community.

Notice the change in URL for public pages and private pages:

Public page URL: `http://neighborhood.cignex.com/en_GB/web/neighbourhood/home`.

Private page URL:

`http://neighborhood.cignex.com/en_GB/group/neighbourhood/about-us`.

The public page URL contains web and private page URL contains group. So this way, you can have the same page name in both public and privates pages. Also, private page URL will be accessible only to users who are a member of the community, otherwise it will redirect to the login page.

What just happened?

You have just created public and private pages in communities of the Neighbourhood site. You have also created child pages under top-level pages. This is the basic requirement of any website and starting point in site creation. You have used the Manage Pages portlet from the **Pages** link under the **Content** section of **Control Panel**.

The Manage Pages interface can also be accessed in other ways as well:

♦ To manage the current page which you are viewing on the site select the **Page** option from Dock.

♦ To manage pages of any community, use the **Communities** link from the **Portal** section of **Control Panel** and select the **Manage Pages** option from the **Action** button for the community whose pages you want to manage.

♦ To manage pages of organizations, use the **Organization** link from the **Portal** section of the **Control Panel** and select the **Manage Pages** option from the **Action** button for the organization whose pages you want to manage.

♦ To manage pages of the current logged-in user, you can use the **My Pages** link from the **Personal** section of the **Control Panel**.

The Manage Pages interface is very user friendly and powerful for page management. Now let's understand the Mange Page interface in more detail. It has three top-level menu items as follows:

♦ **Public Pages**—You can manage public pages for current communities/organizations using this interface. **Public Pages** has three sub menu items.

- **Pages**—This menu item allows you to manage pages. It has the **View Pages** button which allows you to see how pages will appear in the real site. It has the page navigation tree which allows you to see the complete page hierarchy. It also has an option to expand or collapse a specific page tree. If you have selected the root element, which is the community or organization name, then it will show two options, **New Page** to add a new page and **Display Order** which allows you to define the order in which pages will be displayed on the site. If you have selected any page, then it will show three options, **Page**, **Children**, and **Look and Feel**. The **Page** option will define page-level attributes. The **Children** option will allow you to add child pages to the current selected page. The **Look and Feel** option will allow you to set the theme specific to current selected page.

- **Look and Feel**—This feature will allow you to set a theme for a set of pages, that is, communities or organizations level. It allows you to set theme for Regular Browsers and Mobile Browsers. It also has a feature to provide custom CSS, which will be added after the theme for Regular Browsers.

- **Export/Import**—This is a very important and useful feature. It allows you to export pages in a Liferay-specific archive format known as LAR (Liferay ARchive). You can export either public or private pages at a time for a specific community or organization. Similarly, you can import a LAR file generated from a community or organization of another site's community or organization. You can also import pages between communities and organizations of the same site. This is very useful for site migration from one Liferay server to another Liferay server. Export functionality not only exports pages but it also includes portlet setup on each page. Also, it can include data of portlets, permissions, theme, categories, and so on. A similar configuration is available when you perform import to define what should be imported from the LAR file.

 There is a limitation in the export/import feature of Liferay. It is version dependent, which means you cannot export/import LAR files between different versions of Liferay.

- **Private Pages**—You can mange private pages using this interface. Sub menu items of private pages have the same functionality you have seen for public pages.

- **Settings**—This interface allows you to provide various community/organization-level settings related to pages. This feature will be visible when you access the Manage Pages interface from the **Control Panel**. It does not appear when you access the Manage Pages interface from **Docbar | Manage | Page**. You already learned about them in *Chapter 3, Understanding Portal Basics and Theming*.

In the next section, we will explore page-level attributes.

Have a go hero – other top-level and child pages

Do you see yourself as someone who can add pages to communities? Do you feel you have gained knowledge of the basics of Liferay page management? Let's check it out. You should now add some more public and private pages' communities and organizations of the Neighborhood site:

- **Daily Tips** public page in the CIGNEX Neighborhood community
- **Online Games** public page in the Sports and Games community
- **Coming Events** public page in the Cricket Players community
- **Vegetable Schedule** public page in the Gardening DIY community
- **Breaking News** public page in the Neighborhood Exchange community
- **Our Videos** private page in the Neighborhood Exchange community
- **Photo Sharing** private page in the Neighborhood Exchange community
- **Active Motions** private page in the Neighbors Congress organization
- **Your Opinions** public page in the Neighbors Congress organization
- **Security Information** private page in the Security Council organization
- **Security Monitoring** private page in the Security Council organization
- **Neighborhood Prosperity** public page in the Chamber of Commerce organization
- **Arbitration Notice** public page in the Neighborhood Arbitration Committee organization

 You can add pages to the organization in exactly the same way you did for a community. Select organization from the **Content** tab and then select the **Pages** link to go to the Manage Pages interface for the organization.

Setting page-level attributes to define page characteristics

You have just created pages in the last section. Liferay has a rich set of page-level attributes. Page-level attributes means a set of properties associated with each page and they define the characteristics of the page. They also provide very useful functionalities to the site administrator.

Let's explore them.

You will now change the HTML title and Friendly URL of the User Registration page created under the CIGNEX Neighborhood Community. We will also cover what Friendly URL is in a later part of this section.

Time for action – providing a HTML title and friendly URL for a page

1. Log in as default portal administrator and go to **Control Panel**.

2. For CIGNEX Neighborhood Community, click on the **Pages** link. It will open the Manage Pages interface. On that, click on the **User Registration** page from the page tree. It will show you a content area with three menus, **Page**, **Children**, and **Look and Feel**. By default, the **Children** menu will be selected. Now click on the **Page** menu item.

3. You will then be brought to a screen as shown in the following screenshot, where page-level attribute will be visible for User registration page. In the **HTML Title** field, enter **Registration**.

4. Now in the **Friendly URL** field, you can see non-editable URL with format **http://neighborhood.cignex.com/web/neighbourhood** as shown in the following screenshot, which will be followed by a textbox with value **/user-registration**. Change this textbox value to **/registration**.

5. Then you can scroll down and click on the **Save** button at the bottom of the screen. It will stay on the same page with a **Your request processed successfully** message on top of page to indicate that the information has been updated successfully.

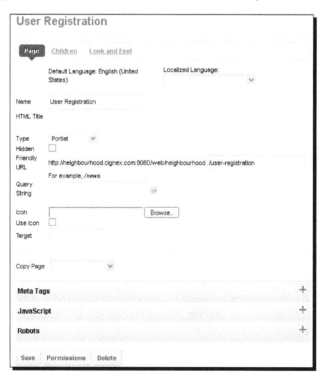

What just happened?

You have changed the **HTML Title** and **Friendly URL** attributes of the **User Registration** page using the Manage Pages Portlet.

Let's learn about the important page-level attributes. Liferay provides the following page-level attributes to each page:

◆ **Default Language** and **Localized Language**: This drop-down is used for the localization of **Name** and **HTML Title** fields in various languages for each page. This helps in localization of your site in languages available in the portal. You can also configure the available languages list using **Control Panel | Portal | Portal Settings | Display Settings**.

◆ **Name**: This is the name of the page and it will appear in the **Menu** item on the site. You can provide the name of the page for **Default Language** as well as any localized language.

◆ **HTML Title**: It appears on the title bar of the browser window. You can provide the name of the page for **Default Language** as well as any localized language.

◆ **Type**: This attribute defines the type of content this page will hold. Liferay provides the following options for the type of page:

   ❑ **Portlet**—This is the default type of page and it allows you to put portlets on pages. The structure of portlets on pages will be defined by the layout template assigned to a page. This is the most recommended and widely used type of page in Liferay.

   ❑ **Panel**—This type of page can hold a number of applications and access is provided through the menu. Use this type if you want a feature to navigate between the Liferay portlets.

   ❑ **Embedded**—Use this type to show an external website through iframe. It's a quick way to integrate external website on your site.

   ❑ **Web Content**—This type of page shows single content created using Liferay Content Management System (CMS). We will explore more on Liferay CMS in the next chapter.

   ❑ **URL**—This type of page is used for linking to another page. They don't have any content on the page. The page name will appear on the menu and clicking on it will take you to the URL associated with this page.

   ❑ **Link to Page**—This is a special scenario of the URL type where you can link one page to another page rather than external URL. The page will appear on the menu and clicking on it will take you to the page associated with this page.

- **Hidden**: Select this checkbox if you want to make the page invisible and it will not appear in the menu. You can access such a page by its friendly URL directly. Also, you can redirect to this page from other pages.

- **Friendly URL**: This attribute allows you to define the user friendly URL for a page, which you can use at various places on the site or post on an external site to provide a link to this page. This URL field is relative to the community URL. This features helps in SEO for the site.

- **Query String**: Use this attribute to pass any query string parameter to the page.

- **Icon**: To display the page-level icon.

- **Use Icon**: This icon will be displayed only if this checkbox is enabled.

- **Target**: It behaves similar to the target attribute of the `<a>` tag of HTML. It takes a value like `_new` to open the page in a new window, `_self` to open in the current window, and so on.

- **Copy Page**: This allows you to copy the content of any other page to this page.

- **Meta Tags—Keywords**—You can define keywords which will be added to HML when this page is being accessed. This is a useful feature for Search Engine Optimization (SEO). It also gives a feature for the provided language specific keywords as well.

- **JavaScript**—You can add custom JavaScript to be executed when this page gets loaded by providing under this attribute.

 Reflect on the page management required for your site. What modifications would you make to what has been discussed in this chapter so far to suit your site?

Pop quiz – true or false?

State whether the following statements are true or false:

1. Private pages are accessible to all types of users.
2. Page URL can be changed using the Friendly URL attribute.
3. Themes can be assigned to individual pages.
4. Hidden pages will appear on the menu.

Exploring the User section

You have just learned about page management in Liferay. Another important aspect of building a site would be users. Users are always considered to be the central data points for any portal. They are the consumer of all the functionality developed and frankly speaking, they are the reason sites are being developed. Can you think of any site which has been developed and doesn't have any users? (Excluding scarped site development projects.) Liferay provides an easy-to-use and feature-rich user management portlet as a built-in functionality.

Before we create a user, we need to perform configuration to enable automatic addition of Summary and Requests portlets to users' pages.

Configuration for user pages' default porltets

In this section, we will do configuration to add the Summary portlet on the default public page and the Requests portlet on the default private page of the user. This configuration is required before we create users so that these portlets appear on a user's public and private pages. They are required for the Chat functionality, which will be discussed in *Chapter 8, Exploring Communities*.

1. Stop the Liferay Portal server, if it is running.

2. Locate the `liferay-portal-6.0.6\tomcat-6.0.29\webapps\ROOT\WEB-INF\classes\portal-ext.properties` file in the root directory where you installed Liferay Portal server.

3. Open the `portal-ext.properties` file in text editor and add the following properties at the end of the file and save it.

   Add the following two properties to `portal-ext.properties`:

   # This property will add three portlets Summary, Blogs, and Search to the first column of default public page of new users:

   ```
   default.user.public.layout.column-1=1_WAR_
   socialnetworkingportlet,82,3
   ```

   # This property will add four portlets Requests, Language, Dictionary, and Directory to the first column of default private page of new users.

   ```
   default.user.private.layout.column-1=121,82,23,11
   ```

4. Start Liferay Server.

Let's get started with creating users.

Creating an administrator user to manage the Neighborhood site

To manage any site in Liferay, common practice would be to create a user with an Administrator role rather than using the default portal administration. Having separate administrator user for each site enables more defined delegation model and access control. In order to do this you would need to create a new Liferay user for yourself and assign an administration role.

Let's get started with creating a new user.

Time for action – creating a user and assigning an administrator role

1. Log in as a portal administrator and go to **Control Panel**.

2. On **Control Panel**, Scroll down to the **Portal** section and click on the **Users** menu item. It will bring you to the User Management portlet of Liferay.

3. On the **Users** screen, click on the **Add** link. It will open a screen to add a new user as shown in the following screenshot.

4. On the **New User** screen, enter the following values as shown in the following screenshot:

   - **Screen Name: jeffm**
   - **Email Address: jeff.mcclure@cignex.com**
   - **First Name: Jeff**
   - **Last Name: Mcclure**
   - **Birthday: 23 May 1980**

These five are mandatory fields to create any user in Liferay.

5. Click on the **Save** button from the right-hand side menu items. It will add a new user and show a screen with detailed profile information for the user.

6. Next step would be to set the password for user. By default, Liferay generates random password and sends to the e-mail address provided during user creation. On the user profile screen, from the right-hand side menu, click on **Password** under the **User Information** section.

7. It will bring you to the password management screen as shown in the following screenshot. Enter **test123** in the **New Password** and **Enter Again** fields. Then scroll down and click on the **Save** button on the right-hand menu. It will save a new password for this user.

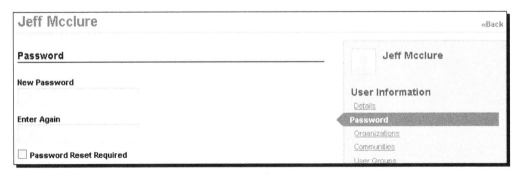

8. Now on the right-hand side menu, click on the **Roles** link from the **Details** section. By default, **Power User** should be assigned to user under the **Regular Roles** section. Click on the **Select** link from the **Regular Roles** section. It will open a pop-up with **Regular Roles** listed. Select the **Administrator** role link from that list. It will close the pop-up and bring back to the roles screen with two roles for your user—**Power User** and **Administrator**—as shown in the following screenshot:

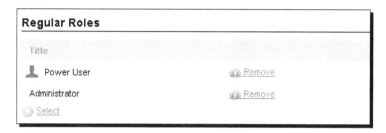

9. Now you should save the changes you made in user roles by clicking on the **Save** button on the right-hand side menu. This will assign administrator rights to your newly created user.

Now let's log in with a newly created user and verify whether administrative privilege is assigned or not.

1. First, log out from the default Liferay administrator and then log in as **Jeff Mcclure** (**jeff.mcclure@cignex.com / test123**).

2. Since the user is logging in for the first time and you have enabled **Terms of Use** (as discussed in *Chapter 4, Tips and Tricks—Advanced Configuration*). User will be presented with the **Terms of Use** screen and click on **Accept**. It will bring you to the **Password Reminder** screen. Choose the first question and enter **Mike** in the **Answer** field and click on the **Save** button. You will then land on the default home page. Let's go to the **Control Panel** to verify administrative access of this user. On the home page, go to the **Manage** menu and click on **Control Panel**. It should take you to the **Control Panel**.

3. Verify that the **Personal**, **Content**, **Portal**, and **Server** sections of the Control Panel are visible and accessible to your user as shown in the following screenshot:

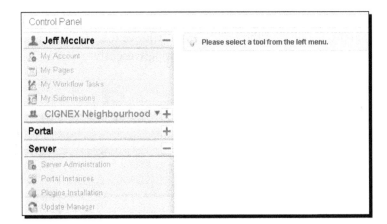

What just happened?

You have just seen the User Management portlet of Liferay in the **Control Panel** and created a new user then changed the password. After that, you assigned the administrator role to the new user. Then, you logged in to Liferay with that user and accessed **Control Panel** to confirm all the administrative functionalities are available to him.

Let's explore more on Liferay User Management. In Liferay, users are created under Portal instance and not directly under any community/organization. Users are associated with communities and organizations. This allows you to associate a user with multiple communities and organizations.

A Liferay server can have more than one portal instance. Each portal instance can have a set of users, communities, organizations, roles, and so on.

To create a new user in Liferay, you need to provide five mandatory fields as follows. If you leave any of them empty during user creation, it will show the appropriate error message.

- **Screen Name**
- **Email Address**
- **First Name**
- **Last Name**
- **Date of Birth** (however, this field will never be empty as it is a calendar gadget)

Screen Name is a unique identifier for users in Liferay along with e-mail address, that is you cannot duplicate screen name for users. Also, you can use screen name for login just like e-mail address. However, for that you need to change the authentication mechanism from e-mail address to screen name at **Control Panel | Portal | Portal Settings | Configuration | Authentication | General | How do users authenticate dropdown**.

There are two other menu items in the user creation screen on the right-hand side menu as shown in the screenshot with the **New User** page.

- **Organizations**—This allows you to assign users to a specific organization during creation
- **Pages**—This allows you to choose specific page templates for a user's public and private pages

Each new user gets public and private pages. You can access it from the **Personal** section—**My Pages** link of the **Control Panel** or from the **Go To** menu of Dockbar.

Liferay also sends **Account Creation Notification** to a new user on the e-mail ID provided during creation, if the mail server is properly set up and the provided e-mail address is valid. You can configure the content of this e-mail at **Control Panel | Portal | Portal Settings | Configuration | Email Notifications interface**. You have already done this in *Chapter 4, Tips and Tricks—Advanced Configuration*. This interface also allows you to change the content of **Password Changed Notification** and **Password Reset Notification**.

You have also seen the User Management Portlet interface which provides the following features:

- **Add/Edit User**—Allows you to create a new user and edit the user profile of the existing user.
- **Search User**—Allows you to search users using various filter options.
- **Deactivate/Delete User**—When you deactivate a user, he/she will no longer be able to log in to the site but their details are not be deleted. This feature is useful to disable users for a specific timeline. **Delete User** will delete the user with all details from the system. You can delete a user only if it is deactivated. A deactivated user can be searched by selecting **No** for the **Active** drop-down in the **Advance Search Options**.
- **Impersonate User**—This feature allows you to access the site as another user, to verify how the site appears to that user and also to check the permissions granted to the user.
- **Permissions**—This feature allows you to manage permission for a specific user.
- **Manage Pages**—Takes you to manage pages of a user's public and private pages.

Editing the user profile

Liferay provides each user with a profile that contains various personal details. You can access the profile of any user from the User Management Portlet. The current logged in user can also access his/her own profile from the **My Account** link in the **Personal** section.

You will now modify the profile details for the user created in the last section and explore the sections of the user Profile.

Time for action – modifying user details

In this section, you will edit the **Title** and **Middle name** of the user created in the last section. Also, you will specify an additional e-mail address for the user. After that, you will select the preferred language for the user.

1. Log in to your site with **jeff.mcclure@cignex.com / test123** and go to **Control Panel**.

2. In **Control Panel**, from the **Portal** section you should click on the **Users** link. It will open the User Management Portlet and show you a list of existing users.

3. From the list of users, click on the **Actions** button for **Jeff Mcclure** user. It will open a pop-up with three actions: **Edit**, **Permissions**, and **Manage Pages**. Click on the **Edit** link. It will open a profile for that user. The user profile in Liferay has been divided into **User Information**, **Identification**, and **Miscellaneous** sections as shown in the following screenshot. By default, the **User Information—Details** menu will be selected, which allows modifying basic demographic information for user.

 The current logged in user can also go to user profile from the **My Account** link in **Control Panel** or clicking on the username displayed on the right-hand side of the Dockbar.

4. Now select **Mr.** from the **Title** drop-down and enter **Tony** in the **Middle name** field. You should notice that on the right-hand side is (**Modified**) text in green next to the **Details** menu. This is a useful feature to indicate which sections have been modified but not saved. After that click on **Additional Email Addresses** from the **Identification** section on the right-hand side menu. On that screen, enter **jeff.cignex@gmail.com** in the **Email Address** field.

5. Next, click on **Display Settings** from the **Miscellaneous** section. It will take you to the screen where you can modify the preferred language for the user. From the **Language** drop-down select **English (United Kingdom)**.

6. Now from the right-hand side menu, click on the **Save** button to save all modified details for the user and bring you back to the same screen with the **Your request processed successfully** message.

What just happened?

We just modified some of the personal details through the User Profile interface. Let's learn a bit more about the User Profile interface of Liferay.

The User Profile interface has been divided into **User Information**, **Identification**, and **Miscellaneous**. Each of these sections contains various links to perform specific operations. They have been mentioned along with their usage in the following table:

Section	Link	Usage
User Information	Details	Contains the basic demographic information such as e-mail address, screen name, first name, last name, and date of birth. This information can be modified using this link.
	Password	Sets the password for the user.
	Organizations	Assigns the user to specific organizations.
	Communities	Assigns the user to specific communities.
	User Groups	Assigns the user to specific user groups.
	Roles	Assigns the user to specific roles.
	Pages	Access the user's private and public pages.
	Categorization	Assigns tags and categories to the user.
Identification	Addresses	Adds one or more addresses for the user. You can also classify addresses as Business, Personal, Other.
	Phone Numbers	Adds one or more users' phone numbers. You can associate type with each phone number.
	Additional Email Addresses	Adds more e-mail addresses for the user, if they have other provided in the **Details** link.
	Websites	Adds one or more user websites. You can associate the type with each website like Blog , Business, Personal, Other
	Instant Messenger	Adds user's instant messenger screen name for various instant messenger services.
	Social Network	Provides user ID for various social networking sites such as Facebook, MySpace, Twitter, and so on.
	OpenID	Provides the user's OpenID.
Miscellaneous	Announcements	Subscribes for various announcements on site and communication mechanism.
	Display Settings	Allows setting preferred language and time zone for user. Also, allows setting a greeting message to appear on Docbar when a user logs in.
	Comments	Adds any comment for the user.
	Custom Fields	All the custom fields configured for the user asset will appear here. The user can provide values for them. We will explore more on custom fields in a later section of this chapter.

Assigning users to Neighborhood communities and organizations

In this section, you will create a regular user and associate user to Neighbourhood communities and organizations. A user can be associated with more than one community/organization and for each of them auser can have a different set of community/organization roles.

Let's do it.

Time for action – assigning a user to communities and organizations

1. Log in to Liferay using administrator user (**Jeff Mcclure**) and go to the **Control Panel**.

2. First, you will add a regular user to the site. Click on the **Users** link from the **Portal** section and click on the **Add** button. It will open a screen similar to the **New User** screen.

3. Enter the following data in the fields:
   - **Screen name**: **markb** , **Email Address**: **mark.bensar@cignex.com**
   - **First Name**: **Mark**, **Last Name**: **Bensar**, **Birth date**: **12, January, 1960**

4. After that, click on the **Save** button. It will add a new user and show the profile of the user.

5. Now click on the **Password** link from the **User Information** section and change the password for **Mark** to **test123**. Also, select the **Password Reset Required** checkbox. This will ensure that the user will be asked to change the password on first login. Click on the **Save** button to save changes.

6. Now go to **Portal | Communities**. Click on the **Action** button next to **CIGNEX Neighbourhood** community. It will open a pop-up menu. Click on the **Assign Members** menu item. It will open a screen similar to the one shown in the following screenshot, from where you can add/remove users in a community. There are two sections, **Current** and **Available**.

7. Click on the **Available** link and select the checkbox for the **Mark Bensar** user from the list of users and click on **Update Associations**. You will be staying on the same screen and the success message **Your request processed successfully** will appear on top to indicate that user association has been done. It will associate Mark to this community and he gets a community member role.

8. Now click on the **Current** link. It should show the **Mark Bensar** username in the list of users associated with the community as shown in the following screenshot. Also, notice that you can also add organizations and **User Groups** as members of the community. Similarly, assign this user to the **Sports and Games**, **Cricket Players**, **Gardening DIY community**, **Neighbourhood exchange**, and **Around the Corner** communities.

9. Next you should explore user association to organization by assigning **Mark** to **Neighbours Congress** organization. Moreover, it is similar to what you did for communities. Click on **Control Panel | Portal | Organizations**. Click on the **Actions** button next to the **Neighbours Congress** organization. It will open a pop-up; click on the **Assign Members** menu item. It will open a screen similar to the following screenshot for communities but with a few less options than operations available for the community. Using the **Available** link associate the user to this organization as you have done for the community. After association Mark gets organization member role for Neighbourhood Congress organization.

10. Similarly, assign this user (**Mark Bensar**) to the **Security Council**, **Chamber of Commerce**, and **Neighborhood Arbitration Committee** organizations.

What just happened?

We just associated the **Mark Benser** user to communities and organizations of Neighborhood site.

Let's explore a bit more on user association to communities and organization. Once you associate a user with community/organization, he/she gets a member role for that community/organization. Also, now the user can access public and private pages of community/organization from the **Go To** menu of the Dockbar as shown in the following screenshot:

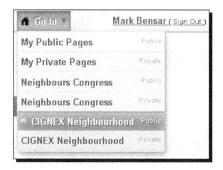

Public pages of any community/organization will be available to all users (including guest users, that is non registered users) of the site irrespective of whether the user associated with community/organization or not.

However, private pages of a community/organization will be available only to users who are members.

For communities, apart from users, you can associate organizations and user groups as well as members. In that case, all the users belong to organizations, and user groups become members of the community. In the case of organizations, you can only associate users.

One more point to remember is that even though organizations are hierarchical, it does not mean that a user in the top-level organization can access all the sub organizations. A user has to be a member of specific organizations to access their private pages.

There is an alternative way as well to associate a user to communities and organizations. It can be done by logging in as the site administrator and going to the user profile of any user from the User Management Portlet. Then on the right-hand side menu, use the links **Communities** and **Organizations** under the **User Information** section and select the communities and organizations you wish to make user a member of.

Once the user is associated with a community/organization, you can assign roles to define what he/she can do in the community/organization. We will do this in later sections of this chapter.

Have a go hero – adding additional users to site

Do you now feel comfortable with user management in Liferay? Are you now ready to assign users to communities/organizations? Let's check it out. In this exercise, you need to add some more users in the Neighborhood site for families staying in Neighborhood. You need to log in as site administrator and use User Management Portlet to add users, and using their user profile change their password and assign them to Communities and Organizations.

Details of users and their community/ organization association are mentioned in the following table. Make sure you keep the password for all the users as **test123**. Also, all users should be associated to the CIGNEX Neighborhood community.

Screen name	Email Address	First Name	Last Name	Birth date (DD/MM/YYYY)	Communities	Organizations
Jennyb	jenny.bensar@cignex.com	Jenny	Bensar	17/05/1965	Neighborhood Exchange	Neighbors Congress
Paulb	paul.bensar @cignex.com	Paul	Bensar	8/05/1985	Neighborhood Exchange	Security Council
Riab	ria.bensar @cignex.com	Ria	Bensar	14/12/1990	Sports and Games	Chamber of Commerce
Royc	roy.crow @cignex.com	Roy	Crow	12/02/1970	Neighborhood Exchange	Security Council
Jiac	Jia.crow @cignex.com	Jia	Crow	23/03/1972	Gardening DIY	Neighborhood Arbitration Committee
Jeffc	Jeff.crow @cignex.com	Jeff	Crow	18/07/1990	Cricket Players	Security Council
Siac	Sia.crow @cignex.com	Sia	Crow	27/09/1992	Sports and Games	Chamber of Commerce

Disabling the option to register for the site for guest users

In the previous section, you created users for the Neighborhood site using Administrator user. However, Liferay does allow guest users to create accounts on their own. It works well with a public facing Internet site or social-networking portal or media site, and so on where a guest user is allowed to register and use more functionality of the site. However, this feature does not work out in all situations, such as with an Internet site for a specific organization, like our Neighborhood site. In those scenarios, we would like only validated users to have an account on the site. So, we should disable the option that allows guest users to create an account and leave user creation to administration.

Let's see how to do that.

Time for action – disabling the Register option for a guest user

1. Access the Neighborhood site and click on the **Sign In** link on the top right-hand side. It will take you to the **Sign In** portlet. Notice the **Create Account** link at the bottom of the **Sign In** portlet which indicates that a guest user can create a new account on the site. Now log in as site administrator user (**jeff.mcclure@cignex.com / test123**) and go to **Control Panel | Portal | Portal Settings**.

2. Now on the portal settings screen, click on **Configuration | Authentication**. It will open a screen as shown in the following screenshot with the **General** tab selected, by default.

3. You can see various configuration options for authentication. Each of them is very important and useful. The option which is of interest to you right now is **Allow strangers to create accounts?**. Uncheck this option to disable a guest user from creating an account. After that, you should click on the **Save** button from the right-hand side menu to save the changes.

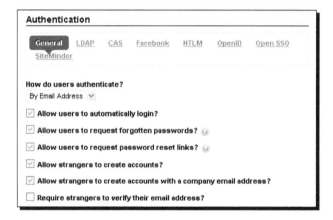

4. Now, you should sign out from the current logged in user and click on the **Sign In** link. You will then be brought to a screen with the **Sign In** portlet. But now in the bottom section of this portlet, there will not be the **Create Account** link. This will ensure that the guest user can no longer create an account by themselves in the Neighborhood site.

What just happened?

We just disabled the account creation option for guest users by themselves. It's required in the Neighborhood scenario as only legitimate Neighborhood users should have an account on the site. Each Neighborhood user has to now request the administrator offline to create his/her account, then the site administrator will create his/her account after verification.

We can also achieve this by setting `company.security.strangers=false` in the `portal-ext.properties` file.

Pop quiz

1. Which of the following can you add as a member of the community?

    a. User only

    b. User, User group only

    c. Organization only

    d. User, User group, Organization

2. When would you prefer to disable the guest user account creation?

    a. With a public facing website social media site

    b. With a public facing media website

    c. With a organization specific website

    d. In all the websites

3. Which are the mandatory fields to create a new user?

    a. Screen Name, First Name, Last Name

    b. Screen Name, First Name, Last Name, Email, Birth Date

    c. Screen Name, Email

    d. Screen Name, Email, Birth Date

Exploring role/permission management in Liferay

After creating pages and users, the next logical step would be to define appropriate roles and permissions. We will do that in this section.

Managing adequate access control is one of the most important requirements of any system. In order to have proper access control, you should define various roles with permissions to perform specific actions and assign these roles to users. Once you, the user, have a certain role it means that the user can perform all the actions permitted by that role. For example, if you want to enable **user1** to create a blog entry then first you have to create the **BlogEntryCreation** role (you can give it any name) with **Create Blog Entry** permission and then assign **user1** to the **BlogEntryCreation** role. Now when the user goes to the blog portlet, he/she will be able to add a new blog entry.

In Liferay, you can define permission for almost all the actions. Actions in Liferay are basically of the following types:

- Portal-level actions (for example, **Create Community**, **Create User**, and so on)
- Portlet instance-level actions (for example, **View permission for specific blog portlet instance**)
- Portlet-level actions (for example, **For blog portlet**, **Add blog entry**, and so on)
- Resource-level actions (for example, **View permission for specific blog entry**, and so on)

In this section, we will cover the following items:

- Create a new portal scope role to manage pages of the Neighborhood site
- Assign a user to the default Community/Organization Administrator role
- Create a new Community /Organization scope role and define permissions for it
- Define resource-level permissions
- Define portlet instance-level permissions

Let's start by creating a role for the site designer.

Creating a role to manage pages of the Neighborhood site

In an earlier section, you created a new user with an administrator role to manage the Neighborhood site. However, having a single administration user to manage the whole site is not be a very feasible and scalable option. Also, making every user site administrator is not feasible. In ideal site design, you should have only a handful of users with the administrator role. Create roles to manage specific areas, that is roles to manage pages, roles to manage content, and so on. Once the roles are created, the administrator will assign these roles to other users, which will enable the administrator-specific areas of the site. This approach creates a more robust and scalable administrator, and more powerful access control on the site.

Now let's start defining access control for the Neighborhood site by creating new roles.

Time for action – creating a role to manage pages

1. Log in to Liferay as site administrator (**Jeff Mcclure**) and go to **Control Panel** | **Portal** | **Roles**. You will be then brought to the **Role Management** screen as shown in the following screenshot:

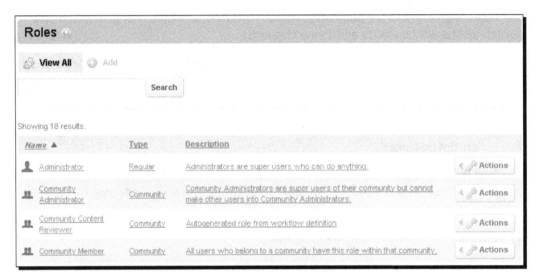

2. As you can see, there exists a set of roles. Some of these roles are default roles which have special meanings. We will explore the default roles in a later section of this chapter. Now click on the **Add** link from the top menu to open the screen to add a new role as shown in the following screenshot. Enter the following details for the fields on this screen:

> ❑ **Name**: **SiteDesigner**
>
> ❑ **Title**: **Site Designer** (Notice the **Other Language** link; it is useful to provide a title in different languages.)
>
> ❑ **Description**: **Role to Manage Pages of the Neighborhood site**
>
> ❑ **Type**: **Regular** (This property is about the scope of the role. **Regular** type is known as **Portal Role**. You will create **Community** and **Organization** type role in later sections.)

3. Now click on the **Save** button. It will add a new role and take you back to the listing of roles. Have a look at the newly added a role in the list.

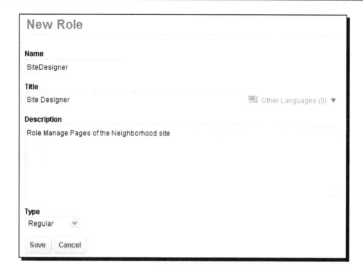

4. Now you should define permissions for this role. Click on **Actions | Define Permissions** for the Site Designer role.

5. You will be then brought to a screen where you can define permissions for this role. In the **Add Permissions** drop-down, there are various sections (**Portal, Content, Applications,** and **Control Panel**) and each of them contains a set of actions. Now, select **Communities** from the **Portal** section from the drop-down. You will see a list of actions available for **Communities**; select the checkbox for the **Manage Pages** action and then click on the **Save** button located at the bottom of page. You will see a success message, **The role permissions were updated** on top of the page to indicate that the operation was successful. Again, click on **Add Permission | Portal | Organizations**. Enable the checkbox for **Manage Pages** and click on the **Save** button located at the bottom of the page. This should add two permissions to the role as shown in the following screenshot, **Permission to Manage Pages of Communities** and **Permission to Manage Pages of Organizations**:

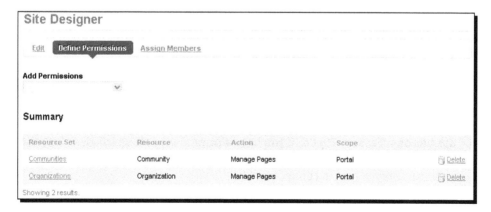

6. You should then click on the **Assign Members** link to assign users to this role. You will then be brought to a screen to assign members to this role. On that screen, click on the **Available** link and select **Mark Bensar**. After that, click on the **Update Associations** button to confirm this association.

7. You have so far created a **Site Designer** role, defined **Manage Pages** permission for this role, and assigned **Mark Bensar** user to this role. This means **Mark** should now be able to manage pages of the communities and organizations for which he is a member of. To verify that **Sign Out** from the current user and **Sign In** as **Mark Bensar** (**mark.bensar@cignex.com** / **test123**) and go to **Control Panel**.

8. You can see the **CIGNEX Neighborhood** community selected in the **Content** section, by default, and only the **Pages** link visible in that section. Click on that link; it will show you the **Manage Pages** interface. **Mark** can also manage pages for other communities/organisations by selecting them from the **Content** section. This concludes that the **Site Designer** role allows users to manage pages of communities and organizations they are a member of.

What just happened?

We just created a regular role, **Site Designer** and gave this role the permission to manage pages for communities and organizations. After that, we assigned **Mark Bensar** user to this role. Finally, we logged in as **Mark Bensar** and verified if he can manage pages.

Let's try to understand a bit more about **Role Management** in Liferay.

Liferay permissions cannot be directly assigned to a user but through **Roles**. It helps to remove tight coupling between users and specific permission. So roles are very integral and important part of permission management in Liferay. There are three types for scope of roles in Liferay:

♦ Portal role—The roles under this category would be applicable across the whole portal. That is, if you have a portal role which gives **Create Blog** permission, then the user with this role can create a blog across all the communities/organizations for which he/she is a member of.

♦ Community role—The roles under this category can be assigned to a user for a specific community. That is, if you have a community role which gives **Create Blog** permission, then the user is assigned with this role for community XYZ. Now, the user can create a blog in community XYZ.

♦ Organization role—The roles under this category can be assigned to a user for a specific organization. That is, if you have a community role which gives **Create Blog** permission, then the user is assigned with this role for community XYZ. Now, the user can create a blog in community XYZ.

In this section, you have seen that role management is facilitated through the **Roles** link of the **Portal** section in the **Control Panel**. You can perform the following operations in role management:

- ◆ **Create Role**—Allows you to create a new role with either **Portal**, **Community**, or **Organization** scope.

- ◆ **Edit Role**—Edit any existing role. Notice that you can change the scope of a role during edit.

- ◆ **Assign Members**—You can add users, communities, organizations, and user groups to the role.

- ◆ **Define Permission**—Allows you to define various portal-level and portlet-level permissions to the role. These permissions defines what this role can do.

- ◆ **View Users**—Shows all the users who have this role. This helps you to find out whether the role has a specific user or not.

In Liferay, there are a few out-of-box roles known as default roles. Each of these roles has a special meaning and a user cannot delete them. Let's explore them.

Portal scoped roles

- ◆ **Administrator**—This role is for admin users. It has all the permissions to perform any operation on the site.

- ◆ **Guest**—This role is for guest users (a non-registered user who visits the site). It contains the minimal permission required for guest. You can add / remove permission to this role to define access for guest users.

- ◆ **Power User**—This role is automatically given to the newly registered users as per the default configuration. However, you can change this default association configuration. This role allows users to manage their public and private pages. You can also define more permissions for this role.

- ◆ **User**—This role is the most basic role, which can be assigned to the registered user. Ideally, this role is used in the default association of roles for new user when you want to restrict users from managing their public and private pages. You can use this role in public facing website, where you don't want your registered user to have their personal pages.

- ◆ **Owner**—This role is automatically given to the creator of the asset and gives him total control of the asset. For example, if you create a blog, you get the **Owner** role for that blog entry. This role gives you all the permissions on assets for which you are an owner.

- ◆ **Omniadmin**—This is an internal role, which is not available on the list of roles in the roles management portlet. The **Omniadmin** users can administer the portal's core functionality: gc, shutdown, and so on. The **Omniadmin** users must belong to the default company. You can set which company to make the default company by using `company.default.web.id=liferay.com`. Multiple portal instances might be deployed on one application server, and not all of the administrators should have access to this core functionality. You cannot define **Omniadmin** users via the **Control Panel** but need to set the `omniadmin.users` property in `portal-ext.properties` with the IDs of users who are **Omniadmin** users. You can also leave this field blank, if users who belong to the right company and have the **Administrator** role are allowed to administer the portal's core functionality.

Community/Organization roles

- ◆ **Owner**—The creator of the Community/Organization gets this role, by default. You can assign another user to this role as well. Users with this role are super users for their community/organization and they can assign the **Administrator** role to other user.

- ◆ **Administrator**—Users with this role are also super users for the community/organization and can perform any operation. However, they cannot make another user an **Administrator** of communities/organizations. Remember that this **Administrator** role is different from that of the **Portal** scope, which has administrative privilege across the site and they can also make other users site administrators.

- ◆ **Member**—When a user becomes a member of any community/organization, he/she will get this role for that community/organization. It allows the user to view the private pages of the community/organization.

Apart from the preceding default roles, Liferay allows you to create any number of custom roles and assign permission to them based on the site requirements.

In this section, we have assigned roles directly to a user. However, you can assign roles to user groups as well and it is a very useful approach as you would not require to go to each user and assign a role. Instead, you can group users who have similar interests in a user group and assign roles to the user group. This will ensure that each user in user group will get the role.

Let's now assign default community/organization-specific roles to the users.

The decision regarding which type of role is to be created depends on various situations, and here are some basic hints:

If you want to create a global permission, go for **Regular** role.

If you want to create a permission specific to Organization or Community, then go for Organization- or Community-specific role.

If you need access control for the portal-specific functionality, then go for the **Regular** role.

These are just guidelines; you would be the best judge to create which type of role based on the requirement of your site.

Assigning users to community/organization administrator role

In the previous section, you have created portal scoped roles to delegate some of the **Site Administrator** responsibility. Now, you can perform more delegation by creating a community/organization specific to an administrator. It's an optimized design in the real-world scenario as well, as it reduces the burden of the **Site Administrator** and provides the model for delegation.

Also, in the previous section, you got a brief introduction to the community/organization **Administrator** role. Let's now assign it to the user.

Time for action – assigning community/organization Administrator role

In this action, you will make **Mark Bensar** the administrator for the CIGNEX Neighborhood community and Neighbors Congress organizations.

1. Log in as **Site Administrator (Jeff Mcclure)** and go to **Control Panel | Portal | Communities**. Now, for the **CIGNEX Neighbourhood** community click on **Actions | Assign User Roles**. It will take you to a screen with available community role listing as shown in the following screenshot.

2. Now, you should click on the **Community Administrator** link from the listing and it will take you to a screen where you can assign members to this role. This screen will be somewhat similar to screenshots shown in earlier sections. Now select the **Mark Bensar** user from the **Available** link and click on **Update Associations**. This will assign him the **Administrator** role for this community.

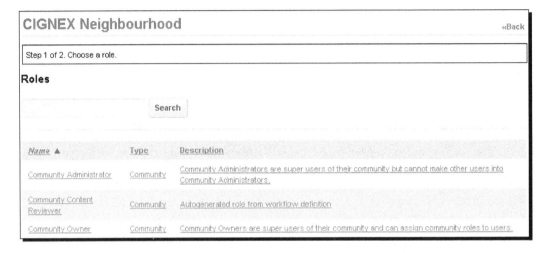

3. Similarly, let's now assign the **Organization Administrator** role to **Mark Bensar** for Neighbors Congress organization. Click on **Control Panel | Portal | Organizations**. Now for the Neighbors Congress organization, click on **Actions | Assign User Roles**. It will bring you to a screen with the list of organization roles.

4. You should then click on the **Organization Administrator** role link to assign users to this role. It will take you to the **Assign Members** screen. Now, select **Mark Bensar** user from the **Available** link and click on **Save**. This will assign him the **Administrator** role for this organization.

What just happened?

We just assigned a user the **Administrator** role for a specific community/organization. Now, the user can perform various administrative functions on that community/organization except that he/she can't make other users **Administrators**.

There is also an alternate way where you can assign community/organization roles to a user. As a site administrator, you can go to the user's profile and click on the **Roles** links under the **User Information** section to assign community/organization roles.

Let's now create custom community/organization roles.

Have a go hero – creating a community role to grant blog creation permission

In the previous section, we assigned default roles to users. However, they will not be enough to define fine-grained permissions. For a community, you would want to allow a set of users to perform a specific action. As an example, you want only a set of users to have blog creation permission for specific community. So, creating a regular role won't help here as it will give that permission to the user for all the communities/organizations him/her is a member of. So creating community-specific roles gives permission to user for only communities for which he/she got the role.

You should create a community-specific role which gives permission to create blogs and assign it to the user. You can achieve this in the following steps:

1. Create a new **Community** type role with name **Create Blog**.

2. Define the following permissions for this role. Give permission to **Access in Control Panel**, **Add Entry** for **Blogs**, **View** and **Update** for **Blog Entry** as shown in the following screenshot:

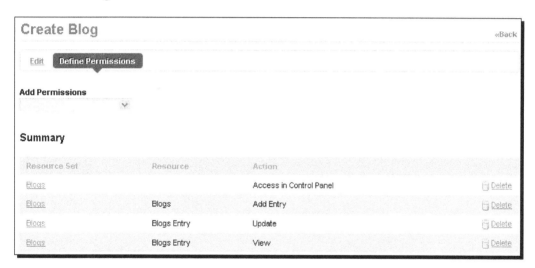

3. Assign this role to the **Roy Crow** user of the Neighborhood Exchange community. You should assign this role to the user using the **Roles** link available in the user profile. After assigning the role, it should look similar to the following screenshot:

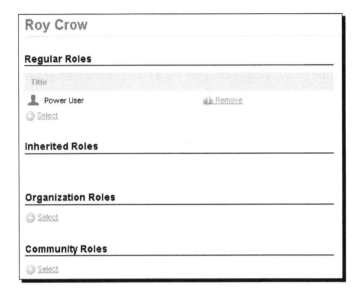

4. After that, log out as **Site Administrator** and log in as user **Roy Crow**. In Docbar, **Go To** menu, select **Neighbourhood Exchange Public** link. After that, select **Control Panel** from the **Manage** menu. On **Control Panel**, you will see the **Neighbourhood Exchange** community selected in the **Content** section and under that you should click on the **Blogs** link. You will see a screen similar to the following screenshot. It should have permission to **Add Blog Entry**.

What just happened?

We just created a new community role for bloggers and assigned permissions to add a blog entry. After that, we assigned this role to **Roy Crow** of the **Neighbourhood Exchange** community. Finally, we logged in as **Row Crow** and verified that the user has got permission to add new blog entries. This shows it works.

More on permissions

In Liferay, you can define permission for almost every action you perform. Actions and resources are the two main concepts of Liferay Permission System. Actions could be **VIEW**, **EDIT**, **ADD**, and so on. Resources could be the **My Communities** portlet on the page, **Page** in the **CIGNEX Neighbourhood** community. In Liferay, **Permissions** are defined as a combination of an **Actions** and **Resources** pair. Some examples of **Permissions** are:

◆ **VIEW** action for the **My Communities** portlet

◆ **EDIT** action for **Page**

You can achieve this by the **Define Permissions** interface as shown in the **Create Blog** screenshot. This interface is used to assign permissions to the roles.

This interface has the **Add Permissions** drop-down. This drop-down has various sections and each section has a list of items under it when you click on any of the item. It will show you the actions associated with that item. It has the following sections:

◆ **Administration** (only for the **Community** or **Organization** type role)—This section contains only one item **Community Administrator** against which you can define permission. It allows you to define permissions for **Community**, **Page**, **Page Template**, **Site Template**, **Task Proposal**, and **Team**.

◆ **Portal** (only for **Regular** type role)—This section allows you to define permissions for the portal-level resources. It allows defining permission for general portal actions, such as **Add Community**, **Add Organization**, **Add Role**, and **Export User**. Also, it allows defining permissions for **Communities**, **Organizations**, **Users**, **Roles**, and so on.

◆ **Content**—This section allows you to define permissions for asset types available in Liferay, for example, blogs, wiki, message board, bookmark, web content, tags, and so on. Let's take the example of the blogs item under this section. It allows you to define permissions for top-level actions, such as **Add Entry**, **Subscribe**, and blog entry-level permissions like **View**, **Update**, **Delete**, **Add/Update/Delete Discussions**, and **Permissions**. Similar permissions for other asset types are available under this section.

The name of one of the items of this section, Docbar, does not match the permission it allows to define, which allows you to define permission for Assets, Category, and Category Vocabulary. This item should have been named **Category** to be more appropriate for the permission it defines. Now you know where to find the permission for **Categories**.

◆ **Applications**—This section allows you to define a portlet-level permission for most of the out of box portlets of Liferay, such as **Activities**, **Alerts**, **Asset Publisher**, **Blogs**, **Web Content**, **Wiki**, and so on. Let's take an example of the **Blogs** item under this section. It allows defining permissions for actions like **Access** in the **Control Panel**, **Add to Page**, **Configuration**, and **View**. Similar permissions can be defined for the other portlets using this section.

◆ **Control Panel**—This section allows you to define permissions for various portlets available in the **Control Panel** like **Blogs**, **Bookmark**, **My Account**, **My Pages**, and so on.

Defining resource-level permissions

In the previous section, we assigned permissions to the roles through the **Define Permissions** interface. However, certain resource-specific permissions cannot be assigned to a role directly using this interface. Examples of such permissions are **View**, **Edit**, and **Delete** permissions for specific blog entry, or you can define **View** permission for a specific page. This feature is very useful in a scenario where you want to restrict content to a targeted set of users. Generally, site uses this feature to market their premium content.

In Liferay, this can be achieved by the **Permissions** link provided as actions for each resource. This allows you to define permission for a specific resource entry.

Let's now define resource permission.

Time for action – defining permissions for a bookmark entry

In this section, you will create new a bookmark entry in the **CIGNEX Neighbourhood** community and define permissions for it.

1. Log in as the Neighborhood site administrator and go to the **Control Panel**. In the Control Panel, click on the **Bookmarks** link from the **Content** section for the **CINGEX Neighbourhood** community from the left-hand side menu. It will bring you to the **Bookmark** portlet.

2. After that, click on **Add Bookmark** from the right-hand side menu. It will open a screen to add a new bookmark. Enter the following data on the screen:

- ❑ **Name**: **Google**.
- ❑ **URL**: **http://www.google.com**.
- ❑ **Comments**: **Google URL**.
- ❑ **Permissions**: You can set permissions for this bookmark at the time of creation as well. Liferay allows setting the basic permission for any resource at the time of creation. You should make this bookmark viewable to all users, so select **Anyone (Guest Role)** in **Viewable by** drop-down.

3. Now click on the **Save** button.

4. New bookmark entry will appear in the bookmark listing. Now, click on the **Action** button; this will open a pop-up with three options, **Edit**, **Permissions**, **Delete** as shown in the following screenshot. Click on the **Permissions** menu item. It allows you to define permission for this resource entry:

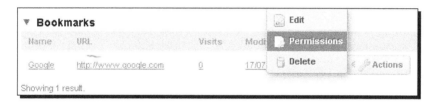

5. It will open the permissions management screen for this bookmark entry as shown in the following screenshot. On the left-hand side, all the **Regular** and **Community** roles will be displayed. In the rest of the column heading, permission available for bookmark entry will be visible. That is, **Delete Permissions**, **Update**, and **View**.

6. Give all the four permissions to the **Create Blog** role and remove the **View** permission for **Guest**. After that, click on the **Save** button. It will save the changes and bring you back to the same screen with the success message.

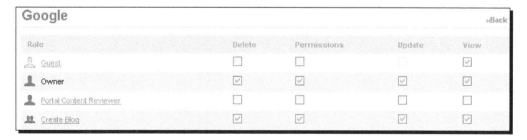

7. After that click on the **Back** link from the right-hand side. You will then be brought back to the bookmark listing screen. Now, any user with the **Create Blog** role will able to delete, update, define permission, and view this **Google** bookmark entry in the **Bookmark** portlet and guest users will no longer be able to see this entry.

What just happened?

We just created a new bookmark entry in the **CIGNEX Neighbourhood** community. During creation, we set permissions that are viewable to all the users. After that, we discussed the permission interface for this bookmark entry and gave **Edit**, **Delete**, **Permission**, and **View** permissions to the **Create Blog** role and removed the **View** permission from **Guest**. This will ensure that the user with the **Create Blog** role will be able to modify this bookmark entry but not other bookmark entries, if you add any.

In Liferay, you can define resource-level permissions from two places:

♦ During creation—Most of the resource types allow you to define permissions for resource at the time of creation. This permission will allow you to define the basic access control for the resource.

♦ **Permissions** link in the **Action** menu—This is a more advanced and effective way to define permissions for any resource. It has a very user-friendly interface which shows all the available actions for resource entry and the available role list for which you can define permissions.

Liferay also provides ways to define permissions dynamically using the **Permissions** interface. You can also define permissions for top-level resource actions in portlets (for example, **Add Bookmark** permission for the **Bookmark** portlet) using the **Permissions** link available as part of the portlet as shown in the following screenshot for the **Bookmark** portlet:

You can also define permissions for individual portlet instances of a specific portlet. For example, if you want to make a specific instance of the **Bookmark** portlet, visible only to the users with a specific role, then you can define permissions for this portlet instance using the **Permissions** link available under the **Configuration** option in the **Portlet** title bar, as shown in the following screenshot:

Using this **Permissions** interface, you can define permissions like **Access in Control Panel**, **Add to Page**, **Configuration**, and **View**. These are standard permissions available to most of the portlet instances. The **Access in Control Panel** permission will allow the user to access this portlet in the **Control Panel**. The **Add to Page** permission will allow the user to add this type of portlet to a page. The **Configuration** permission will allow the user to modify configuration of this portlet. The **View** permission will define who can view this portlet when added to the page. Even though the user has access to the page, if they don't have **View** permission for a specific portlet then that portlet will not be visible to the user.

So we saw that in Liferay, permissions can be assigned at various levels:

♦ Portlet-level permission—Permission on a specific portlet instance like the **View** permission for any portlet

♦ Top-level resource action permission—Permission for top-level actions such as **Add Entry** in blogs

♦ Resource entry-level permission—Permission for actions on individual resource entries, such as **Edit** or **Delete** permission for individual blog entry

These permissions can then be grouped under roles and roles can be scoped to be applicable for the entire portal or specific community or specific organization. After that, users will be assigned roles so that they get permission to perform specific actions on the portal.

 Reflect on the permission system required for your site. Take a moment and sketch out the permission model for your site. What type of roles will you create for your site? Define user-role mapping for your site.

Have a go hero – defining the View permission for the Bookmark portlet

You will need to add the **Bookmark** portlet to the **Daily Tips** page on the **CIGNEX Neighbourhood** community. After that, define the **View** permission of this portlet to users with the **Create Blog** role. The portlet should not be visible to other community members and guest users.

 You can define portlet-level permission using the **Permissions** link action under the **Configuration** link on the portlet title bar.

Pop quiz

1. What are the various types of roles?

    a. Community

    b. Organization

    c. Community, Organization

    d. Community , Organization , Portal

2. **Community** type role gives user permission for action to user in:

    a. Complete portal

    b. All the community

    c. Community for which the role has been granted

    d. None of the above

3. In Liferay, you can assign permission at:

    a. Portlet instance level, top-level resource level, Resource entry level

    b. Portlet instance level only

    c. Portal instance level and resource entry level

    d. None of the above

4. Which of the following operations can't the **Community Administrator** role perform in the community?

    a. Managing community pages

    b. Assigning members

    c. Assigning other user administrator role

    d. Modifying community details

Summary

We learned a lot in this chapter about page management, user management, and permission management. We have added pages, users, and roles to the Neighborhood site.

Specifically, we covered:

- ◆ Page management
    - ❑ Public and private Page creation in communities and organizations
    - ❑ Page-level attributes to define characteristics of individual pages
    - ❑ Features of the **Manage Pages** portlet
- ◆ User management
    - ❑ Creating an administrator user to mange the Neighborhood site
    - ❑ User profile modification to change the demographics and password
    - ❑ Associate users to community and organizations, so users can access those communities and organizations
    - ❑ Disabling of site registration for guest users to allow other users to register by themselves
- ◆ Permissions management
    - ❑ Creating roles
    - ❑ Assigning the community/organization administrator role to a user to mange them
    - ❑ Creating community-scope role
    - ❑ Defining resource-level permissions

After learning about page management, user management, and permission management, we're ready to look at the Content Management System (CMS) of Liferay, which is the topic of the next chapter.

7
Creating and Publishing Content

In the last two chapters, we have learned how to create communities and organizations in Liferay Portal. We have also learned how to add public and private pages in communities and organizations. In this chapter, we will learn how to create and publish information using the web content portlet and other portlets of Liferay Portal.

Specifically, we will learn how to use the following portlets:

◆ Web content portlet

◆ Web content display portlet

◆ Document library portlet

◆ Image gallery portlet

◆ Asset publisher portlet

Using the aforementioned portlets, we will populate the portal pages at the neighborhood site with content. In this way, we make the neighborhood site an interesting place for the users to stay.

Content management preview

Liferay Portal has rich and strong functionalities for online content management. Before we take up its content-related portlet applications, we will review some concepts in content manipulation.

Analyzing online content

Content shown on a web page can be classified as follows:

♦ Text

♦ Images

♦ PDF files and files of other formats

♦ Videos

The images, formatted files, and videos are relatively static – they do not change very often. Some texts, such as online advertisements, do not change very often either. Other texts, such as the quantity of a certain pair of shoes at `http://www.zappos.com/`, change very often – they are relatively dynamic.

Organizing content

Liferay Portal uses different portlets to manage different types of content.

For static content, Liferay Portal provides the following applications:

♦ Document library portlet that is used to upload video, audio, image, PDF, Excel, and other files.

♦ Image gallery portlet that is used to upload image files specifically

♦ Web content portlet that is used to create and edit web content

♦ Web content display portlet that is used to create, edit. and present web content

♦ Asset publisher portlet that is used to show all static content

Liferay Portal uses other portlets such as chat portlet to manage dynamic content. Users also write custom portlets to present frequently updated content.

Liferay Portal has version control over its content. When you use the document library portlet to upload the same file for the second time, both the original and the new file are saved, with different version numbers; after you edit web content and save the changes, the new content is saved with a higher version number.

Purpose of Liferay content management

The content management system in Liferay Portal is for a user to create, update, and publish content on the run. The user can use a What-You-See-Is-What-You-Get (WYSIWYG) editor to achieve this. No programming is needed. The user can set up a whole site using the content management application by clicking and typing.

Uploading images

First we will take a look at the image gallery portlet. We will use this portlet to upload image files for the content that we are going to create.

The image gallery portlet is used to upload and manage image files. You can create hierarchical image folders and save the uploaded images in them. The maximum size of an image file that you can upload is 10 megabytes. You can upload image files of the following file extensions:

- `.bmp`
- `.gif`
- `.jpeg`
- `.jpg`
- `.png`
- `.tif`
- `.tiff`

 You can set the size of an uploaded image file to be unlimited in a `portal-ext.properties` file. You can also update the `portal-ext.properties` file to allow files of all file extensions to be uploaded.

A user can access the image gallery portlet in the **Control Panel**.

Time for action – uploading an image file

Suppose that a house is on sale in the neighborhood. As the portal administrator, you need to upload the image of this house to the neighborhood site to facilitate its sale. You can take the following steps for the neighborhood site:

1. Log in as portal administrator.
2. Hover over the **Manage** link and click on the **Control Panel** link.
3. Click on the **Image Gallery** link to open the portlet.
4. Click on the **Add Folder** link on the right-hand side and create a **Neighbor** folder.
5. Open the **Neighbor** folder and click on the **Add Image** link.
6. Follow the on-screen instructions to upload a **house_on_sale.png** file on your local computer into the **Neighbor** folder.
7. Click on the **<<Back** link.

Here is what you get:

What just happened?

You have just uploaded a house image with the image gallery portlet to Liferay Portal. That image is saved in a **Neighbor** folder. Next time you can just navigate to this folder and use this image in a piece of web content.

Pop quiz

Which of the following statements are correct about content management in Liferay Portal?

    a.   A non-technical user can learn to use the content management system of Liferay Portal

    b.   You use an HTML editor to generate content

    c.   The image gallery portlet has file organization and versioning functionalities

    d.   All of the above

Have a go hero – uploading another image

Now click on the **Add Image** link again to upload another image into the **Neighbor** folder. Click on one of the images. What do you see?

Creating web content

Web content is a section of a web page that includes text, images, and links. We use the web content portlet to create content in Liferay Portal. This portlet has a WYSIWYG editor to assist a user in content generation. It also has the following features:

- Multi-language: This allows a user to create the same content in different languages and save it in the database
- Structure: This allows a user to define input fields for separate pieces of content
- Template: This can be used to arrange content pieces and generate dynamic content
- Permission: A user can define which users have access to this content
- Scheduled publishing: A user can set the display date of a piece of content
- Categorization: The content creator can associate content with a category
- Tagging: The content creator can apply multiple tags to a piece of content—this facilitates searching
- Versioning: The portlet automatically applies a new version to a piece of content
- Workflow for content approval: When workflow is enabled for web content, it has to be reviewed and approved before it is published

For ease of description, we disable workflow for web content in this chapter. Thus we create, approve, and publish web content on the same web page.

We will create content for the following public pages of the **CIGNEX Neighborhood** community:

- **Welcome**: This is the first page of the community, which is also the default page when a user accesses this community
- **Registration**: This page is for a neighbor to create an account for himself at the neighborhood site
- **House on Sale**: Users come to this page to find the house in the neighborhood for sale
- **Daily Tips**: This page contains small pieces of advice for neighborhood residents

We will also create content for the following two pages:

- **Planting Schedule** in the Gardening DIY community
- **Arbitration Notice** in the Arbitration Committee organization

We assume that necessary image files have already been uploaded to the neighborhood site.

Regular web content

We will now create a simple piece of content to populate the **Welcome** page.

Time for action –adding content to the welcome page

Suppose that you are the portal administrator. Go to the `http://neighborhood.cignex.com/web/guest/home` page. Follow these steps:

1. Log in and go to the **Control Panel**.

2. Click on **Web Content**.

3. Click on the **Add Web Content** button.

4. Enter **WELCOME-MESSAGE** in the **Name** field.

5. In the **Content** field, which is a What-You-See-is-What-You-Get (WYSIWYG) editor, enter **Welcome to Our Neighborhood** as the title.

6. Highlight the title, centre it with the WISIWYG editor, change its font size to 28, change its font color to deep green, and make it bold.

7. Beneath the title, enter an image by clicking on the image icon in the WYSIWYG editor.

8. Click on **Browse Server | CIGNEX Neighborhood | Neighborhood**.

9. Click on **welcome_house.png** file – this image will be chosen.

10. Click on **OK**. Centre the image by clicking on the centre icon in the WYSIWYG editor:

11. Enter more text as the welcome message.

12. Change the paragraph font size to 18.

13. Leave the default permissions as they are, so that anyone can view this content.

14. Click on the **Publish** button at the bottom of the page.

The welcome message content is created. Now, on the next page find the content in the list and click on the **Actions** button | **Preview** – you will see how it looks in a separate browser window.

> The aforementioned WYSIWYG editor is a ckeditor, whose detailed information can be found at `http://ckeditor.com/`. By default Liferay Portal uses the ckeditor for creation of web content, blogs, message board messages, and wikis. The portal administrator can also configure Liferay Portal to use fckeditor, liferay, simple, or TinyMCE editors.

The WYSIWYG editor—as an HTML editor—can pose a risk to the Liferay Portal site. It may be used to launch cross-site-scripting or phishing attacks. It is important to allow only trusted users to access the ckeditor.

What just happened?

You have successfully used the web content portlet to create a piece of content. That content is a regular kind of web content. Most web content is regular web content.

Web content with a structure and template

Some people may want to give their content a certain layout – they may want their images to be on the left-hand side while their description text is on the right-hand side. They can achieve this in the following two ways:

1. Using the table functionality that comes with the WYSIWYG editor (which is the same as in any other HTML editors and will not be explained here)

2. Using a content template

The content template and content structure are two features that come with the web content portlet – you may have noticed the **Structure** link and the **Template** link in the last screenshot.

The content structure defines the input field names and types for pieces of content. These input fields will show in the creation of a piece of web content that is associated with this structure. The content creator input values for these input fields. These values will be retrieved in the content template.

In the content template, Velocity variables are used to retrieve values entered in the creation of the web content. So the content template can mean Velocity template. At the same time, the content creator can insert HTML tables in the template to arrange pieces of content. In this sense, the content template is also a layout template.

Let us see the web content, structure, and template combined in action.

Time for action – creating a structure

We will create a structure first:

1. Go to **Control Panel | Web Content**.

2. Click on **Structures | Add Structure**.

3. In the **ID** field enter **HOSALE-STRUCTURE**.

4. In **Name** field, enter **HO Sale Structure**.

5. Click on the **Add Row** button and add the following rows:

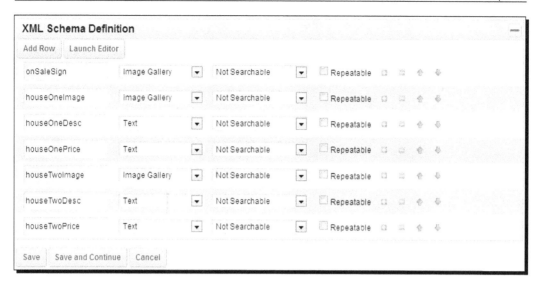

6. Leave the default permissions as they are.

7. Click on **Save**.

You will return to a page where the **HOSALE-STRUCTURE** structure is displayed in a list.

What just happened?

You have successfully created the **HOSALE-STRUCTURE** structure. This structure has seven variables. For the Text type variables, you will enter text as their values; for the Image Gallery type variables, you will enter Uniform Resource Locators (URL) to image files as their values. Those image files have been uploaded through the image gallery portlet or are uploaded through the WYSIWYG editor on the run.

A structure will be used by one or more templates.

Time for action – creating a template

It is time to create a template:

1. Go to **Control Panel | Web Content**.

2. Click on **Templates | Add Template**.

3. In **ID** field, enter **HOSALE-TEMPLATE**; in the **Name** field, enter **HO Sale Template**.

4. For **Structure**, click on **Select** and double-click **HOSALE-STRUCTURE**.

5. For **Script**, click on **Launch Editor**.

6. When an editor window pops up, clear all content in the editor box, and paste in the following content:

```
<table border="0" cellpadding="8" cellspacing="0" width="50%">
  <tr>
    <td></td>
    <td><img src="$onSaleSign.getData()" alt="On-sale image"
    height="150" width="150" /></td>
    <td></td>
  </tr>
  <tr>
    <td><img src="$houseOneImage.getData()" alt="On-sale house
    image" height="200" width="200" /></td>
    <td>$houseOneDesc.getData()</td>
    <td>$houseOnePrice.getData()</td>
  </tr>
  <tr>
    <td><img src="$houseTwoImage.getData()" alt="On-sale house
    image" height="200" width="200" /></td>
    <td>$houseTwoDesc.getData()</td>
    <td>$houseTwoPrice.getData()</td>
  </tr>
</table>
```

7. Click on **Update**.

8. Leave the default permissions as they are.

9. Click on **Save**.

On the next page, you will find the **HOSALE-TEMPLATE** template listed in a table.

What just happened?

You have successfully created the **HOSALE-TEMPLATE** template. As you have noticed, the template just created divides the presentation into three columns with an HTML table element. The content is displayed in respective rows and columns.

You can also notice the `$houseTwoPrice.getData()` expression in the preceding HTML markup. This expression gets a value from the `houseTwoPrice` variable, which has been declared in the **HOSALE-STRUCTURE** structure. Where does its value come from? It comes from the content to be created.

The aforementioned `$houseTwoPrice` variable is a Velocity Template Language (VTL) variable. Liferay Portal has used VTL for rendering dynamic content in themes and web content. Liferay Portal calls the Velocity engine Application Programming Interface (API) to interpret this variable and get its values. An interested reader can refer to `http://velocity.apache.org/` for more information about VTL.

Time for action – creating template-based content

Carry out the following steps to create a piece of content that uses the **HOSALE-STRUCTURE** and the **HOSALE-TEMPLATE**:

1. Go to **Control Panel | Web Content**.

2. Click on **Add Web Content**.

3. In the **Name** field, enter **HO-SALE-ARTICLE**.

4. Under **Template** label on the right-hand side, click on **Select**.

5. When a window pops up, click on **OK**.

6. Choose **HOSALE-TEMPLATE** – the page re-loads and its content changes:

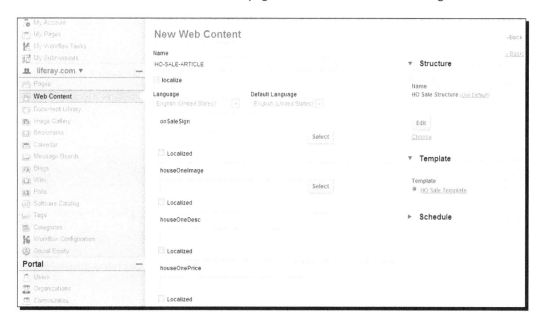

7. Click on **Select** for **onSaleSign**.

8. When a window pops up, click on the folder where you have uploaded the on-sale sign image.

9. Click on the **Choose** button for the on-sale sign image file – a URL to the image file is set as the value of the **onSaleSign** field.

10. Select or enter values for other variables as defined in the **HOSALE-STRUCTURE** structure.

11. Click on **Publish**.

The **HO-SALE-ARTICLE** content is created.

What just happened?

As you can see, the creation of this piece of content is different from that of the general content – you are restricted to entering values in just seven input fields. You are not concerned with style or other common content as defined in the template.

There are three advantages to the creation of web content based on structure and template:

1. Uniformity: As the content's look-and-feel can be defined in the template, all web content based on the same template has the same look-and-feel.

2. Maintainability: If the content creator changes the style definitions in the template, all web content based on this template will have an updated look-and-feel.

3. Flexibility: The content creator can modify the values for input fields as defined in the structure to update the web content.

Migrated web content

If you are upgrading your web site to Liferay Portal and you want to move some static content from your previous site to your new site, it is easy to do it with the web content portlet.

Time for action –migrating static content from an existing site using the web content portlet

We use the source code mode of the WYSIWYG editor to accomplish this:

1. Open your previous site with a browser.

2. In the menu bar, click on **View** | **Source**, you will see the HTML markup of the page.

3. Find and copy that part of the content that you want to migrate to Liferay Portal (some sample HTML mark-up follows):

```
<h1 class="section-heading"> Announcements & Alerts </h1>
<h2> West Coast Symposium - September 2011</h2>
<p> Liferay's third annual <a href="http://liferay.
com/wcs2011">West Coast Symposium</a> will be held in
<strong>Anaheim, California on September 21-22, 2011</
strong>. The Symposium is a great opportunity for learning,
knowledge sharing, and networking. <a href="http://liferay.com/
wcs2011">Registrations are now open</a>!</p>
```

4. Go to **Control Panel | Web Content | Add Web Content**.

5. In the **Name** field, enter **MIGRATED-CONTENT**.

6. Click on the **Source** button in the WYSIWYG editor; now the editor changes into source code mode.

7. Paste the copied HTML markup into the editor box.

8. Click on the **Source** button again to check the effect.

9. Leave the default permissions as they are.

10. Click on **Publish**.

You will find the **MIGRATED-CONTENT** content in content list on the next page.

What just happened?

The source code mode of the WYSIWYG editor is a very handy tool for you to migrate static content from a previous site. You can add style to the HTML markup and adjust spacing between the elements.

Pop quiz

1. Which of the following statements are correct about web content creation?

    a. You can create a piece of content in several steps

    b. If you create a piece of content when you are in a certain community, that piece of content only shows in that community by default

    c. You can save or publish a piece of content at the end of the creation process

    d. All of the above

2. Which of the following statements are true about content structures?

    a. You can specify permission for a structure as you do web content

    b. A structure limits information to be entered by a user for a piece of content

    c. A structure field can be of text, image gallery, or selection list type

    d. All of the above

3. Choose the statements that you think are correct about content templates:

    a. Like page layout template, the content template can be used to define the locations of content pieces in the web content

    b. A template is based on a structure. When the structure changes, the template may also need to be changed accordingly

    c. The Velocity template language is the default language for template creation

    d. All of the above

4. Why is content based on structure and template useful?

    a. It can have a uniform look-and-feel

    b. Its style can be updated in the same template

    c. It is flexible for the content creator to update the content

    d. All of the above

5. Which of the following features belong to the WYSIWYG editor?

    a. You can change the color of text in the editor

    b. You can insert a link in your content

    c. You can add a smiley icon in your content

    d. All of the above

Have a go hero – exploring the content creation process

The web content portlet has a lot of other optional functionalities. Some of the functionalities are useful in content management while others are useful for different requirements on various projects.

Suppose that you are still on the web content portlet page. Try to change the number of items displayed in the web content list.

Suppose that you want to examine the display of a piece of content just created. Find a way in the web content portlet to do this.

The web content portlet supports multi-language content. Try to create multiple pieces of content in different languages and save them in the same web content.

During web content creation, a portal administrator can directly upload an image through the WYSIWYG editor. Find a way to do this.

Displaying web content

Liferay Portal has a web content display portlet for showing the static content that we created in the last section. The web content display portlet is a simple portlet. You add this portlet onto a page and specify through configuration the content to show in this portlet. During runtime this portlet will go to the database and fetch the content and render it.

We will add this web content display portlet to the public and private pages of the communities and organizations created at the neighborhood site.

Let us go to the `http://neiborhood.cignex.com/web/guest/home` page, which is the **Welcome** page of the CIGNEX Neighborhood community. This community has four public pages:

- **Welcome**
- **Registration**
- **House on Sale**
- **Daily Tips**

We will populate each of these pages with static web content that we have created with the web content portlet.

Welcome page

The **Welcome** page is the default page that a user will come to when he accesses the **CIGNEX Neighbourhood** site. We will place a welcome message and a log-in portlet on this page.

Time for action – adding content to the Welcome page

Here's how you do it:

1. Suppose that you have logged in as the portal administrator. Click on **Manage | Page Layout**, and a window pops up with 10 pre-defined layouts.

2. Select the **2 Columns (70/30)** layout and click on **Save**.

3. Remove the **Hello World** portlet if it is there.

4. Move the **Sign in** portlet to the right-hand side column.

5. Hover over the **Add** link. Click on **Web Content Display** – the web content display portlet is added to the left-hand side column of the page:

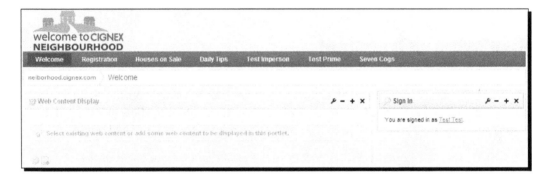

6. Click on the gear-shaped icon on the left-hand side of the portlet at the bottom.

7. Click on **WELCOME-MESSAGE**. Click on **Save** – the content is displayed.

8. Click on the wrench icon on the right-hand side of the portlet on the top.

9. Click on **Look and Feel** – a window pops up.

10. Uncheck **Show Borders** – we want to hide the top bar of the web content display portlet.

11. Click on **Save** and close the pop up window.

12. Refresh the page – the portlet title bar is gone.

Now sign out. Here is how the **Welcome** page looks:

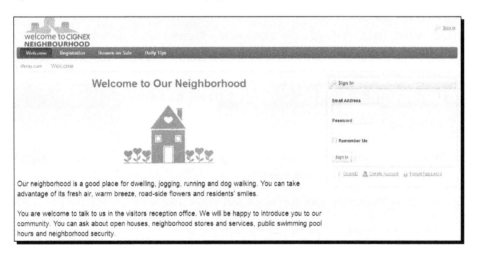

What just happened?

You have just successfully added content to the default page of the **Guest** community at the **CIGNEX Neighborhood** site. Now any user who comes to this site will read the welcome message. He can also log in to the site through the **Sign in** portlet.

Houses-on-Sale page

Two houses are on sale in the neighborhood. Besides placing an on-sale post in front of each of the houses, the Neighbors Congress requires you—the portal administrator—to promote their sale online. You are supposed to attract nice and amiable buyers who have financial capability to pay for the houses.

Time for action – selling houses online

This time you will use the **HO-SALE-ARTICLE** content, which is based on a structure and template.

Go to the `http://neiborhood.cignex.com/web/guest/houses-on-sale` page and perform the following steps:

1. Click on **Manage | Page Layout**.

2. When a window pops up, select **1 Column** and click on **Save**.

3. Close the pop up window.

4. Click on **Add | Web Content Display** – the portlet is added onto the page.

5. Click on the gear-shaped icon at the bottom of the portlet and select the **HO-SALE-ARTICLE** – the content is shown in the web content display portlet.

6. Remove the portlet title bar.

7. Here is how the page will look like:

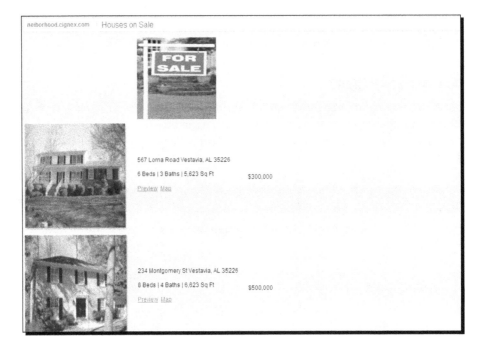

What just happened?

You have successfully added the house-on-sale post to the neighborhood site! You can tell that the house images, house addresses, and house prices are listed in three separate columns respectively, as is defined in the **HOSALE-TEMPLATE** template.

Registration page

On the registration page, we allow visitors to create an account at the **CIGNEX Neighborhood** site.

Time for action – populating the registration page

Here's how you do it:

1. Apply a **2 Columns (50/50)** page layout.

2. Add the **Sign In** portlet in the left-hand side column; add an introduction message in the right-hand side column using the web content display portlet.

Here is how the page will look:

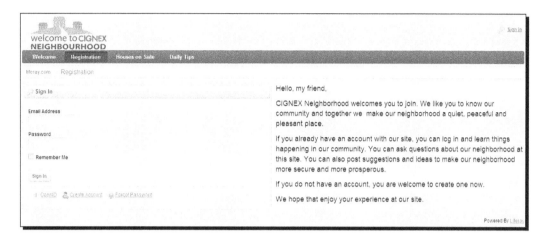

What just happened?

The **Registration** page has been populated with account-creation functionality and content. Now a visiting user can click on the **Create Account** link to create an account at the neighborhood website for himself.

Pop quiz

What do you think is true about content display in Liferay Portal?

- a. By choosing a piece of content in the web content display portlet, you tell the portlet the ID of this piece of content
- b. Each web content display portlet can only hold one piece of content
- c. You can add multiple web content display portlet instances onto a page
- d. All of the above

Have a go hero – tweaking content display

In the preceding examples, we hide the portlet title bar of the web content display portlet, which is good. However, in some situations, we need the portlet title bar with a custom title. Find a way to customize the portlet title for the web content display portlet.

The web content display portlet also allows a user to create a piece of content for it on the run. Find a way to create a piece of content using the web content display portlet.

Uploading documents

You can view a video online. However, you should first upload the video to a server first so that other users can access it through a URL. Liferay Portal provides a document library portlet for us to upload video files and file in other formats to the application server that Liferay Portal is running in.

The document library portlet is used to create folders and upload documents. It is a central place for document management in Liferay Portal.

If you go to a community, use the document Library portlet to create a folder and upload a file into it, the folder and the file are only visible in the document library portlet when you stay in that community. If you change a community and open the document library portlet, you will not see that folder and file – the folders created and files uploaded through the document library portlet are specific to a community or an organization.

The document library portlet is in the Control Panel. By default, only the portal administrator can use it. Other users can use it through custom configuration.

The document library portlet will save the uploaded files on the server machine in the local file system. This design ensures faster retrieval of the files.

By default, you can upload files with any extensions through the document library portlet. You can limit the file extension types in the `portal-ext.properties` file.

Time for action – uploading a video file

Here's how you do it:

1. Suppose that you are the portal administrator. Log in and go to the **Control Panel**.

2. Click on **Document Library | Add Folder**.

3. In the **Name** field, enter **NeibourDoc**.

4. Click on **Save** – a **NeibourDoc** folder is created.

5. Click on the **NeibourDoc** folder name.

6. Click on **Add Document**.

7. Browse to a **swfupload_f8.swf** video file and click on **Open**.

8. Click on **Upload Files** – the file is successfully uploaded.

9. Click on **<< Back** – you can see the uploaded file shown in the **NeibourDoc** folder.

Here is the screenshot of the resulting page:

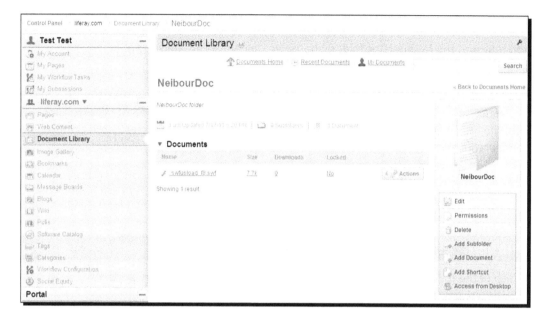

What just happened?

You have created a folder and uploaded a video file into it – it is so easy to use the document library portlet! You can create web content to refer to this video file. This means that you can now present this video online.

Can the document library portlet be used to upload other kinds of files? Let us try a Portable Document Format (PDF) file.

Time for action – uploading a PDF file

You can also use the document library portlet to upload a PDF file. Try uploading an arbitration notice PDF file using the following steps:

1. Remain in the **NeibourDoc** folder and click on **Add Document** again.

2. Browse the local file system and find an **arbitration_results.pdf** file. Click on **Open**.

3. Click on **Upload Files**. Click on **<< Back**, and the **arbitration_results.pdf** file is uploaded successfully.

4. Click on the **arbitration_results.pdf** file name.

5. Find a **URL** input box and copy the value in it.

6. Click on **<< Back** to **NeibourDoc**.

You return to the **NeibourDoc** folder where two uploaded files are shown.

What just happened?

By default, a user with proper permissions can upload files with any kind of file extension with the document library portlet. However, the file extensions can be restricted through configuration in the `portal-ext.properties` file.

The URL field value that you just copied is like this: `http://neiborhood.cignex.com/documents/10157/529b95af-5d6d-41a9-b2c5-9421e4e9be70`. We will refer to this URL later in a piece of web content.

Pop quiz

Which of the following statements are true about the document library portlet?

    a.   You can upload a file to the server and later download it to another computer

    b.   You can add as many sub-folders as you need under any folder that you have permission for

    c.   You can set up the permissions for each folder and file as necessary

    d.   All of the above

Have a go hero – find out more about file uploading

The files that you have just uploaded are in the local file system on the server. Now go to the `${liferay.home}/data/document_library/` directory on your computer. What do you find there?

Now go back to the user interface of the document library portlet. Open the **NeibourDoc** folder. Add the **arbitration_results.pdf** file into the folder again – the original file will be overwritten. Click on the **arbitration_results.pdf** file name link. Go to the **Version History** section. What do you find there? Has file versioning been enforced in the document library portlet?

On the same page above **Version History**, find a **Your Rating** label with five grayed-out stars beneath it. What is this for? Try it out.

Find a **Comments** section under **Version History**. This is the place where you can add some comments about this document. Try to add a comment.

You can configure Liferay Portal through the `portal-ext.properties` file so that the files uploaded through the document library portlet are saved in the Liferay Portal database instead of the local file system.

Showing a PDF file link in web content

Do you remember that we added content to the **Arbitration Notice** private page of the **Arbitration Committee**? The related parties of the arbitration can browse that page to get the arbitration results. Usually, they will also like to keep a copy of the arbitration notice as a PDF file. So, if we can provide a link to a PDF file of the arbitration notice, it will be convenient for the related parties and the site will be more user-friendly. How can we embed such a link in web content to the PDF file? In the preceding section, we uploaded that PDF file to the Liferay Portal server and made it accessible to the members of the Arbitration Committee. Now we update the arbitration notice content to add to it a link to the PDF file.

Time for action – embedding a link for a PDF file

Go to the `http://neiborhood.cignex.com/group/arbitration-committee/arbitration-notice` page and perform the following steps:

1. Click on the pencil icon on the left-hand side corner at the bottom of the web content display portlet – the WYSIWYG editor opens for editing.

2. Create a new line at the bottom of the web content.

3. Click on the link icon in the editor tool bar – a window pops up.

4. In the URL input box, enter **neiborhood.cignex.com/documents/10157/529b95af-5d6d-41a9-b2c5-9421e4e9be70**.

5. Click on **OK** – the pop up window closes, and the URL shows as the link name.

6. Update the URL link name by clicking on the **Source** button in the editor toolbar.

7. Browse to the end of the HTML markup for the web content and find markup as follows:

   ```
   <a href="http:// neiborhood.cignex.com /documents/10157/529b95af-
   5d6d-41a9-b2c5-9421e4e9be70"><span style="font-size:
   14px;">http:// neiborhood.cignex.com /documents/10157/529b95af-
   5d6d-41a9-b2c5-9421e4e9be70</span></a>
   ```

8. Change the markup into the following:

```
<a href=" /documents/10157/529b95af-5d6d-41a9-b2c5-
9421e4e9be70"><span style="font-size: 14px;">Arbitration Notice</
span></a>
```

9. Click on **Publish**:

You will find the next page as shown in the following screenshot:

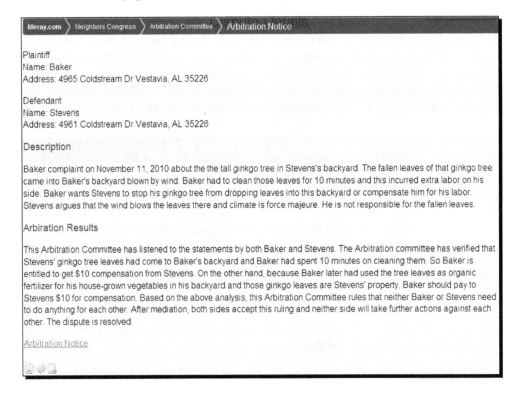

What just happened?

You have just integrated two content management portlets – you embedded a link in a piece of web content that points to a file uploaded through the document library portlet.

Click on the **Arbitration Notice** link at the bottom – a browser window pops up with the arbitration notice PDF file.

Which of the following statements is true about content management portlets?

    a.   If you edit a piece of content through the web content display portlet, the new version will show in the portlet while the old version will still be saved in the database

    b.   For every file you upload through the document library portlet, a URL to that file is generated automatically in Liferay Portal

    c.   Both of the above

Have a go hero – checking file permissions

The `arbitration_results.pdf` file is uploaded in the **Guest** community. Why can you still view it when you come to the **Arbitration Committee** organization? Go back to the **Guest** community and check the permissions for the `arbitration_results.pdf` file in the document library portlet.

Enabling comments for web content

In the web content display portlet, we can enable comments for published web content. This feature is useful in collecting users' reviews about a proposal. Suppose that the neighborhood is considering construction of a public leisure park for the community. The **Neighbors Congress** declares this project for the residents' comments. How can we start such an online event?

Time for action – enabling comments for content

Assume that you have logged in as the portal administrator:

    1.   Go to the public page at the **Neighbors Congress** organization at `http://neiborhood.cignex.com/web/neighbors-congress/proposed-projects`.

    2.   Change the page layout to **2 Columns (70/30)**.

    3.   Add a web content display portlet onto the left-hand side column of the page.

    4.   Click on the **Add Web Content** icon.

    5.   Enter **PUBLIC-GARDEN-ARTICLE** in the **Name** input box.

    6.   Enter the content of the neighborhood project.

    7.   Leave the default permissions as they are.

8. Click on **Publish** – you are back on the **Proposed Projects** page.

9. Click on the wrench-shaped configuration icon on the right-hand side of the portlet title bar.

10. Click on **Configuration**.

11. Check **Enable Comments** and click on **Save**.

12. Close the pop up window.

You will find **No comments yet. Be the first** at the bottom of the web content display portlet as shown in the following screenshot:

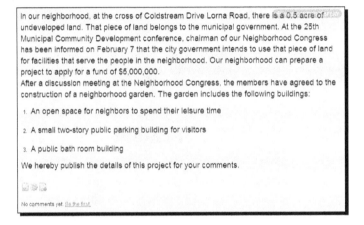

What just happened?

You have just started an online event by enabling the comment feature of the web content display portlet. If you have an account at the neighborhood site and you are a member of the **Neighbors Congress**, you can now log in and enter comments about this public garden project.

Pop quiz

Which of the following statements is true about the content commenting feature?

    a. As a portal administrator, you can enable both rating and comment for a piece of content

    b. If you are not a member of an organization, you may not be able to add comment about content displayed on the page of that organization

    c. Both of the above

Have a go hero – adding comment about content

Try clicking on the **Be the first** link and add a comment about the neighborhood project.

Disclosing decrypted Congress documents

The **Neighbors Congress** makes those Congress documents public that have gone past the encryption deadlines. It publicizes these documents on its decrypted documents page.

Time for action – displaying documents

Suppose that you are the portal administrator:

1. Log in and go to the **Decrypted Documents** public page at `http://neiborhood.cignex.com/web/neighbors-congress/decrypted-documents`.

2. Change the page layout to **1 Column**.

3. Add a web content display portlet on the page.

4. Click on the **Add Web Content** icon and add a description for the page.

5. Add a document library display portlet below the web content display portlet.

6. Click on the **CongressDocHome** folder name – you will see a page similar to the following screenshot:

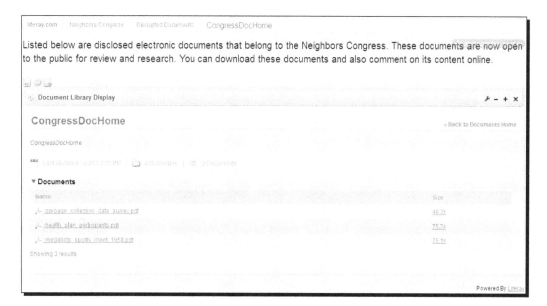

What just happened?

You have successfully used the document library display portlet to start a research environment with the decrypted Congress documents.

Pop quiz

Which of the following statements are true about the document library display portlet?

    a.   It shows files uploaded through the document library portlet in the same community or organization

    b.   The portal administrator can select the root folder for the documents to be displayed

    c.   By default commenting is enabled for the uploaded files

    d.   All of the above

Have a go hero – adding comments

Suppose that you are a member of the **Neighbors Congress** and you are doing research on these decrypted neighborhood documents. You want to express your views on the content of these documents. Please use the features in the document library display portlet to achieve this.

Managing content

The **Neighbors Congress** is a non-profit organization. Below it there is a **Security Council**. This Security Council is responsible for residents' security in the neighborhood. It is also responsible for maintaining order at the neighborhood site.

Suppose that you are a member of the neighborhood Security Council who has the portal administrator role. You are in charge of content management at the neighborhood site.

Reviewing web content

A lot of web content has been created in the guest community. Everything is fine. However, we still need security personnel to supervise web content creation and update. How can this be done?

Liferay Portal has a web content list portlet that shows a list of all the web content created in a community. By clicking on the name of a piece of content, you can see the whole content.

Time for action – using the web content list portlet

Follow this procedure to add the web content list portlet:

1. Go to the **Web Review** page at `http://neiborhood.cignex.com/group/guest/web-review`.

2. Change the page layout to **1 Column**.

3. Hover on the **Add** link. Click on the **More ...** link.

4. In the **Content Management** category, add the web content list portlet to the page.

5. Close the **Add** drop-down menu – you will find the web content list portlet as follows on the page:

6. Click on the wrench-shaped icon at the upper right-hand side of the web content list portlet – a configuration window pops up.

7. For **Web Content Type**, select **General** – most web content created is general type web content.

8. For **Display per Page**, select **10**.

9. Click on **Save**. Close the popup window.

The page will appear as shown in the following screenshot:

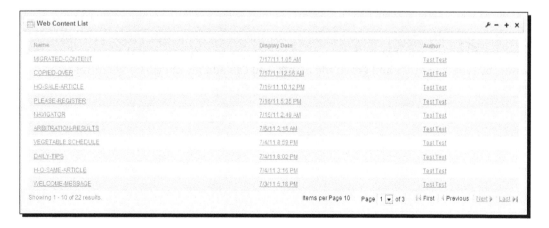

What just happened?

You have added the web content list portlet onto a private page of the **Guest** community and configured it to list 10 pieces of content on one page. Now you can click on the name of any web content and check if it contains anything obsolete, offensive, or politically wrong.

Pop quiz

Which of the following statements is true about the web content list portlet?

- ◆ By default, it only displays content created in the community or organization where it is added
- ◆ By configuration you can filter the content to be displayed
- ◆ Both of the above

Have a go hero – filtering content

Click on the wrench-shaped icon. Click on the **Configuration** link. In the pop-up window, find **Structure** and click on **Select** below it. In the next pop-up window, click on **HOSALE-STRUCTURE** – the second pop-up window closes. Click on **Save**. Close the first pop-up window. What is the change in the list of displayed content?

Monitoring other content

There is also other content like uploaded files to monitor in the **Guest** community. We will do this with the asset publisher portlet of Liferay Portal. The asset publisher portlet publishes a mixture of images, documents, blogs, and web content. It provides each asset a **Read More >>** link to show its content. It also offers an **Edit** link for updating the asset.

When you add the asset publisher portlet onto a page in a community, it will list all the assets added in that community.

The asset publisher portlet contains a lot of functionalities to manage these assets. By configuration, you can choose the asset selection type, specify scope of the assets, filter the assets by type and order and group the assets. You can add file conversion features to an asset and enable ratings and comments for the asset.

Time for action – adding the asset publisher portlet

Suppose that you have logged in as the portal administrator:

1. Go to the **Info Monitoring** page at `http://neiborhood.cignex.com/group/guest/info-monitoring`.

2. Change the page layout to **1 Column**.

3. Hover over the **Add** link and click on the **Asset Publisher** link – this adds the asset publisher portlet onto the page.

You can see that PDF files, video files, web content, and image files are all displayed in the asset publisher portlet, as follows:

What just happened?

You have added the asset publisher portlet onto the Info Monitoring private page of the **Guest** community. All assets added in this community are shown in the asset publisher portlet.

Pop quiz

Which of the following statements are true about the asset publisher portlet?

    a.   You can select assets manually for it to display

    b.   You can add blogs, bookmarks, calendar entries, documents, images, and web content

    c.   By configuring the asset type, you can show only web content

    d.   All of the above

Have a go hero – updating content

Click on the **arbitration_results.pdf** file link – the content of this PDF file is shown in the browser window. Suppose that there is something inappropriate in this PDF file or a user has complained about its content. Take actions to replace this file with a new version.

Converting web content to formatted files

Remember that we have a **Planting Schedule** page in the **Gardening DIY** community? That page has an article about when to plant which vegetables in the backyard. Some housewives or farming fans may like a copy of that article in their pocket when they work in their backyard. So it would be handy if there was a feature to convert this Planting Schedule into a PDF file. In this way we can convert the content, download the PDF file to our computer, and print it. Liferay Portal has this file conversion feature for its content. This feature has been enabled in *Chapter 4, Tips and Tricks-Advanced Configuration*. It relies on the OpenOffice service that was started in *Chapter 1, Planning Your Portal*.

Time for action – adding a file conversion feature

Suppose that you want to add this feature on the **Planting Schedule** content:

    1.   Log in as portal administrator and go to the **Gardening DIY** page at `http://neiborhood.cignex.com/web/gardening-diy/planting-schedule`.

    2.   Click on the wrench-shaped icon at the upper right-hand side corner of the content.

    3.   Click on **Configuration** – a window pops up.

    4.   For the **Enable Conversion To** part, check **DOC** and **PDF** – this will enable the features of converting the web content to a Word document and to a PDF document.

    5.   Click on **Save** and close the configuration window.

Now the web content display portlet will show two file conversion icons as in the following screenshot:

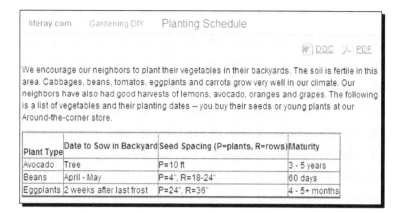

What just happened?

You have just added the file conversion feature to the **Planting Schedule** content. Now these two conversions will be available to all the users, because this page is a public page in the **Gardening DIY** community.

Pop quiz

Which of the following statements are correct about the file conversion feature in the web content display portlet?

    a.   This feature relies on an OpenOffice service

    b.   By default, the OpenOffice service is listening at port 8100

    c.   File conversion can also be added in the document library portlet

    d.   All of the above

Have a go hero – performing conversion

Click on the **DOC** and the **PDF** links to convert the web content into a Word document and a PDF document.

Summary

We learned a lot in this chapter about content creation and publishing in Liferay Portal. Specifically, we covered:

◆ Using the image gallery portlet to upload and manage image files

◆ Creating regular content and content based on a template using the web content portlet

◆ Configuring the web content display portlet to show web content on a portal page

◆ Uploading and managing all kinds of files through the document library portlet

◆ Integrating files uploaded through the document library portlet with the web content display portlet

◆ Monitoring online content through the asset publisher portlet

◆ Converting web content into a PDF file using OpenOffice service

We also discussed content versioning, adding comments to content, and rating content.

Now that we have learned about content creation and publishing with pre-installed portlets, we are ready to populate portal pages with custom portlets, which is the topic of the next chapter.

8
Exploring Communities

In the previous chapter, we learned about Content Management features provided by Liferay. We explored portlets for the Web Content, Images, and Document Management.

In this chapter, we will learn about some preinstalled portlets and custom portlets. We will also explore out-of-the-box Search and Chat portlets provided by Liferay. You will also learn about Open Social Widget integration.

In this chapter, we shall:

- ◆ Learn how to install and add Flash Portlet to play games in a Sports and Games Community
- ◆ Use Web Content Display Portlet to announce cricket matches
- ◆ Learn to use YouTube Portlet to share videos
- ◆ Share Neighborhood photos and view them as a slide show using Image Gallery
- ◆ Explore Chat functionality to chat with other members
- ◆ Learn how to integrate Open Social widgets in Liferay
- ◆ Learn to use Bookmark Portlet to share useful links with the Neighborhood Site
- ◆ Learn how to conduct polls using Polls Portlet
- ◆ Learn to change the language of the Neighborhood site using Language Portlet
- ◆ Learn how to display Breaking News on Neighborhood site using the What's New custom portlet
- ◆ Explore search functionality provided by Liferay

So now it's time to build more Neighborhood pages; let's do it.

Prerequisite

Before you get into this chapter, you need to make sure that all the following prequisites are taken care of:

- In *Chapter 6, Managing Pages, Users, and Permissions,* you should have created all the mentioned private pages for communities/organizations of the Neighborhood site. You will need to use them in this chapter.

- In *Chapter 6,* you should have done the configuration as mentioned in the section, *Configuration for User Pages Default Portlets* to add the Summary Portlet on public pages of users and Members Portlet on private pages of users. After that, you should have created users in *Chapter 6,* so that all the user public and private pages have these portlets.

 Please note that in this chapter, Administrator refers to the Neighborhood Site Administrator created in *Chapter 6,* that is, jeff.mcclure@cignex.com / test123.

Setting up an online game using Flash Portlet

Games can be added to Liferay sites in multiple ways. You can either use Iframe Portlet to configure a website for games, or you could use Flash Portlet and configure it with a flash game. In this section, you will learn about the usage of Flash Portlet to play games. The first step would be to install Flash Portlet, as it is not part of the default installation, and then configure it with a flash game file.

Let's get started.

Time for action – setting up an online game using Flash Portlet

1. Log in to the Neighborhood site as **Site Administrator**.

2. Hover the cursor over the **Manage** menu, and click on the **Control Panel** link.

3. Click on **Plugins Installation** from the **Server** section. It will take you to the **Plugins Installation** screen.

4. On this screen, click on the button **Install More Portlets**. It will take you to the following screenshot:

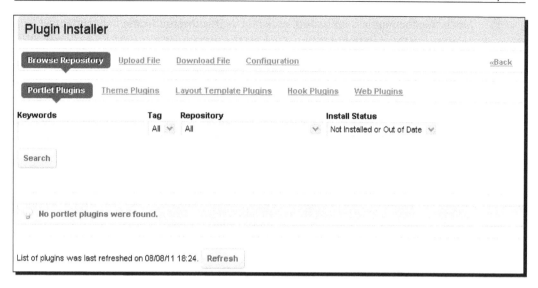

5. Click on **Upload file**, and browse for the portlet war file, `flashportlet-6.0.10.1.war` in the downloaded code for this book.

6. After clicking on **Install**, it will upload a war file to the Liferay server, and deploy it for you. At the end of the successful deployment, you will see a message in tomcat log, as shown in the following screenshot to indicate successful deployment:

7. Now, before you add a Flash Portlet to the page, you will need to add a flash file for the Baseball game to **Document Library**. You will then configure this game in the Flash portlet. Select the **Sports and Games** community in the content section, and then click on **Document Library**.

8. You have already seen the **Document Library** interface in *Chapter 7*. Now, click on **Add Document** from the right-hand side menu, and add the flash file `pinchhitter2.swf` (you can find this file in the downloaded code for this book) as the document.

9. Once the document is uploaded, click on the **Documents Home** link, and it will take you to the document listing. Click on the document `pinchhitter2.swf`. It will open a detail view for the document. Copy the full URL from the URL field and paste it to a temporary location. You can open Notepad and paste it there. You will need to use this URL in Flash Portlet configuration. This URL refers to the path of this flash file.

10. Now, click on **Pages**, and it will open the manage pages interface, where you need to click on **View Pages**. This should take you to the **Sport and Games** community. Then click on the **Online Games** page.

11. Now, you should click on the **Add** menu from the top menu, and click on **More**. It will open a popup with all portlets available. In the popup search box, enter the word **flash**. It will show you Flash Portlet, as shown in the following screenshot. Click on the **Add** button next to add Flash Portlet on the page:

12. Once Flash Portlet is added, the next step is to configure it and provide the location of the flash file to be played. Open configuration for Flash Portlet, as shown in the following screenshot.

13. In the **Movie** field, enter the URL, which you had copied to Notepad as mentioned in step 9 of flash file. You can also specify **Flash Attributes** and **Flash Variables**, if you want to change default behavior or pass a parameter to flash. In this scenario, we will leave them as they are, as shown in the following screenshot. Now, click on the **Save** button to save the configuration, and close the popup:

14. You should then see the **Pinch Hitter2** game from
`http://www.addictinggames.com` in Flash Portlet. You just need
to click on the **Play** link, and start playing. Don't get addicted to it,
as there is more to learn in further sections of this chapter.

What just happened?

You have set up an online game, using Flash Porltet on the Neighborhood site. Flash
Porltet also provides an option to specify **Flash Attributes** and **Flash Variables** to change
the behavior of the movie being played. **Flash Attributes** allow providing attributes for
alignment, background color, height of movie, looping option, and so on. **Flash Variables**
allow sending variables to the movie, in order to change the state of the movie.

Have a go hero – displaying a Vegetable schedule

Now, since you have set up the game, and have enjoyed playing, try changing some of its
attributes to change the default behavior of the movie. Change height to 400 sec as the
behavior of the portlets. Try changing the background color.

Adding Web Content Display to announce a cricket match

Most of the websites that you will develop will have a lot of static content to share
information. In this section, we will learn how to create static content and display it on the
page. We will now announce a cricket match, which is going to be played in Neighborhood,
using **Web Content Display** Portlet in this section.

Time for action – announcing a cricket match

1. Log in to the Neighborhood site as **Site Administrator**.

2. Hover the cursor over the **Manage** link in **Dockbar**, and click on the **Control Panel** link.

3. In the **Content** section, select the **Cricket Players** community.

4. Now, you should click on the **Web Content** link, and it will open Web Content Portlet. In that, click on the **Add Web Content** button. It will open the interface to add new web content.

5. You should then enter **Cricket Match** in the **Name** field. Now, under the **Content** section, click on the **Source** button item in the WYSWYG editor, and enter the following HTML code in it:

```
<p>
    <span style="font-size:22px;"><strong>Cricket Match </strong></
span></p>
<p>
    We have organized cricket match on this weekend in ground area.
Details have been mentioned below</p>
<table border="1" cellpadding="1" cellspacing="1" style="width:
181px; height: 93px;">
    <tbody>
        <tr>
            <td>
                Date</td>
             <td>
                03 Dec 2011</td>
        </tr>
        <tr>
        <td>
                Venue</td>
            <td>
                Neighbourhood Ground</td>
        </tr>
        <tr>
            <td>
                Team1</td>
            <td>
                Block-A</td>
        </tr>
        <tr>
            <td>
```

```
            Team2</td>
        <td>
            Block-B</td>
        </tr>
    </tbody>
</table>
<p>
So come and enjoy the match.</p>
```

6. Now, you should click on the **Source** button again to see how content will be visible to the end user. The **Source** button is very useful when you want to create content with existing HTML.

7. Now, scroll down and then click on the **Publish** button to publish this web content. It will take you to the web content listing, and you can see newly created web content in the listing.

8. After creating the web content, you should go to the **Cricket Players** community page, and make this content visible. Click on the **Pages** link from the menu on the left side under the content section. Make sure you have the **Coming Events** page available as you created in *Chapter 6*. If not then create a new public page, **Coming Events**. You should then click on the **View Pages** button. It will open a new tab and will show you pages of the **Cricket Players** community.

9. Now, you should add the **Web Content Display** Portlet using the **Add Application** popup to the **Coming Events** page.

10. On the **Web Content Display** Portlet, click on the **Select Web Content** icon   . It will open a popup to select content. In content listing, select **Cricket Match** and the content will be visible, as shown in the following screenshot. After that, click on the **Save** button, and close the configuration popup. Now, you can see information about a cricket match being displayed on the page web content:

What just happened?

You have just created web content for a cricket match, under the **Cricket Players** community. After that you added Web Content Display Portlet to the **Coming Events** page, and configured it with **Cricket Match** web content to show details about the upcoming cricket match.

Web Content Display Portlet is very useful to show static content, and it also has a feature which allows an admin to create new content directly from the portlet by clicking on the **Add Web Content** link. This portlet also allows you to edit content directly from the portlet, by clicking on the **Edit Web content** link. This feature is very useful to editors who might not want to keep going to **Control Panel**, find content, and then modify it.

 Take a moment and think of all the static web content you need for your website and identify pages on which they need to be placed.

Using Video Portlet to share Neighborhood videos

One of the most important features of any intranet or public facing site is sharing videos, as videos are very effective collaboration mechanisms. In this section, we will see how easily you can share videos in Liferay site. We will use Video Portlet provided in the downloaded code of this book to achieve that.

Let's do that now.

Time for action – sharing Neighborhood videos

1. Log in to the Neighborhood site as **Administrator**.

2. Hover the cursor over the **Manage** link and click on the **Control Panel** link.

3. Click on **Plugins Installation** from the **Server** section. It will take you to the **Plugins Installation** screen.

4. On this screen, click on **Install More Portlets**. It will take you to the screen where you can install portlets, as shown in following screenshot.

5. Click on the **Upload** file and browse for the portlet war file, `youtube-portlet-6.0.10.1` in the downloaded code for this book.

6. After that, click on **Install**. It will upload the war file to the Liferay server and deploy it for you. At the end of a successful deployment, you will see a message in the tomcat log as shown in the following screenshot to indicate successful deployment:

```
14:43:52,734 INFO  [PortletHotDeployListener:220] Registering portlets for youtube-portlet
14:43:52,859 INFO  [PortletHotDeployListener:369] 1 portlet for youtube-portlet is available for use
```

7. Now, you should select the **Neighbourhood Exchange** community, and click on the **Pages** link. Now, on manage page interface, click on the **Private Pages** from the top menu. You should then click on the **View Pages** button to go to community private pages.

8. Click on the **Our Videos** page. Now, you will add a video portlet on this page. Open the **Add Application** popup, and search for the word **YouTube**. You will see the **YouTube** portlet under the **Entertainment** category. Click on the **Add** link, which will add the portlet to the page.

9. You should now remove portlet borders to make it look better to end users. Click on **Look and Feel** from the portlet title bar menu. It will open the **Look and Feel** configuration popup. By default, the **Portlet Configuration** menu item will be selected. In that, uncheck the **Show Borders** checkbox and save it. Now, close the **Look and Feel** popup, and refresh the page for changes to take effect.

10. Now, click on the link **Please configure this portlet** to make it visible to all users. This will take you to the portlet configuration, as shown in the following screenshot.

11. In configuration, enter the `http://www.youtube.com/watch?v=vQ4CQxnt61E` link in the **URL** field, and click on the **Save** button. If you are connected to the Internet, it will bring up the video in the preview section, as shown in the following screenshot. Now, close the configuration popup.

12. You can now click on the play button to view this video. Similarly, you can add more instances of video portlets and show more videos to users. Each video should first be uploaded on YouTube.

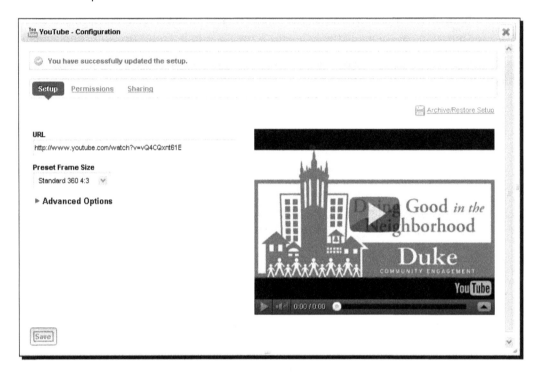

What just happened?

You have just added a video player in the community page, and configured it with the Neighborhood site video. You can similarly upload more videos on YouTube, and share them on your site using this portlet. This approach allows you to share selective videos very easily with your site users.

This video portlet also has advanced settings, which are available in the configuration tab of the portlet. Some of the most important ones are as follows:

- ◆ Present Frame size: This allows you to change the quality of the video
- ◆ Player Color, Border Color: This allows you to change the color of the player and border
- ◆ Auto Play: This allows you to start playing automatically
- ◆ Loop: This allows you to keep playing the same video again and again
- ◆ Enable Fullscreen Option: This allows the user to view in full screen

Another option for video sharing is through video streaming portlets, which allow you to upload videos in the document library and stream using streaming portlets. But Liferay does not provide any video streaming portlet out of the box. You would need to either develop it or buy one from a vendor.

Sharing Neighborhood photos using Image Gallery

Photo sharing is one of the most critical and important requirements of any social website. In this section, we will learn how to share photos with community members using Image Gallery Portlet. You have already learned about Image Gallery Portlet in the previous chapter. In this section, we will explore the slide show feature of Image Gallery Portlet. It is built using Alloy UI (`http://alloy.liferay.com/`) slide show tag libraries.

 Make sure that you have done the first point from the *Prerequisite* section mentioned at the beginning of this chapter.

Time for action – sharing Neighborhood photos

1. Log in to the Neighborhood site as **Administrator**.

2. Hover over the **Manage** link and click on the **Control Panel** link.

3. From the **Portal** Section, click on the **Communities** link.

4. In the community listing, under the **Neighbourhood Exchange** community, click on **Private Pages**. It will take you to the private pages of the community.

5. In the **Navigation** menu, click on the **Photo Sharing** page, and add Image Gallery Portlet using the **Add Application** menu.

6. Now, click on the **Add Image** button from the right-hand side menu in the portlet. It will open flash uploader to upload images. Click on the **Browse** link, and it will open **File selector** for you. Now, select three files: `neighbourhood-aerial-view.jpg`, `neighbourhood-street-view.jpg`, and `neighbourhood-house-view.jpg` from the folder for *Chapter 8* in the downloaded code for this book.

7. Once you have selected all three files, click on **Upload Files** to complete the uploading process. Once the upload is done, click on the **Back** link to go back to the main portlet view. It should now show three images as shown in the following screenshot:

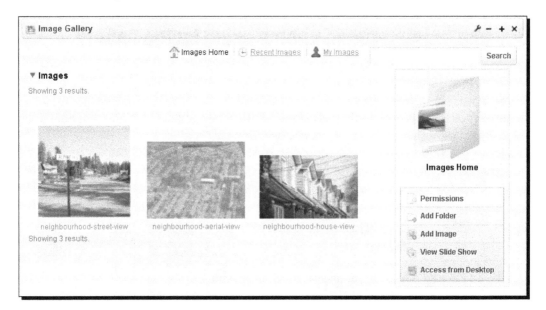

8. Now click on **Permissions**, and verify that only community members have view permission apart from the owner.

9. You are now done with uploading images. The next step is to log in as a normal community member, and verify how an image appears to a community member and check the slide show feature. Log in as user, jenny.bensar@cignex.com / test123 (in *Chapter 6*, you should have created this user and made her the member of Neighborhood Exchange community. If these steps have not been carried out, then refer to *Chapter 6* and create this user).

10. After logging into the site, click on **Neighbourhood Exchange Private Pages** from **Go to menu** in **Dockbar**.

11. After that, you should click on the **Photo Sharing** page. Once the page is loaded, you will see the **Image Gallery** Portlet with three pictures. Click on the first picture; it will open the overlay popup with the picture visible as shown in the following screenshot. Now, click on the next arrow icon to go to the next image. There is also a previous arrow icon to go back to the previous image:

12. Alternatively, you can click on the **View Slide Show** button from the right-hand side menu to view the slide show.

13. It should open a popup to show images in a slide show as shown in the following screenshot. By default, it will loop through all the images one by one. However, you also have the option to stop automatic looping by clicking on the **Pause** button. In that scenario, you can also move between images using the **Previous** and **Next** button:

14. You also have the option to set the number of seconds. Each image should be visible in the slide show using **Speed** dropdown. In the **Speed** dropdown, by default, 3 will be selected. Change it to 6. You can observe that now each image will be shown for six seconds before the next image comes up. Change that value to 1, and you will observe that now the image changes after one second.

What just happened?

You have added the **Image Gallery** Portlet to the private page of the **Neighbourhood Exchange** community. You have also added three images to the community. After that you have logged in as a normal user and verified that only the slide show feature is available. You have navigated between different images and also seen the out of the box slide show feature provided by the **Image Gallery** Portlet. Also, these images can be used in conjuction with Web Content, images from Image Gallery can be embedded into Web Content.

Navigation feature between images, when you click on it has been implemented using the `aui-image-gallery-viewer` module of Alloy UI tag libraries. Alloy UI (`http://alloy.liferay.com/`) is a Liferay community project, which is built on top of YUI3 libraries (`http://developer.yahoo.com/yui/3`), provided by Yahoo!. Earlier versions of Liferay used custom UI tags, which internally were using Jquery. Alloy UI is gaining momentum, and the tag libraries are powerful and very easy to use. You have seen the power of Alloy UI in image navigation. You can use this module in a custom portlet and incorporate the image navigation feature on the set of images.

Reflection

Take a moment and think of photo sharing in your site. How would you do that? Does Image Gallery portlet suffice with minor changes, or would you need to develop a custom portlet? In the case of a custom portlet, what are the features that you need to include, for example, showing images which have specific tags?

Pop quiz – multiple choice

Alloy UI is based on:

    a.   Google Web Tool kit

    b.   query

    c.   YUI3

    d.   None of the above

Exploring chat functionality to enable chat between Neighborhood members

In this section, we will explore Liferay's out of box chat functionality. Chatting is a very useful collaborative feature in the intranet scenario, where employees can collaborate over chat. Liferay Chat Portlet is shipped as a plugin, which by default will be added to the bottom of each page. Liferay Chat will require some setup, which will allow members to add other members as friends and start chatting.

Let's explore it.

Time for action – exploring chat functionality

1. Prerequisite: Make sure you are done with point 2 in the *Prerequisite* section given at the beginning of this chapter. If you have not done that then you have to log in as **Administrator** and get the public pages of **Roy Crow** and then add **Summary** Portlet. Then you have to go to the private pages of **Roy Crow** and add Requests Portlet.

2. Log in as **Site Administrator** and go to **Control Panel**.

3. First, you would need to add **Members** portlet to each community, which will show current community members. It will help users to invite their friends by clicking on their public profile and sending friend requests. In the content section, select the **CIGNEX Neighbourhood** community, and click on the **Pages** link under it.

4. Add new public page members under it.

5. Now, you click on the **View Pages** button, which will take you to public pages of this community. Click on the **Members** page from the menu.

6. Now, we will add a **Members** portlet in this page. Click on the **Add** menu from top bar, and click on the **More** link. It will open the **Add Application** popup with a listing of all the portlets. Now, you should add the **Members** portlet found under **Social category to page**. It will show all the available members of the community.

7. Similarly, create the **Members** page and add the **Members** portlet for all the other communities mentioned as follows:
    - ❑ Sports and Games
    - ❑ Cricket Players
    - ❑ Gardening DIY
    - ❑ Neighborhood exchange
    - ❑ Around the Corner

8. The step would be to make users friends, so they can start chatting. Go to the
Members page of the **CIGNEX Neighbourhood** community. In Member listing,
the user **Roy Crow** should be there (since we had added him to this community in
Chapter 6; if not, go back to *Chapter 6* and perform this operation). Now, click on
the link on his name. It should take you to the Public Profile of **Roy Crow**, as shown
in the following screenshot:

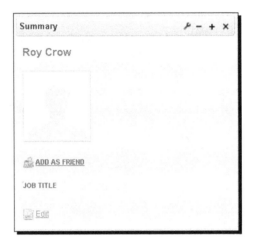

9. Click on the **Add as Friend** link, and it will send a friend request to Roy.

10. Now you should log in as **Roy Crow**, and go to his private pages. You should be able
to send a friend request in Requests portlet as shown in the following screenshot.
Now you should click on the **Confirm** link to add Administrator as a friend. Now Roy
and the Administrator can start chatting with each other.

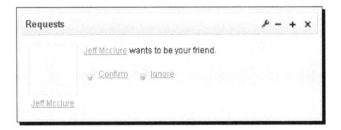

11. After adding both users, add friends. To simulate chatting, you should open two
different browser clients (from Firefox, Internet Explorer, Chrome, and Safari).
In one browser you should log in as **Administrator** and in another browser,
log in as **Roy Crow**.

12. Now in the browser with **Administrator** logged in, you should be able to see **Roy Crow** as an online friend in the bottom-right corner under the **Online Friends** popup, as shown in the following screenshot. Now, you should click on the name **Roy Crow** and send him the message, **Hi, how are you?**

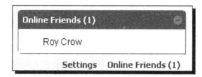

13. Open the browser where **Roy Crow** is logged in, and you should be able to see the message from **Administrator** in the bottom-right corner. You can then reply as **Row Crow** and enjoy chatting.

What just happened?

You have just explored chat functionality provided by Liferay. You have made **Administrator** and **Roy Crow** friends, and simulated chatting between them. You have also seen chat interface provided by Liferay. It contains the following features:

- **Online Friends**: This popup shows your current online friends and allows clicking on them to start chatting. Clicking on the names of any of your friends opens a new window with their name where you can chat with them.

- **Settings**: This popup allows you to perform basic settings for chat. It allows you to set user status. Also, gives the option to not be available for chat, since, by default when a user logs in, he/she appears on the online friends list of other users. Also, there is the option to disable sound while chatting.

Apart from chat in this section, we have also seen three other out of box portlets provided by Liferay that is, Members, Summary, and Requests.

Members Portlet is a very useful portlet to show the current member of the community or organizations. It can be put on either of them. It also allows you to go to a public profile of each of the members. It also supports pagination, which is helpful in the case of large numbers of users. By default, pagination is set to show five users per page. You can modify this by doing source level customization of this portlet. We will not discuss customization of the portlet as it is a bit early for you to get into the details of source code level customization of Liferay out of box portlets.

You have also seen Summary Portlet of Liferay. This portlet shows the following details of the user:

- Name of user
- Portrait of user
- Option to add user as a friend if you are on the public page of the user
- Job title of user
- Activity details
- Open to edit user profile if you have rights to do so

One more portlet which we discussed in this section is the Requests portlet. This portlet is found in the **Social** category in the **Add Application** popup. It is also an out of box portlet provided by Liferay. This portlet shows all the current pending requests on which user has to take action. It is best to be put on private pages of the user. In this section, we had seen that **Roy Crow** had accepted a friend request from the Administrator through this portlet.

Pop quiz – True or false

1. Request portlet shows requests from users who want to be your friend:
   a. True
   b. False

2. Using chat portlet you can appear offline to your friends even though you logged into the site:
   a. True
   b. False

Integrating Open Social Gadgets in Neighborhood site

So far you have seen portlets being installed and added to pages to perform various functions in the Neighborhood site. In this section, we will explore a new concept called **Open Social Gadgets**. These apps are developed using **Open Social API** (http://www.opensocial.org/), which allows them to run on various sites such as hi5, LinkedIn, MySpace, Netlog, Ning, orkut, and Yahoo!. Open Social gadgets are available as XML files; you can either refer to them at another website or host them on your own site. Liferay provides support for Open Social Apps out of box by integrating the Open Social container based on **Shindig** (http://shindig.apache.org/), which can hold Open Social Apps. In this section we will configure a few Open Social Apps in the Neighborhood site.

Time for action – integrating Open Social Gadgets

1. Log in to your Liferay site as default **Administrator**.

2. On your home page, go to the **Manage** menu and click on **Control Panel**.

3. In **Control Panel**, scroll down to the **Portal** section and click on the **Open Social menu** item. It will bring you to the Open Social interface.

4. Click on **Add Gadget** and enter the name as **Cinco Online Games** and URL as `http://www.labpixies.com/campaigns/cinco/cinco.xml` (Labpixies is a google company, which provides a lot of interesting Open Social Apps free for use), as shown in the following screenshot. Now click on the **Save** button:

5. Now, Gadget is ready for use. Next step would be to go to the **Community** page and add gadget. Since it's a game gadget, you should add this to the **Sports and Games** community. In content section, select the **Sports and Games** community, and click on the **Pages** link. Now, you should click on the **View Pages** button. Now from menu, click on the **Online Games** page.

6. Liferay adds all the Open Social apps under a special category called **Open Social**. Open the **Add Application** menu and go to the category **Open Social**. You should see the **Cinco Online Game** application and add it to the page.

7. As shown in the following screenshot, it will display the game in the content section. Also, you will notice that it has title bar options just like portlets. This allows you to configure this widget just like portlets for look and feel and permission.

8. This game is very simple; you have to place five balls of the same color in a line and they will disappear. You can move any ball from one place to another by clicking on a specific ball, and then clicking on its end position.

9. The game will be over when the board is full and you can not move any balls. You can restart the game any time by clicking on the refresh icon in the bottom bar. Enjoy playing.

10. Now, let's add some more gadgets. We will add a gadget for weather, which allows you to configure it just like portlets. Go to **Control Panel** and click on the **Open Social** link from the **Portal** section. Then click on the **Add Gadget** button.

11. Enter **Name** as **Weather Gadget** and URL as `http://hosting.gmodules.com/ig/gadgets/file/109162539679639397174/weather.xml` and click on **Save**.

12. Now, let's add this gadget to the welcome page of the **CIGNEX Neighbourhood** community. Select **CIGNEX Neighbourhood** in the content section and click on the **Pages** link. After that, click on the **View Pages** link. By default, the **Welcome** page will be selected.

13. Using the **Add Application** menu, add the **Weather Gadget** to this page. By default, it will show the weather of New York. You should then click on the configuration from the top menu to configure this portlet. In the configuration popup, enter **Mumbai** as **Location**, change scale to **C** and give the title as **Mumbai City**. To save changes, click on the **Save** button and close the configuration window.

14. On Weather Portlet, you will see the weather of Mumbai, as shown in the following screenshot:

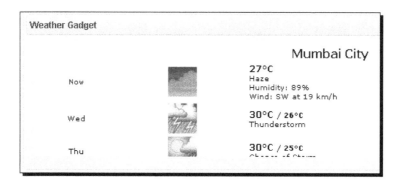

What just happened?

In this section, you have integrated external gadgets into Liferay. You first created gadgets by providing the name and URL of the gadget. After that you placed gadgets on pages, just like portlets, to use them. You also configured the Weather Gadget just like you configured the portlets.

Let's understand a bit more about Open Social Gadgets. From now on, Open Social Gadgets will be referred to as gadgets in this chapter. Gadgets are the future of the Web, as they are easy to build, share, and use. They are being developed using client-side technologies such as HTML, JavaScript, and so on. Also, they use Open Social API, which is supported by many websites, allowing them to easily get embedded in various websites and access friends and update details on social networking platforms. Gadgets are highly popular in social networking sites as they provide various tools and games, and so on, to end users. However, gadgets will work on sites which support Open Social API and provide an Open Social container to host gadgets. The best place to get Open Social Gadget is `http://www.google.com/ig/directory`.

Now in Liferay, support for the Open Social gadgets has been included by integrating the Shindig container. This container is the reference implementation of Open Social API. Liferay also provides functionality to gadgets similar to portlets, like title bar menus such as Look and Feel, Configuration, and so on. It also allows you to add gadgets. Internally, Liferay also stores user data created by gadgets in its own database. So, for example if you have a game, which stores user scores, those scores will be stored on Liferay database locally, rather than on gadget provider server.

In this section, we have used an external URL to refer to gadgets. Alternatively, you can download an XML file and store it on the local server and provide that URL during creation. Either you can put the XML file on the web server, or alternatively you can upload to Document Library as a document and reference it by URL.

Creating bookmark of useful links using Bookmark Portlet

Sharing useful links between site members is necessary. In this section, we will share various useful links with Neighborhood members using Bookmark Portlet. Bookmark portlet allows you to manage various bookmarks.

Let's look at this in detail.

Time for action – creating bookmarks of useful links

1. Log in to your Liferay site as default **Administrator**.

2. Go to **Control Panel**, and select **Neighbourhood Exchange** in the content section. Select the **Pages** link and create a new public page, **Useful Information**.

3. Now click on the **View Pages** button to go to the public pages of this community. Now you should click on the **Useful Information** page from the menu.

4. After that add **Bookmarks** portlet to the page using the **Add Application** popup.

5. In the bookmark portlet on the right-hand side menu, click on the **Add Bookmark** link. You will see a screen like the following screenshot to add a new bookmark:

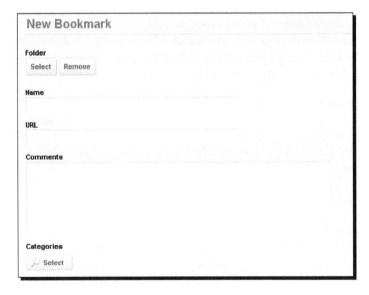

6. Enter the following details on screen:

    ❑ Name: **Do and Dont:Neighbours Relations**

    ❑ URL: `http://realestate.findlaw.com/neighbors/home-neighbors-overview.html`

7. Now, click on the **Save** button at the bottom to save this entry.

8. It will add a new entry in the list. Similarly add one more entry, described as follows:

    ❑ Name: **Kids - Handwriting Guidelines**

    ❑ URL: `http://www.nellieedge.com/articles_resources/GuidelinesHandwriting.html`

9. Then click on the **Save** button from the bottom to save this entry.

10. Now, log out from Administrator and log in as jenny.bensar@cignex.com / test123. You should have created this user in *Chapter 6* and assigned it to the **Neighbourhood Exchange** community.

11. Once you are logged in, click on the **Go To** menu, then click on **Neighbourhood Exchange Public Pages**. After that, click on the **Useful Information** page; you will see a bookmark portlet with two links.

12. Click on the Title link for the first entry. You will be taken to a details view of the bookmark entry, as shown in the following screenshot. Clicking on the link will take you to the actual URL:

What just happened?

You have just added bookmark portlet to the page, and created two bookmark entries as admin. After that, you have logged in as the normal user used as a bookmark entry.

Let's understand this in more detail. Bookmark Porltet allows you to organize bookmarks in folders structure. It's possible to create a folder and sub folder structure as per requirement. This will allow you to manage bookmarks in a more structured manner. Also, it gives flexibility to define access rights at folders level to implement ACL on bookmarks. You can alternatively define permission at the bookmark entry level as well.

For each bookmark entry, you can provide the following information:

◆ **Name**: This is used to enter the name of the bookmark entry

◆ **URL**: This is used to provide the link of the URL which this bookmark is representing

◆ **Comments**: This is used to enter comment or descriptions for the bookmark entry

◆ **Categories**: This is used to assign a category to the bookmark entry

◆ **Tags**: This is used to assign tags to the bookmark entry

◆ **Permissions**: This is used to set permission regarding who can access this bookmark entry

Bookmark listing has one more interesting feature—visits, which shows how many times this entry has been visited. This information is very useful for the Administrator to gather information on the popularity of a specific bookmark entry.

Apart from this, Bookmark Portlet has two more features:

◆ **Recent Entries**: This link shows the list of recently added bookmark entries. This is a useful feature when Bookmark Portlet has quite a big number of entries.

◆ **My Entries**: This link shows the list of entries added by currently logged in user. This feature helps the users to manage their personal bookmark entries.

Bookmark Portlet also has the feature to search entries from the list of entries. This is really helpful to quickly find the required bookmark entry.

Now, let's explore a bit on configuration options provided by Bookmark Portlet. You can open the configuration screen from the portlet title bar menu option. It will look as shown in the following screenshot. Configuration has been divided into two sections, **Folder Listing** and **Bookmark Listing**.

In **Folder listing**, the following options have been provided:

- **Root Folder**: This allows you to select a folder whose sub folder and bookmark listing will be shown in this instance of Bookmark Portlet
- **Show Search**: If this checkbox is selected, search functionality will be shown in the Bookmark Portlet
- **Show Subfolders**: If this checkbox is selected, subfolders will be shown to the current selected root folder
- **Folders Per Page**: This is the pagination feature for folders
- **Show Columns**: This feature allows you to choose which metadata information about folders will be shown to the end user

In **Bookmark Listing**, the following options have been provided:

- **Documents Per Page**: This shows the number of bookmark entries to be shown for each page
- **Show Columns**: These features allow you to choose metadata information about bookmark entries to be shown to the end user

This configuration option allows each Bookmark Portlet instance to show different information, based on the needs of the site:

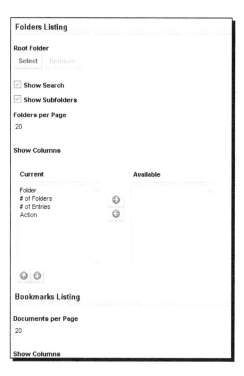

Conducting polls in the Neighborhood site using Polls Portlet

Liferay provides another useful feature to conduct Polls on your website. Polls allow you to provide an easy way to your user for participation. Liferay has given out of box portlets to create and display Polls. These polls can have various options, and can also maintain result of Polls. Polls feature is also very common and an interesting feature to increase the traffic of the site.

Let's understand how to use the Polls functionality in the Neighborhood site.

Time for action – creating bookmarks of useful links

1. Log in to your Liferay site as default **Administrator**.

2. Go to the **Control Panel** and select **Neighbourhood Exchange** in the content section.

3. Now, click on the **Polls** link from the left-hand side menu. You will be shown the **Polls Management** screen.

4. You should then click on the **Add Question** button. It will take you to the screen where you can add new questions, as shown in the following screenshot:

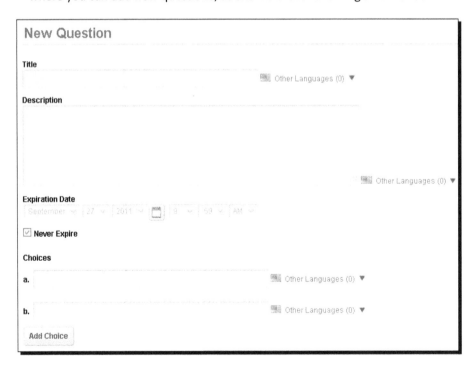

5. Add new poll based on the following information:

 ❑ **Title: Choose a place for annual trip?**

 ❑ **Description: As per our yearly tradition, this year also we are organizing one week holiday trip. We need your suggestion in selecting a destination. Please choose one option.**

 ❑ **Expiration Date**: Select **March, 31, 2012**

 ❑ **Never Expires**: Unselect this checkbox.

 ❑ **Choices**: Enter **Hawai**, **Las Vegas**. Then click on **Add Choice** and add **Goa, Dubai**, and **Paris**.

6. Now, click on the **Save** button to create a new poll. After saving, it will appear in the listing.

7. Now, since we have added a poll, the next step would be to publish on site where users can participate in polls. So, go to the private pages of the **Neighbourhood Exchange** community, and click on the **Gossip** page.

8. Now, using the **Add Application** menu, add **Polls Display** Portlet from the **Content Management** category onto the page.

9. Click on the configuration link from portlet body to configure this portlet to display polls. In drop-down, select the poll you created in previous steps. After selection, save changes and close configuration popup. You will see that **Polls Display** Portlet will show poll configured.

10. Now, log out as **Administrator** and log in as normal community member Jenny Bensar (jenny.bensar@cignex.com /test123). Go to **Neighbourhood Exchange** community privates pages, and click on the **Gossip** page. As shown in the following screenshot, the poll will be visible on the page:

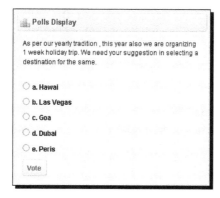

11. Now, select your favorite destination, and click on **Vote**. You will then see the current result of the poll in the portlet body. You are allowed to submit your view only once for one poll.

12. Since more information is available to the Administrator for analysis, logout as the community member and login as the **Administrator**. You should then go to **Control Panel** and select **Neighbourhood Exchange** in the content section. Now, click on the **Polls** link from the left-hand side menu.

13. You will be shown the list of polls available. Click on **Choose a place for annual trip?**. It will open the screen in which you can see results as **Administrator**, and it will also show users who participated in the poll and their choices.

14. You can also see results in various charts like **Area**, **Horizontal Bar**, **Line**, **Pie**, and **Vertical Bar**. Click on the **Pie** link, which will open a popup with a pie chart.

What just happened?

In this section, you have created a new poll using the **Polls** Portlet in **Control Panel**, under the **Neighbourhood Exchange** community. After that, you have used the **Polls Display** portlet to show that poll to the end user. You have also logged in as the community member and participated in polls and seen results.

Basic information is clear now, let's understand Polls in bit more detail. Liferay provides two portlet for Polls functionality, that is, **Polls** Portlet and **Polls Display** Portlet.

Polls Portlet is embedded in **Control Panel**, and allows you to create polls. These polls are created under the content section, so they are available to a specific community or organization under which they are created. Each poll is represented as a question in Polls Portlet, and it can have two or more choices. This portlet, by default, supports only single answer multiple-choice questions. There is one more feature provided by the **Polls** Portlet to set the **Expiration Date** of any polls, which makes it time-bound. This is very useful in a scenario, where you want to take a decision based on the poll in a certain time frame. **Polls** Portlet in **Control Panel** also shows results and analysis for any polls conducted. It shows total response received and the number of votes for each choice, who has voted against which option. Also, there are various charts available for each poll to perform more detailed analysis.

Polls Display Portlet is used to display polls on website pages. It is an instantiable portlet, which means you can configure multiple instances of it to conduct multiple polls across the site. **Polls Display** Portlet shows all the options available for a poll to users and allows them to select one of them. Once the users submit their opinion to the poll, they cannot change it or resubmit it.

Pop quiz – multiple choice

Which type of question does Polls Portlet support?

    a.   Multiple choice with single answer

    b.   Multiple choice with multiple answers

    c.   Both of the above

Have a go hero – creating more polls

Create one more poll to find out which Hollywood actor you like most. Options could be Tom Hanks, Tom Cruise, Leonardo DiCaprio, Pierce Brosnan. **Expiration Date** should be set to one month from the current date. You should then put this poll on the **Gossip** page of the **Neighbourhood Exchange** community.

Changing language of Neighborhood site using Language Portlet

In this era of globalization, language should not be a barrier to sharing information. Keeping that thought in mind, Liferay has always been very powerful in terms of its localization support. The latest version of Liferay supports 33 languages out of the box. Most of these translations are done by either the community, or sponsored by customers. Liferay also supports changing interface from one language to another on the fly, using Language Portlet. Liferay also provides a very nice interface, through which you perform translation of Liferay in your language. You can access that interface using `http://translate.liferay.com`.

Time for action – changing language using Language Portlet

    1.   Log in to your Liferay site as the default **Administrator**.

    2.   On the welcome page using the **Add Application** menu, add the **Language** Portlet from the **Tools** category. You will be see the **Language** Portlet, as shown in the following screenshot. It displays flags of all the countries whose languages are supported. Move the mouse over a flag and it will show you the information regarding the language and country.

3. This portlet also provides the option of showiing less number of languages for user selection through configuration. Also, it has configuration option to change the display style of listing of languages. Open the configuration popup. It will look as shown in the following screenshot.

4. From the **Languages** drop-down, move all the languages from the current to available box except for **English (United States)**, **English (United Kingdom)**, **Hindi(India)**, **German(Germany)**, **Spanish(Spain)**, as shown in the following screenshot. Also, change Display Style from icon to **Select Box**. Now, click on **Save**, and close the configuration popup.

5. Now, in the portlet there will be a drop-down with only five languages. You can switch between the languages by selecting it from the drop-down. Select **Hindi (India)** in the dropdown, and the page will be reloaded with the interface changed to Hindi. You may still find pages named in English, because they are data items and need to be localized in the **Control Panel**.

6. Change it back to **English (United States)** in the drop-down. This way, you can easily change between languages:

What just happened?

In this section, we have learned about the **Language** Portlet, which allows changing the language on the fly. It also provides a feature to show only the subset of available languages.

Language Portlet is an important feature when your site will be accessed across the globe. It helps change language interface on the fly. A more advanced way is to use this portlet to embed it in Theme, so it will appear on every page.

Apart from the **Language** portlet in Liferay, there are other ways as well to change language for the user. Users can do that by setting the language in their personal profile. Also, you can enable language detection from the browser for the guest user by enabling the following property in `portal-ext.properties`:

```
#
# Set this to true if unauthenticated users get their preferred
language
# from the Accept-Language header. Set this to false if
unauthenticated
# users get their preferred language from their company.
#
locale.default.request=true
```

This way the guest user can see the website content in their preferred language.

Have a go hero – change user language

Set the user language of the user Jenny Bensar to Spanish, and verify the interface in Spanish. Once done, change back to **English (United States)**.

Hint: Do this by modifying the display setting in the profile of the user in **Control Panel**.

Displaying breaking news as a carousel on the Neighborhood site

In this section, we will set up the portlet to show breaking news in the Neighborhood site dynamically, as soon as they get generated by the content writer. All the breaking news will be displayed as a carousel (like slide show one by one). We will deploy a portlet, which will display this news based on tags.

Time for action – displaying breaking news as a carousel

1. Log in to your Liferay site as default Administrator.

2. On your home page, go to the **Manage** menu and click on **Control Panel**.

3. Click on **Plugins Installation** from the **Server** section. It will take you to the **Plugins Installation** screen. On this screen, click on **Install More Portlets**. It will take you to the screen where you can install portlets as shown in the section, *setting up an online game using Flash Portlet.*

4. Click on the **Upload** file and browse for portlet war file **content-rotator-portlet-6.0.10.1** in the downloaded code for this book.

5. After that, click on **Install**. It will upload the war file to the Liferay server and deploy it for you. At the end of a successful deployment, you can see messages in the tomcat log to indicate successful deployment.

6. The next step is to create breaking news. You need to create them as web content (which you have learned in *Chapter 7, Creating and Publishing Content*). Breaking news will be published under the **Neighbourhood Exchange** community, so you should create web content under the same community. Select **Neighbourhood Exchange** in the content section, and click on **Web Content**. You will be shown the screen to create new web content.

7. Click on the **Add Web Content** button. It will show you the screen where you can create new web content. One point that you should take care of while creating breaking news web content is that all the web content should have the tag of breaking news.

8. Enter the following details in that screen:

- ❑ **Name: Our neighborhood won the best neighborhood in the city award**
- ❑ **Content: Today at the city awards, our neighbourhood won the best neighborhood awards. The awards function was hosted by Civic Authority of Society, and each neighbourhood was evaluated in various performance criteria, such as, Cleanliness, Security, Law and Order.**

  It is a great moment for our neighborhood. Let's celebrate this occasion on 13 Feb 2012, Saturday by meeting at the Main Lawn area.
- ❑ **Categorization – Type: News**
- ❑ **Categorization – Tags: breakingnews**

9. Now, click on the **Publish** button at the bottom to create this web content.

10. In a similar way, add two more breaking news items as web content with the following details:

- ❑ Web Content 1:
- ❑ **Name: Testing BreakingNews2**

- ❏ **Content: This breaking news is for testing purposes. It shows the second breaking news.**
- ❏ **Categorization – Type: News**
- ❏ **Categorization – Tags: breakingnews**
- ❏ Web Content 2:
- ❏ **Name: Testing BreakingNews3**
- ❏ **Content: More on breaking news. This is added for testing purposes. It shows the third breaking news.**
- ❏ **Categorization – Type: News**
- ❏ **Categorization – Tags: breakingnews**

11. Now that we have created news, the next step would be to display it on the page using content rotator portlet. Click on the **Pages** link from the content section. After that click on the **View Pages** link, it should take you to the public pages of the **Neighbourhood Exchange** community. You should be able to see the **Breaking News** page in the menu. Click on it.

12. Now, using the **Add Application** popup, add the **What's New** Portlet from **CIGNEX** Portlets category. This portlet will show you a carousel for all the three breaking news, as shown in the following screenshot. You can also switch manually between breaking news by numbered navigation provided in the bottom-right side of the portlet.

 If the portlet does not show any content then restart your tomcat server once. Sometimes due to caching problems it does not show content.

13. After that, go to **Control Panel** | **Neighbourhood Exchange** | **Web Content** | **Add Web Content** with the following details:

- ❏ Web Content 3:
- ❏ **Name: Testing BreakingNews4**
- ❏ **Content: This is the fourth breaking news to test dynamic addition of content.**
- ❏ **Categorization – Type: News**

- Categorization – Tags: breakingnews

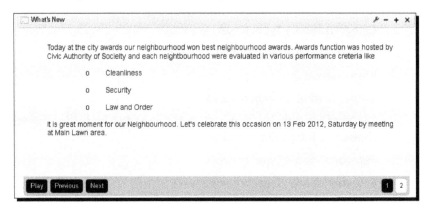

14. Now, go back to the breaking news page of **Neighbourhood Exchange** and you will see newly added news appearing in the carousel.

15. In a similar way, you can remove any news from the carousel by removing breakingnews tags from any web content. After that, content will not appear in the **What's New** portlet.

What just happened?

In this section, you have installed **What's New** portlet to show the Breaking News of the Neighborhood community. This portlet dynamically picks up latest content tagged as **breakingnews** to show as Carousel.

Let's understand the working of this portlet. It has two parts which are as follows:

- First, we have to log in to search all the content with the tag breakingnews. It will accumulate all the content and provide us a list to view layer.

- In the view layer, we have used works on tag lookup and fetching web content based on tags. It also uses the `jquery.jshowoff` plugin (`http://ekallevig.com/jshowoff/`) to show content in slide show mode.

If you are more curious about code, you can extract the war file, and the code is embedded in for your reference.

Defining a search on the Neighborhood site

Searching is the core functionality required for any site. It allows the end user to find required information from the site, without having to manually look on the site. In this section, we will learn about the searching functionality provided by Liferay. Liferay provides two out-of-the-box portlets for search functionality, which are as follows:

- ◆ Search Portlet: This portlet searches everything in the entire content's web content, blogs, Wikis, and message boards.

- ◆ Web Content Search Portlet: This portlet searches only web content.

Let's explore it.

Setting site wide search on the Neighborhood site

First, we will explore Liferay Search Portlet, which is capable of searching in every asset type (for example, Wikis, blogs, web content, bookmark, and so on). Let's see it in action.

Time for action – searching all content

1. Log in to your Liferay site as default **Administrator**.

2. In the **CIGNEX Neighbourhood** community welcome page, open the **Add Application** menu, and add **Search** Portlet from the **Tools** category to the page.

3. In this portlet, you can search either **Everything** (which includes all the communities and organizations), or **This community**, which limits search to the current community. It also contains textbox, where you can enter search keyword. Enter **Neighbourhood** in the search textbox, and select **Everything**. Now click on the search icon.

4. It will then show you the search results, such as, Result page, groups results asset wise, that is, number of Web content, number of blogs, number of Wikis, and so on. Also, it will show **Search** portlets, search in Blogs, Bookmark, Calendar, Directory, Document Library, Image Gallery, Message Boards, Web Content, and Wiki. It also shows highlighted result of the keyword searched, as shown in the following screenshot:

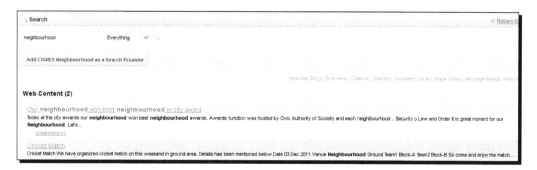

5. Each search result shows a title with links to full view of the content, abstract of the content, and also associated tags with the article, as shown in the previous screenshot. Now, click on the first result title, which will take you to full view of the content, where you can read article in full.

6. You can click on **Return to Full Page** to go back to the page from where you started the search.

What just happened?

You have just added the search portlet on the welcome page of the **CIGNEX Neighbourhood** community to perform a site-wide search. You have also performed the search to see the interface for the search results and features provided by it.

Liferay internally provides search using Lucene API (`http://lucene.apache.org/java/docs/index.html`). Lucene is a java-based search API project hosted under Apache. Liferay uses lucene API to create indexes of content in Liferay and search. Liferay also provides functionality to re-index all the search indexes, or any specific asset type.

Liferay Search Portlet provides feature to search within all the asset types of Liferay. Scope for search can be provided by the user during searching. **Search** Portlet provides two options to specify scope, mentioned as follows:

- Everything: This option searches within all the contents of Liferay. It searches in all communities and organizations.

- This Community: This option will limit the search within the current community only.

Search Portlet results show all the results that have have matching keywords. More importantly, Liferay shows only search results on which the user has permission. This is a very important feature, as it restricts the user from accessing content for which he/she doesn't have permission. Also, results are combined in sections for each asset type. This allows users to easily find the results he/she is looking for in the respective asset type group. Each result shows a title with links to its full view page, abstract of the content, and tags if any, associated with content.

Liferay Search Portlet is a non-instanciable portlet, which means that you can not add more than one instance to one page. This is because there is no portlet-specific configuration available in **Search** Portlet. So, all the searches various pages will yield the same results.

Setting Web Content search on the Neighborhood site

Web Content Search is another version of **Search** Portlet. This portlet will search only in Web Content and not in other asset types, such as blogs, wikis, and so on. It also provides specific configuration for Web Content to provide effective search results to users.

Let's see it in action.

Time for action – searching for Web Content

1. Log in to your Liferay site as default **Administrator**.

2. Go to the **Neighbourhood Exchange** community, and click on the **Breaking News** page. In this page, you will now see **Web Content Search** Portlet, which will allow the user to search all the news.

3. Go to the **Add Application** popup, and from the **Content Management** category, add **Web Content Search** Portlet. It will look like the Search Portlet you saw in the previous section, *Searching all content*, but without the dropdown to decide scope.

4. Now, change the title of the portlet to **News Search** from **Web Content Search**. You need to click on **Look and Feel**. It will open the **Look and Feel** popup. Select the **Use Custom Title** checkbox, enter **News Search** in the portlet **Title** field and click on **Save**. Then you should close the popup. You will notice that the title of the portlet will be changed to **News Search**.

5. Now, in order to reduce our search to News content only, go to configuration of portlet from portlet title bar menu. The configuration screen will look as shown in the following screenshot.

6. In the configuration screen, select the **News in Web Content Type** dropdown.

7. Uncheck **Only show results for web content listed in a Web Content Display portlet**. Check the box to show the entire news type web content, which has not been put on the site as well:

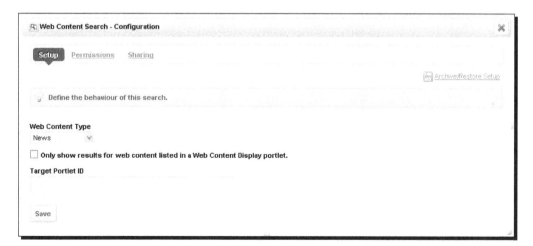

8. Now, click on the **Save** button to save changes. After that, close the configuration and go back to the portlet.

9. You should then enter **Awards** in the search textbox, and click on the search icon. It will take you to the search results page to show results as shown in the following screenshot. Search results contain dynamic highlighting of search results, pagination, title, abstract, score, and the link to all the contents of the document:

What just happened?

In this section, you have added **Web Content Search** Portlet in the **Breaking News** page of the **Neighbourhood Exchange** community. You have then configured the portlet to search on news content types. After that, you have performed a search and seen the search results interface.

Let's have a more detailed look at the **Web Content Search** Portlet. This portlet is similar to the **Search** portlet in terms of implementation, as this portlet also uses Lucene API to perform search internally. Remember, this portlet searches within the current community only.

However, this portlet is search-specific to web content assets only, and it has configuration features, mentioned as follows:

- Content Type: This configuration option is used to limit searches to any specific content type. You can select any content type in the dropdown, and the portlet will search within the content of those types only. If you select blank, then the portlet will search in all the content types.

- Only show results for web content listed in a Web Content Display portlet: As the name suggests, this checkbox, if selected, searches web content listed in a **Web Content Display** portlet on the pages of the community. If not selected then the portlet will search all the web content irrespective of whether they are explicitly put on site, and you can also provide the target portlet ID, where results will be directed.

Also, search results of this portlet are in tabular format showing, title, abstract of content, link to full content, and score of this web content based on its rating. It also provides pagination and the search time it has taken for any performance measurement in the larger system.

Have a go hero – searching only general content

Set up one more Web Content Search Portlet to search in only general content.

Summary

We have seen lots of portlets in this chapter to achieve basic requirements of any website, and learned about their functionality. We have covered out-of-the-box and custom portlets in this chapter. Specifically, we covered the following:

- Learning about Flash Portlet to play any flash file.
- Playing videos from YouTube in the Neighborhood site.
- Organizing various images from Image Gallery to present them as a slide show.
- Overview of out-of-the-box chat functionality provided by Liferay, and demonstrations on how users can chat among themselves.
- Widgets integration in the Neighborhood site.
- Some out-of-the-box portlets like Bookmark and Language.
- Search functionality provided by Liferay. We have explored Search Portlet to perform site-wide search and Web Content Search to search within Web Content only.

Since our communities' pages are ready with out-of-the-box portlets and custom portlets to achieve generic requirements, the next step would be to set up Social Collaboration in our Neighborhood site, which is the topic of our *Bonus Chapter, Exploring Social Collaboration*.

You can download the Bonus Chapter from `http://www.packtpub.com/sites/default/files/downloads/Social_collaboration.pdf`.

9
Setting up an Online Shop

Shopping is one of the key activities we do in our day to day life. Nowadays, we do most of our shopping online. Liferay provides built-in support for setting up an online shop. We can easily configure an e-commerce website and sell our products.

In the bonus chapter, we will learn about the social collaboration features of Liferay. Using blogs, wikis, and the message board portlet, we will see how to configure the Neighbors Congress, Chamber of Commerce, and Neighborhood Arbitration Committee organizations in our CIGNEX Neighborhood portal.

In this chapter, we are going to build an online shop within our CIGNEX Neighborhood portal. By the end of this chapter, you will have learned how to:

- Set up an online store using the Shopping portlet
- Configure tax rates, shipping charges, and payment options for our online store
- Categorize sellable items of our online store
- Create new types of items
- Update stock of sellable items
- Shop from an online store
- Configure offers to increase sales
- Manage online orders

So let's gear up to start our online shop in CIGNEX Neighborhood!

Getting started with online store setup

In this chapter, we are going to set up an online store in the Around the Corner community. Before we begin this chapter, the following steps should already have been performed:

◆ Liferay Portal is installed

◆ Liferay Portal server is running

◆ The Around the Corner community has been created

It is assumed that the user will sign in with the default admin credentials (**test@liferay.com / test**) whenever it is mentioned to sign in as an admin.

Online shop configuration

We have a flower shop in the CIGNEX Neighborhood. We want to provide an online shopping facility for this flower shop, so that people from our neighborhood can order flowers online. In this section, we will first configure our shop step by step.

Page configuration

We will first configure a page to host our online shop. We will create our online shop in the Around the Corner community. We already created the Around the Corner community in *Adding the Community* section of *Chapter 5, Building your First Liferay Site*. So let's configure this page.

Time for action – configuring an online shop page

1. Navigate to the **Control Panel** as an admin.

2. Select the **Around the Corner** community from the drop-down available in the **Content** section.

3. Click on the **Pages** option under the **Content** section. It will open the manage pages interface. We have used this interface to create pages in *Chapter 6, Managing Pages, Users, and Permissions*.

4. Now click on the **Private Pages** tab. The system will display the add page screen.

5. Enter the following details on the screen and click on the **Add Page** button:

   ❑ **Name: Florence Flower Shop**

   ❑ **Template: (None)**

   ❑ **Type : Portlet**

6. Now click on the **View Pages** button.

7. The system will show a blank page.

8. Now, open the **Manage layout** functionality by selecting **Manage | Page Layout** menu option from the Dockbar.

9. Select **1 Column** layout from the manage page layout dialog and click on the **Save** button.

10. Now, open the **Add Application** dialog by selecting **Add | More..** option from the Dockbar.

11. Expand **Shopping Category** from the **Add Application** dialog and click on the **Add** button beside the **Shopping** portlet as shown in the following screenshot:

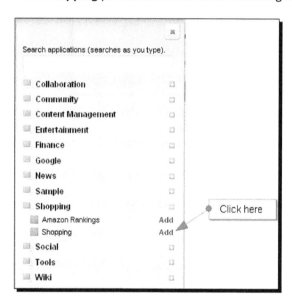

What just happened?

We just configured the **Florence Flower Shop** page within the Around the Corner community. We configured our shop in the private pages area. We did so because we want to ensure that our online shop is accessible to those users who are members of the Around the Corner community.

We also added the **Shopping** portlet to the **Florence Flower Shop** page. The **Shopping** portlet is an out-of-the-box portlet which is a part of the Liferay bundle. We changed the layout of the page to **1 Column layout**.

Payment configuration

Payment is the most important component of an e-commerce system. In the previous section, we set up the **Shopping** portlet on a page. Now in this section, we will configure/change various payment settings of the **Shopping** portlet.

Time for action – configuring tax rate and currency

1. Navigate to the Around the Corner community from the Dockbar as the admin.

2. Now, click on the **Configuration** mode of the **Shopping** portlet as shown in the following screenshot. The system will open the **Configuration** dialog box:

3. Enter the values in the fields as shown in the following screenshot and then press the **Save** button:

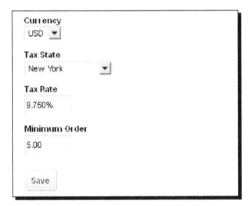

What just happened?

We just configured the **Shopping** portlet to accept the payment in US Dollars. In USA, each state has its own sales tax rate. Sales tax needs to be paid on a total transaction value. That's why we configured the name of the **Tax State**. We also configured sales **Tax Rate** applicable in **New York** State. We configured the **Minimum Order** amount. The order below a certain amount can cause losses due to overhead. To avoid that, the merchant can set a minimum order amount. So, we set 5 Dollars as our minimum order amount.

Payment method configuration

We configured the general payment settings such as **Tax Rate**, **Minimum Order** amount, **Tax State**, and so on. Now, the most important part is the payment method. There are various ways to accept online payments. We can accept payments through credit cards, Internet banking, or PayPal. The **Shopping** portlet supports payments through credit cards or PayPal. In the next section, we will configure the **Shopping** portlet to accept payments through PayPal.

Time for action – configuring payment through PayPal

1. As mentioned in *Appendix A, PayPal Test Account Configuration*, create buyer and seller accounts on the PayPal Sandbox environment. Also, keep note of the buyer and seller account login e-mail addresses. We will use them later in this chapter.

2. Navigate to the Around the Corner community as an admin.

3. Now click on the **Configuration** mode of the **Shopping** portlet.

4. In the **PayPal Email Address** field, enter the PayPal seller login e-mail address which we noted in step 1. Then click on the **Save** button and close the **Configuration** dialog box.

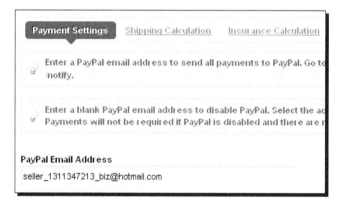

What just happened?

We just integrated our **Shopping** portlet with the PayPal Sandbox environment. We first created an account on the PayPal Sandbox environment. The PayPal Sandbox environment provides a facility to create the merchant and buyer accounts for testing. With the test account, we can test the actual payment workflow without affecting our bank accounts or credit cards.

We then added a pre-configured buyer account with $50 as an initial balance. When we created a buyer account, PayPal automatically associated the dummy bank account with the buyer account. After the creation, it gave a unique sign-in e-mail address to the buyer. We will use this test buyer account to purchase flowers from our shopping portal later in this chapter.

We also added a pre-configured seller account. This seller account represents our shop's account in PayPal. The test seller account is also created with a dummy bank account associated with it. PayPal generated a unique sign-in e-mail ID for our seller account. We then configured this seller account login e-mail ID in the **Payment Settings** configuration of the **Shopping** portlet.

Adding PayPal Sandbox environment support in the Shopping portlet

In the preceding section, we configured PayPal accounts in the Sandbox environment. We will now provide PayPal Sandbox environment support to the **Shopping** portlet.

Time for action – installing a plugin to provide PayPal Sandbox environment support

1. Stop the Liferay Portal server, if it is already running.

2. Locate the `deploy` directory in the root folder where you installed the Liferay portal server:

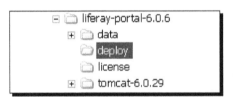

3. Copy `shopping-paypal-ext-6.0.6.1.war` from the downloaded code to deploy the directory located in the preceding step.

4. Now, start the Liferay Portal server.

5. Once the server is up and running, we need to restart the server again as we deployed the `ext` plugin of Liferay. So stop the server and start the server again.

> Once the server is started after step 4, you should see the following message on the server console. You need to restart the server after you see this message:
>
> **INFO [ExtHotDeployListener:188] Extension environment for shopping-paypal-ext has been applied. You must reboot the server and redeploy all other plugins.**

What just happened?

We deployed an extension plugin war file to the Liferay Portal server. This plugin customizes the PayPal integration functionality of the **Shopping** portlet. By default, the **Shopping** portlet is configured to work with the PayPal live environment (`https://www.paypal.com`) only.

We cannot test the payment workflow with the live environment of PayPal. If we perform testing with the live environment of PayPal, then it will make the actual financial transactions between the buyer and seller bank accounts or credit cards. So we deployed an extension plugin to integrate the **Shopping** portlet with the PayPal test environment (`http://www.sandbox.paypal.com`). With this, we can complete the payment workflow for any purchase without affecting the actual bank accounts or credit cards.

> We do not need to install this extension plugin for the production environment. In the production environment, we work directly with `http://www.paypal.com`. This customization is required to simulate the payment process without affecting the actual bank accounts.

What about payment with credit cards?

We have used PayPal as our payment provider. However, what if some shop owner wants to accept payment with credit cards? We can also configure the **Shopping** portlet to accept payment with credit cards. We can configure which credit card brands our shop supports. To configure the supported types of credit cards, we need to open the **Shopping** portlet configuration mode dialog box.

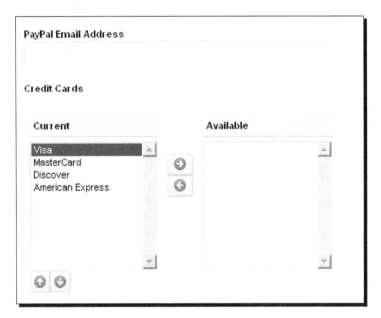

As shown in the preceding screenshot, to accept credit cards directly we need to clear the PayPal e-mail address. The **Available** listbox contains a list of available credit card types. The **Current** listbox contains the credit card types which are supported by our online shop.

If we decide to use credit cards directly, then we need to implement the payment integration ourselves. Liferay only provides an interface to capture and validate the credit card types during the payment workflow.

Shipping cost configuration

Unlike the regular window shopping, online shopping involves shipping costs. The shipping cost is generally applied to the total order amount.

Time for action – configuring the shipping cost

Let's configure the shipping cost calculation for our online shop:

1. Navigate to the Around the Corner community as the admin, and click on the **Configuration** mode of the **Shopping** portlet.

2. Click on the **Shipping Calculation** tab and then enter the values as shown in the following screenshot. After setting the following values, click on the **Save** button.

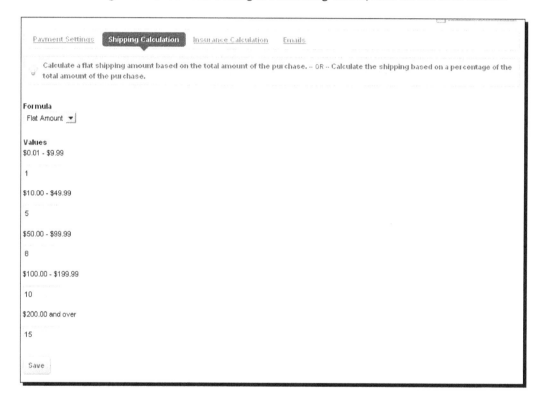

What just happened?

We just configured the shipping cost for our online shop. We configured the **Flat Amount** formula for calculating the shipping cost. Liferay provides five different bands for providing the shipping cost. We have set the shipping cost for all the five bands.

Let's understand the shipping cost calculation with an example. Suppose a buyer orders five different types of flower bouquets in an online order. The total cost of all the five bouquets is coming to around $72. So this order falls in the **$50 - $99.99** band. Hence as per our configuration, we will charge **$8** for shipping.

Setting up an Online Shop

Percentage formula for shipping cost calculation

The **Shopping** portlet also supports a percentage formula for calculating the shipping cost. The percentage calculation is similar to the Flat Amount formula. Instead of applying the flat cost, in this case, it will calculate shipping cost based on the percentage set for a particular band. Let's understand this by an example. Suppose we have the following values in the shipping cost configuration:

- **Formula—Percentage**
- **Values**:
  - **$0.01 - $9.99**—0.01
  - **$10.00 - $49.99**—0.02
  - **$50.00 - $99.99**—0.03
  - **$100.00 - $199.99**—0.04
  - **$200.00 - and over**—0.05

We have set the percent values for each band. If we take the same example where the buyer bought five bouquets and the total purchase amount was $72 then, the shipping cost will come around 2.16 ($72 * 0.03).

Insurance cost configuration

It is possible that during the delivery of purchased goods they get damaged. In such cases, the customer has to bare the damage that happens to the goods unless explicitly specified. To avoid this loss, merchants provide a facility to their customers to add the minimal insurance on the total purchased amount. If goods got damaged during delivery then the merchant provides replacement of the product. The **Shopping** portlet provides a configuration to set the insurance cost.

Time for action – configuring the insurance cost

Let's configure the insurance cost calculation for our flower shop:

1. Navigate to the Around the Corner community and open the **Configuration** mode of the **Shopping** portlet.

2. Click on the **Insurance Calculation** tab and then enter the values as shown in the following screenshot. After setting the values, click on the **Save** button.

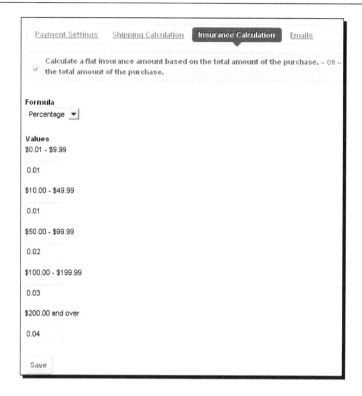

What just happened?

We just configured the insurance cost calculation for our online shop. We configured the **Percentage Amount** formula for calculating the insurance cost. Liferay provides five different bands for providing insurance cost similar to shipping cost calculation. We configured percentage values for all five bands. Let's take an example where the customer bought flower bouquets costing $250. As per our configuration system will calculate insurance cost based on percentage mentioned in fifth band. So in this case insurance cost will be $10 ($250 * 0.04).

Similar to the shipping cost calculation, insurance cost configuration also supports **Flat Amount** formula. In this case, we will charge a fixed amount of insurance when the total purchase amount falls within a particular band.

E-mail configuration

Unlike regular window shopping, where the customer gets confirmation of his/her order face to face, online shopping does not have such an option. So, as a merchant, we need to provide different types of confirmations via e-mail. In most of the scenarios, we need to send confirmation when a customer places an order and a second confirmation needs to be sent when the ordered goods are shipped. The **Shopping** portlet supports both types of confirmations via e-mail. We can personalize the e-mail format as per our needs.

Time for action – configuring the e-mail templates

Let's configure the e-mail formats for our Florence flower shop:

1. Navigate to the Around the Corner community as an admin, and open the **Configuration** mode of the **Shopping** portlet.

2. Click on the **Emails** tab. The system will select the **Email Form** sub tab, by default. Fill up the following details in the given fields and then click on the **Save** button:
   - **Name**: Your name
   - **Address**: Your e-mail address

3. Click on the **Confirmation Email** tab under the **Emails** tab. Enter the following values in the input fields and click on the **Save** button:
   - **Enabled**: Checked
   - **Subject**:

     ```
     Thank you for shopping at Florence Flower Shop. Order Number
     [$ORDER_NUMBER$].
     ```

   - **Body**:

     ```
     Dear [$TO_NAME$],

     Thank you for your shopping at Florence Flower Shop. You
     should receive your order within 2 to 3 working days. Your
     satisfaction is important to us. If you have any questions
     or concerns, please email us at [$FROM_ADDRESS$] or call us
     at 800.999.9999.
     If you would like to give feedback about our products or
     services, please email your comments and suggestions on
     email us at [$FROM_ADDRESS$].

     Order Details:
     Order Number: [$ORDER_NUMBER$]
     Order Amount: [$ORDER_TOTAL$] [$ORDER_CURRENCY$]
     Shipping Address: [$ORDER_SHIPPING_ADDRESS$]

     Sincerely,
     [$FROM_NAME$]
     [$FROM_ADDRESS$]
     http://[$PORTAL_URL$]
     ```

4. Click on the **Shipping Email** sub tab under the **Emails** tab. Enter the following values in the input fields and click on the **Save** button:

❑ **Enabled**: Checked

❑ **Subject**:

```
Your order has been shipped. Order Number [$ORDER_NUMBER$].
```

❑ **Body**:

```
Dear [$TO_NAME$],

Thank you for your shopping at Florence Flower Shop. Your
order has been shipped. You should receive your order
within 2 to 3 working days.

Your satisfaction is important to us. If you have any
questions or concerns, please email us at [$FROM_ADDRESS$]
or call us at 800.999.9999.
If you would like to give feedback about our products or
services, please email your comments and suggestions on
email us at [$FROM_ADDRESS$].

Order Details:
Order Number: [$ORDER_NUMBER$]
Order Amount: [$ORDER_TOTAL$] [$ORDER_CURRENCY$]
Shipping Address: [$ORDER_SHIPPING_ADDRESS$]

Sincerely,
[$FROM_NAME$]
[$FROM_ADDRESS$]
http://[$PORTAL_URL$]
```

What just happened?

We have just configured **From_Name** and **From_Address** for confirmation e-mails. When order confirmation or order shipment e-mails are sent, the system will use the given from name and from e-mail address in the e-mail.

We then configured the order confirmation e-mail and shipping confirmation e-mail formats. We can enable or disable e-mail notification by the **Enabled** checkbox. We also configured the e-mail subject and the e-mail body. We used **[$...$]** dynamic fields in the e-mail subject and body. These dynamic fields will be replaced with the actual value of respective order.

We can use any of the following dynamic fields in the subject and body fields:

Field	Description
[$FROM_ADDRESS$]	From e-mail address. It is the same e-mail address that is set in the **Email Form** tab.
[$FROM_NAME$]	Name of the person who will appear in the from e-mail name field of e-mail. It is the same name set in **Email Form** tab.
[$ORDER_BILLING_ADDRESS$]	The billing address provided by the customer during the checkout process.
[$ORDER_CURRENCY$]	Currency used in the order.
[$ORDER_NUMBER$]	Order number generated by the **Shopping** portlet.
[$ORDER_SHIPPING_ADDRESS$]	The shipping address provided by the customer during the checkout process.
[$ORDER_TOTAL$]	The total order amount or the order.
[$PORTAL_URL$]	Base URL of the portal.
[$PORTLET_NAME$]	Name of the portlet. In our case, it is **Shopping**.
[$TO_ADDRESS$]	E-mail address of the customer. In our case, this will be the logged in user's e-mail address.
[TO_NAME]	Name of the customer. In our case, it is the username of the user who placed the order.

Pop quiz

1. To integrate with PayPal, which e-mail address we need to configure in the **Payment Settings** configuration?

   a. Buyer's PayPal login e-mail address

   b. Company Admin's e-mail address

   c. Merchant's PayPal login address

2. What is the full form of IPN?

   a. Instant Payment Notification

   b. Internet Payment Notification

   C. International Payment Network

3. Which of the following formulas are supported by the **Shopping** portlet for the shipping cost calculation?

    a. Percentage

    B. Flat

    C. Fixed

4. What different types of e-mail notifications are supported by the **Shopping** portlet?

    a. Order Confirmation

    B. Order Status Change

    C. Order Completion

    D. Order Shipping Confirmation

Shopping items

Managing shopping items within an online shop is one of the most important activities for a merchant. It involves item creation, inventory/stock management, pricing, and so on. In this section, we will create shopping items for our flower shop.

Item categories

Let's think how a merchant arranges the items in his/her shop. He/she usually arranges similar products together. This will make his/her life easier. It also helps his/her customers to quickly locate their choice of item. Putting similar items together is nothing but categorization. The **Shopping** portlet provides a way to categorize items. So, before creating the shopping items, let's create item categories first.

Time for action – item category creation

1. As the admin navigates to the Around the Corner community from the Dockbar.

2. Now from the **Shopping** portlet home page, click on the **Add Categories** button.

3. The system will display the add category form. Enter the following details in the form and then click on the **Save** button:

    ❏ **Name: Bouquets**

    ❏ **Description: Here you find beautiful flower bouquets**

    ❏ **Permissions: Anyone (Guest Role)**

4. The system will go back to the **Shopping** portlet home page as shown in the following screenshot and show the **Bouquets** category on the category list:

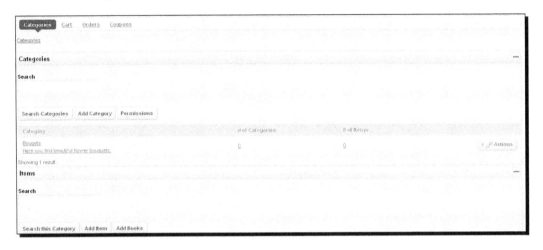

5. Now, click on the **Bouquets** hyperlink shown in the **Category** column. The system will display the **Bouquets** category home page. It looks similar to the **Shopping** portlet home page. The only difference we can notice is the breadcrumb shown on top of the **Shopping** portlet. It now shows **Categories | Bouquets**. It indicates that we are currently on the **Bouquets** category page. Another difference is that instead of having the **Add Category** button we have the **Add Subcategory** button.

6. Click on the **Add Subcategory** button. The system will display the add category form. Enter the following details in the form and press the **Save** button:

   ❑ **Name: Roses**

   ❑ **Description: Here you find all beautiful bouquets covered with roses**

   ❑ **Permissions: Anyone (Guest Role)**

7. The system will go back to the home page of the **Bouquets** category. It will show the **Roses** category in sub category list.

What just happened?

We just created a root category called **Bouquets**. We then added a subcategory in the **Bouquets** root category. We created an item category by providing a name, description, and permissions. The name and description attributes are very much clear from their labels. With the permissions attribute, we can actually configure access of the particular category or subcategory. We selected **Anyone (Guest Role)**, which means anyone can view a particular category. For example, this attribute could be useful if we want to restrict access to only authenticated users on a particular category.

With categorization of shopping items, we can provide an easy way to locate relevant items. The **Shopping** portlet allows us to create a hierarchy of categories. There is no limitation of levels although it is meaningless to create a hierarchy which is deeper than four or five levels.

By default, home page of the **Shopping** portlet displays the root categories in the **Categories** section. We can navigate to the subcategories by traversing through each category. Listing of categories or subcategories provides the following columns in the table:

- ◆ **Category**: This column displays the name of the category and description of the category. It provides a hyperlink to navigate to the home page of that category.

- ◆ **Number of Categories**: This column displays the recursive count of all the subcategories.

- ◆ **Number of Items**: This column displays the recursive count of all shopping items within a particular category.

- ◆ **Action Button**: This column provides a context menu associated with a particular category. The context menu provides three actions, **Edit**, **Delete**, and **Permissions**. As the names of action suggest, the **Edit** action provides a way to edit the category information, the **Delete** action provides a way to delete a particular category, and the **Permissions** action provides a way to define specific permissions for a particular category.

Changing the Parent Category

We can change the **Parent Category** of a particular category after creation. In order to do this, we need to go to the **Category** listing page and then click on the **Edit** action button for that category. The system will show the edit category form as displayed in the following screenshot:

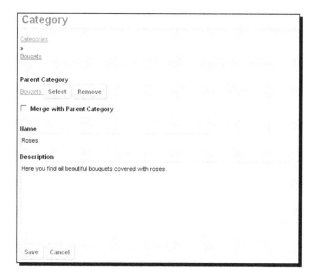

The **Edit category** form is similar to the **Add category** form. We have some more options to change/remove the parent category. As displayed in the preceding screenshot, we are editing the **Roses** category. It also displays the current parent category. In this case, it is **Bouquets**.

So, we have three options which affects **Parent Category** field:

- ◆ **Remove**: The **Remove** button allows the user to remove the parent category.
- ◆ **Select**: To change the parent category, we can use this option. On click of this button, the system displays a dialog to choose parent category. The system displays all the siblings of the current category, by default. We can use breadcrumb to navigate to other category hierarchy levels and choose the parent category.
- ◆ **Merge with Parent Category**: If we enable this checkbox and save the category, then the system will remove the current category and move all the subcategories and items to its parent category.

Have a go hero – define another subcategory

We have created the **Roses** category under the **Bouquets** category. Now it's your turn to define another subcategory named **Mix Flowers** under the **Bouquets** category.

 Remember to follow the same steps. First, you need to open the home page of the parent category and then you will need to use the **Add subcategory** option. As we did before, we will keep permissions as default values.

Shopping items

We have configured the **Category** hierarchy for our flower shop. Now, it's time to configure the shopping items. In this section, we will configure the shopping items.

Time for action – item creation

Let's create our first shopping item:

1. Navigate to the Around the Corner community from the Dockbar as the admin.

2. From the **Shopping** portlet home page, click on the **Bouquets** category to navigate to the home page of the **Bouquets** category.

3. Click on the **Roses** category hyperlink to navigate to the **Roses** category home page.

4. Now click on the **Add Item** button under the **Item** listing section.

5. The system will display and create an item form as shown in the following screenshot. Enter the details in the form fields as shown:

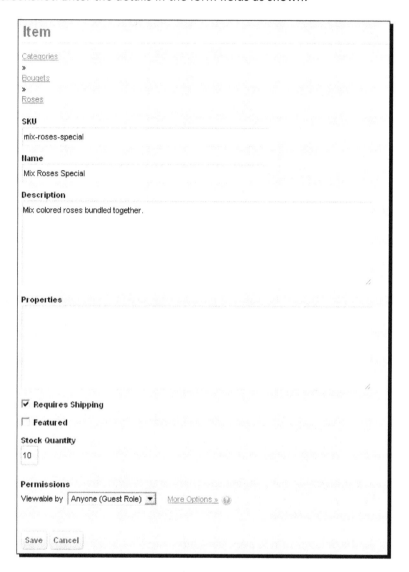

6. Now from the the **Fields** section, click on the **Add Field** button. The system will add three input fields (**Name**, **Values**, and **Description**) in the **Fields** section. Enter the following values in these fields:

- ❑ **Name: Size**
- ❑ **Values: Small, Medium, Large**

7. Now, click on the **Edit Stock Quantity** button under the **Fields** section.

8. The system will open a dialog box to modify the stock quantity for a specific **Size**. Enter the values as shown in the following screenshot and then click on the **Update** button:

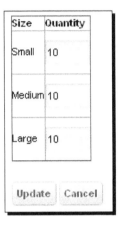

9. The system will move control to the **Add Item** screen. Now, under the **Prices** section enter **12** in the **Price** field and **2** in the **Discount** field. Leave default values in the other fields.

10. From the **Images** section, enable the **Use Small Image** option and then click on the **Choose File** button and locate the `mix-roses-special-small.png` image from the downloaded code.

11. From the **Images** section enable the **Use Medium Image** checkbox and then click on the **Choose File** button and locate the `mix-roses-special-medium.png` image from the downloaded code.

12. From the **Images** section, enable the **Use Large Image** checkbox and then click on the **Choose File** button and locate the `mix-roses-special-large.png` image from the downloaded code.

13. Click on the **Save** button to save the item.

14. The system will now show the home page of the **Roses** category. Under the **Items** section, you can now see the newly added **Mix Roses Special** bouquet item.

15. Now click on the **Mix Roses Special** item row.

16. The system will present the **Mix Roses Special** item page as shown in the following screenshot:

What just happened?

We just added the first item in our store. We added the item from the respective category (**Roses**) home page. We added the item with the following characteristics:

◆ **SKU** (Stock Keeping Unit)

◆ **Name**

◆ **Description**

◆ **Item Variants**

◆ **Item Stock per Variant**

◆ **Item Price**

◆ **Discount on Item**

◆ **Item Image**

After creating our first item, we verified how our item will be presented to our customers. Let's understand the **Item** attributes in detail.

Basic attributes

- **SKU**—SKU stands for Stock Keeping Unit. It's a unique identifier for our shopping item.

- **Name**—Name of the item. It is displayed in the item listing. It is also displayed on the item details page.

- **Description**—The detailed information of the product. The description is displayed on the item listing page and item details page.

- **Properties**—It is used to define the features of a product. For example, if an item can have two properties, **Type** and **Colour**, then we can define these properties by giving the following values in the **Properties** field. These properties are displayed on the item details page as shown in the following screenshot:

- **Requires Shipping**—If this checkbox is checked, then the system will consider this item's price for calculating the shipping cost.

- **Featured**—This attribute indicates whether the item is a featured item or not.

- **Stock Quantity**—This filed defines the available stock of the item. Merchant has to update this field when new stock is available. If the item has fields defined in the **Field** section then the system will remove this attribute. In this case, the system will use the stock defined in the **Fields** section.

- **Permissions**—We can control permission of a particular item for a specific role using this attribute. This is useful when we want to show/hide an item to specific roles.

Fields section attributes

The **Fields** section is used to define variants of the item. For example, our first item comes in three variants **Small**, **Medium**, and **Large** in size. We need to maintain a separate stock for each variant. If there are multiple fields then the stock has to be kept for each combination of two fields. While making a purchase, the customer has to select a value for each field. Let's look at the details of the **Field** section.

♦ **Add Field**—With the use of the **Add Field** button, we can add a field to the item. When we click on the **Add Field** button, the system adds one field row with the following subfields/action buttons:

   ❏ **Name**

   ❏ **Values**

   ❏ **Description**

   ❏ **Delete** button

   ❏ **Edit Stock Quantity** button

♦ **Name**—It is the name of a field. It is displayed as a label of the field in the **Item** details view. In our first item, we defined **Size** as a custom field.

♦ **Values**—It defines a list of the possible values in the specific field. We need to separate each value with a comma. In our first item, we entered **Small**, **Medium**, **Large** in the **Size** field. And so in the item details view, we can see the three options in the **Size** drop-down.

♦ **Description**—It is a description of the field.

♦ **Delete** button—With the use of the **Delete button**, we can remove any field associated with the item.

♦ **Edit Stock Quantity** button—This button is used to define the item's stock. The stock has to be defined for each variant combination. As we have seen for our first item, on a click of this button, the system opened a dialog asking stock for three variants (**Small**, **Medium**, and **Large**). When the item is created with fields, the stock has to be managed with this option.

   If there are multiple fields defined for an item, then we need to enter the stock for each combination of field values. That is, if there are two fields and each field has two options, then we need to enter the stock for four different variants.

Prices section attributes

This section allows us to define the pricing of an item. We can also define multiple price values based on order quantity range. Let's understand the details of each field. By default, the system will add one price row. Each row contains the following fields:

♦ **Min Qty** and **Max Qty**—These two fields define the minimum and maximum range of order quantity for which the given price attributes should be applied. For example, if we define **1** in **Min Qty** field and **10** in the **Max Qty** field, then all the other price attributes of a particular price row will be applied only when the ordered quantity is between 1 and 10. In our first product, we kept the default value (**0**) for both the fields. So in our case, the same price is applied for any order quantity.

♦ **Price**—This field defines the price of the item.

- **Discount**—This field is used to define the percent discount on a product. For example in our first item, we have defined 2 percent discount. When we define discount on an item, the system highlights the discount on the item details page.

- **Taxable**—If this checkbox is enabled, then the system will calculate the sales tax on this item. If this checkbox is disabled, then the system will not calculate tax on this item.

- **Shipping**—In some cases, we may want to decide the shipping cost based on the item and not based on the order. In such a scenario, we can define the shipping cost amount for the item. This shipping cost is multiplied by the item quantity.

- **Use Shipping Formula**—If this checkbox is not enabled, then the item-specific shipping cost will be applied. If this checkbox is enabled, then the system will apply the generic shipping cost as defined in the shipping calculation configuration of the **Shopping** portlet.

- **Active**—This field indicates whether a particular price row is active or not. If it is not active, then that particular price row is not used for calculation.

- **Default**—This radio button identifies the default price row. It is important when there are multiple price rows for an item.

- **Add Price** button—With the use of this button we can add another price row.

Images section attributes

This section allows us to configure the images associated with items. Images are used to present the shopping items. Let's lear about the different fields available in this section:

- **Small Image URL** or **Small Image**—We can specify small images either through a URL or by browsing the image from a local computer. The small image is displayed in the **SKU** column on the item listing page of a specific category as shown in the following screenshot:

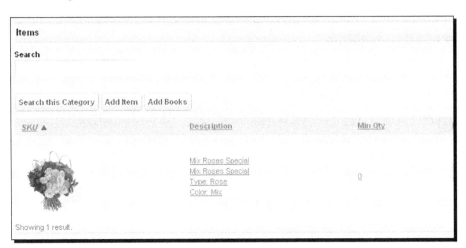

- ◆ **Use Small Image**—If this checkbox is enabled, then only a small image will be displayed in the **SKU** column.

- ◆ **Medium Image URL** or **Medium Image**—We can specify a medium-sized image either through a URL or by uploading the image from a local system. A medium image will be displayed in the item details view.

- ◆ **Use Medium Image**—If this checkbox is enabled, then only the medium image will be displayed on the item details view.

- ◆ **Large Image URL** or **Large Image**—We can specify a large-sized image either through a URL or by uploading the image from a local system. We can view the large size image by clicking on the **See Large Photo (Opens New Window)** hyperlink from the item details view.

- ◆ **Use Large Image**—If this checkbox is enabled then the system will only display the **See Large Photo (Opens New Window)** hyperlink in the item details view.

Have a go hero – defining a complete set of items for our shop

First, we created the shopping item of our flower shop. Now, it is your turn to define the rest of the items of our shop. So, create the following shopping items. Use the following key attribute when creating items. You may use the other attributes if you want:

	SKU	Parent Category	Small Image	Medium Image	Large Image	Price	Stock
1	virgin-white	**Mix Flowers**	`virgin-white-small.png`	`virgin-white-medium.png`	`virgin-white-large.png`	$13	17
2	superb-mix	**Mix Flowers**	`superb-mix-small.png`	`superb-mix-medium.png`	`superb-mix-large.png`	$12	8
3	sunny-yellow	**Mix Flowers**	`sunny-yellow-small.png`	`sunny-yellow-medium.png`	`sunny-yellow-large.png`	$15	5
4	special-red	**Roses**	`special-red-small.png`	`special-red-medium.png`	`special-red-large.png`	$9	12
5	sparkling-pink	**Mix Flowers**	`sparkling-pink-small.png`	`sparkling-pink-medium.png`	`sparkling-pink-large.png`	$8	10
6	plain-yellow	**Roses**	`plain-yellow-small.png`	`plain-yellow-medium.png`	`plain-yellow-large.png`	$11	50

	SKU	Parent Category	Small Image	Medium Image	Large Image	Price	Stock
7	orange-yellow-combo	Roses	`orange-yellow-combo-small.png`	`orange-yellow-combo-medium.png`	`orange-yellow-combo-large.png`	$12	7
8	beauty-blue	Roses	`beauty-blue-small.png`	`beauty-blue-medium.png`	`beauty-blue-large.png`	$16	18
9	colourful-mix	Mix Flowers	`colourful-mix-small.png`	`colourful-mix-medium.png`	`colourful-mix-large.png`	$13	12

Follow the same steps as we did for our first shopping item. You need to use the **Add Item** button to add a new item. You may skip adding the custom field as we did for our fist shipping item.

Pop quiz

1. Which of the following statements are true?

    a. We can create items associated with multiple parent categories

    b. We can create item in the root category

    c. We can change the parent category of any category

2. What is the full form of SKU?

    a. System Key Unit

    b. Stock Key Unit

    c. Stock Keeping Unit

3. Which of the following statements are correct?

    a. We can add more than one field for an item

    c. We can configure price of the item for each field combination

    c. We can configure stock of the item for each field combination

    d. We can configure an item such that the item's price is not used for the shipping cost calculation.

Shopping cart

So far, we have completed the basic configuration of our flower shop. We are now ready to shop from our flower shop. So far, we were navigating as admin user for the configuration of our shop. Admin user is normally used by the merchant to configure his/her shop. To test shopping, we need to have a normal user who is a member of the Around the Corner community.

Have a go hero – creating a login id for our customer

We have already learned how to create a user and associate them as a member of a particular community. So now it's your turn to create a user and associate it with "Around the Corner" community. Make sure you note down the e-mail id and password. In this book, we are referring to `james.desoza@cignexneighbourhood.com` as our customer's e-mail id and test as his password.

 You need to log in as the admin user (`test@liferay.com/test`) and then from the control panel you can create a user and make him the member of the "Around the Corner" community.

Let's do shopping

Now that we created our first customer account, we will start buying bouquets with our customer account. We will understand the shopping process by actually shopping bouquets from Florence flower shop.

Time for action – adding items to the shopping cart

Let's start buying the flower bouquets from our flower shop:

1. Sign in to the Neighborhood portal using the normal user credentials (**james. desoza@cignexneighbourhood.com / test**) and navigate to the Around the Corner community from the Dockbar.

2. From the **Shopping** portlet home page, navigate to the **Roses** category. You need to first open the **Bouquets** category and then you can navigate to the **Roses** category.

3. Now click on the **Mix Roses Special** item from the item list.

4. Now select **Medium** size from the **Size** drop-down and click on the **Add to Shopping Cart** button.

5. The system will open the **Shopping Cart** page as shown in the following screenshot:

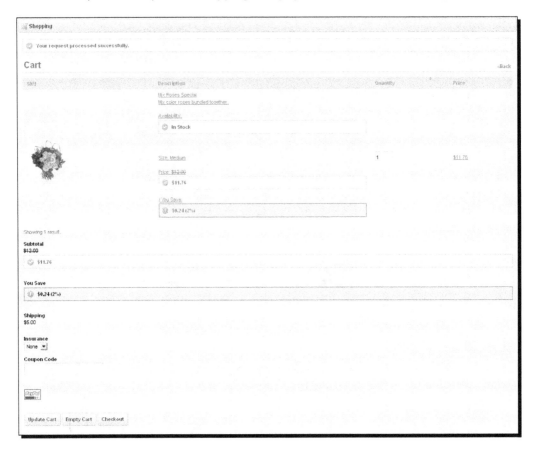

6. To buy two **Mix Roses Special** bouquets, change the value in the **Quantity** input field to **2** and then click on the **Update Cart** button. After updating the cart, the system will come back to the same page.

7. Now click on the **Back** hyperlink from the top-left corner as shown in the preceding screenshot.

8. The system will go back to the **Item** details view of the **Mix Roses Special** item. Now, using the **Next** and **Previous** buttons, navigate to item details view of the **Special Red** item.

9. Click on the **Add to Shopping Cart** button to add the **Special Red** item to the shopping cart. We will order only one bouquet of this type.

What just happened?

We just signed in as a normal user to the CIGNEX Neighborhood portal. To buy some flowers, we opened the Around the Corner community. As we wanted to buy flower bouquets containing roses, we located the **Roses** category under the **Bouquets** category. From a variety of rose bouquets displayed on the **Roses** category home page, we selected **Mix Roses Special** and added it to the shopping cart. To buy two **Mix Roses Special** bouquets, we updated the item quantity in the shopping cart. We then moved back to the item details page for the **Mix Roses Special** item. Using the **Next** and **Previous** buttons, we browsed the other rose bouquets. We then selected another item called **Special Red**. So at the end, we collected three items in our shopping cart.

Now let's understand the process of adding items to the shopping cart in detail.

Item listing view (category listing view)

Before we understand the details of the item listing view in detail let's compare regular window shopping and online shopping. How do we locate items in a shop? We look around sections in the shop. For example, if we want to buy an iPod Case from a supermarket, we look around for electronics section in the shop. Same concept is implemented by the **Shopping** portlet by providing categories. Each shopping item belongs to one parent category. We can locate specific items by browsing items of a specific category.

Now let's look at the details of the item listing view, or category listing view:

- **Breadcrumb**—With the use of breadcrumb within the **Shopping** portlet, we can navigate to the ancestor categories of the currently selected category.

- **Category Listing**—This section displays a list of subcategories of the selected category. We already discussed the category listing table.

- **Items Section**—The **Items Section** displays a list of items that belongs to a selected category. The items table displays the following information:

    - **SKU**—The **SKU** column displays a small image associated with an item. If small image is enabled, then the image will be displayed. If small image is disabled, then the SKU description will be displayed.

    - **Description**—The **Description** column displays name of the item, and description of the item. It also displays properties associated with the item.

    - **Min Qty**—It is the item quantity that a customer has to order.

    - **Price**—The **Price** column displays the price of the item. If a discount is defined for an item then system highlights both the actual price and discounted price of the item.

      ❑ **Action**—It displays the actions available for a specific item. This column is normally displayed to the admin or merchant. There are three actions available on the **Action** button: **Edit Item**, **Delete Item**, and **Permission** configuration.

◆ **Search**—Unlike with window shopping, where it is difficult to search for a specific item, the **Shopping** portlet provides the search functionality. To search for a specific item, we need to enter the search keyword in the search box and then press the **Search this Category** button to search for the specific item.

Item details view

When we do window shopping, we do not purchase any item without looking at it closely. This view simulates something similar. A customer can look at the details of an item. If they like the item, they can put that item in the shopping cart. Let's understand item details and actions available from this view:

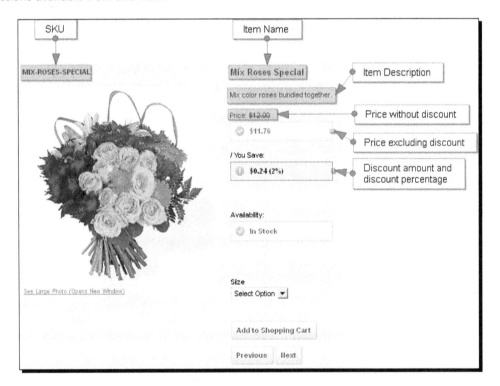

◆ **Breadcrumb**—It provides breadcrumb of items parent category hierarchy. We can navigate to a particular ancestor category by clicking on the breadcrumb link.

◆ **SKU**—As highlighted in the preceding screenshot, system SKU is displayed on the top-left corner.

- **Item Medium Image**—If medium image is enabled for an item, the system displays medium image of the item just below SKU.

- **Item Name** and **Description**—The item name and item description are displayed on top-right corner.

- **Item Properties**—The item properties are displayed just below the item description. Each property is displayed on a separate line.

- **Price**—The item price is displayed below the item properties. If there is any discount on an item, then the system displays a price without discount as highlighted in the preceding screenshot. The system also highlights the discounted price and the discount amount.

- **Availability**—If the item is available in the store, then the system highlights stock availability with a green message. If the item is not in stock, then the system highlights non availability with a red message.

- **Fields**—If there is any field associated with the item, then the system allows the user to select the filed. As shown in the preceding screenshot, we have a **Size** field defined for the item. The user has to choose the value for all the fields when s/he decides to add the item to the shopping cart.

- **Add to Shopping Cart** button—The user can add the item to his/her shopping cart by clicking this button. On clicking this button, the system adds item to the shopping cart and open shopping cart view.

- **Next/Previous** button—The user can navigate to another item's detail view by using these two buttons.

- **See large photo** link—System displays this link when large image is enabled for an item. On the clicking of this link, system opens a new window with item's large image.

Shopping cart view

Before we discuss the shopping cart view of the shopping portlet, let us understand shopping cart concept. Again let's think about the activities that we do in a supermarket:

1. We first pick up a cart or basket.

2. We then visit relevant sections to buy items that we need.

3. We put items in our cart.

4. Sometimes we pick up unnecessary items in our cart and later remove them from the cart.

5. After we choose all our needed items, we go to the payment counter and pay the bill.

The shopping cart concept is the exact simulation of our window shopping behavior. We already performed all of the preceding activities except 4 and 5 through our shopping portlet.

Unlike window shopping, our shopping portlet allows us to keep items in our cart and leave the shop for some time. We cannot do this in window shopping. So now that we are clear with the shopping cart concept, lets understand shopping cart view in detail.

- **Item listing** – As shown in the following screenshot, the system displays a list of items in the cart. Each item row contains the following information:

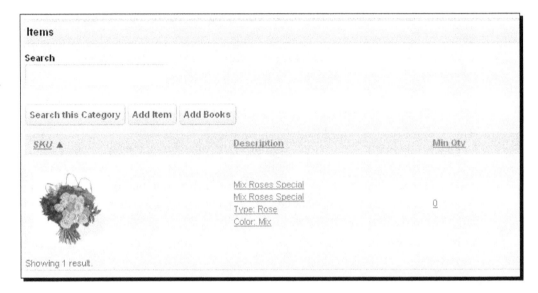

- **SKU** – This column displays a small image of the item if it is enabled. If a small image is not enabled then this column displays SKU.
- **Description** – This field provides the following information about the item:
  - **Item Name**
  - **Item Description**
  - **Item Properties**
  - **Stock Availability**
  - **Item Price**
  - **Discount**

- **Quantity** – This column provides an input field for each item row to view/ modify order quantity. If the minimum quantity and maximum quantity of items is set to 0 then the system will set the default value of this field to 1. To remove any specific item from the shopping cart, we can set this field to 0 and update the cart. If the minimum and/or maximum quantity of the item is set then the system will display a drop-down instead of an input field. In such a case, we can set the quantity range between minimum and maximum quantity of the item.

  - **Price** – This column display the discounted price of one item.

- **Sub Total** – This field displays total price of all the items in the cart. If there is a discount on any item then the system displays the actual subtotal and discounted subtotal. The subtotal is calculated with the following formula:

  ```
  Subtotal = Item Price (Item Discounted Price) * order quantity
  ```

- **Shipping** – This field displays the shipping cost. Shipping cost is calculated based on the shipping calculation formula set in the **Shopping** portlet configuration. Items which do not use the shipping formula are not considered in the general shipping cost calculation. Such items' shipping costs are directly added to the shipping cost based on the general formula.

- **Insurance** – If the insurance calculation formula is set in the **Shopping** portlet configuration then system will show this field. It will be a drop-down with two values (None and insurance cost). By default, the system selects "*None*" in this field. If the customer wants insurance then s/he may change it.

- **Coupon Code** – If the user has any active discount coupon then s/he may provide the value before the checkout. The system will calculate discount as defined by the promotion coupon.

- **Payment Method** – If the payment is enabled through PayPal then the system will show the PayPal logo. If credit card payment is enabled then the system will display supported credit card logos.

- **Update Cart button** – With this button, the user can save changed cart details. These details are kept in the database, and can be kept for a long time. After updating, the cart system will again show the same page.

- **Empty Cart** – This button allows the user to remove all the items from the shopping cart.

- **Checkout** – Once the customer has decided to pay for the items in the cart, s/he needs to click on it and initiate the payment process.

Pop quiz

1. How can we remove all the items from the shopping cart?

   a. We can open the shopping cart page and set quantity as 0 for all the items and save.

   b. We can click on the **Empty Cart** button to remove all the items from the shopping cart.

   c. We can click on the **Remove action** button for each item from the shopping cart page.

2. Which of the following statements are true?

   a. Shopping cart does not keep items in the shopping cart once the user signs out from the portal.

   b. Shopping cart displays the total discount

   c. If insurance calculation is configured for the shopping portlet, by default, it adds insurance cost.

Checkout process

Let's recap actions which we performed while shopping in a super market. Once we pick up all the needed items in our cart where do we go? We go to payment counter to pay the bill. We have picked up the necessary bouquets in our shopping cart, now we must pay the bill.

Time for action – making a payment

Follow these steps:

1. Sign in to the neighborhood portal using the normal user credentials (**james. desoza@cignexneighbourhood.com** / **test**) and navigate to Around the Corner community from the Dockbar.

2. Now click on the **Cart** tab from the top of the shopping portlet. The system will display the shopping cart view with those items which we added to the shopping cart.

3. Click on the **Checkout** button.

4. The system will show the payment details view, asking the user to enter **Billing and Shipping** address details. Enter the following values in the given fields:

- ❏ **Billing Address**
- ❏ **First Name – James**
- ❏ **Last Name – Desoza**
- ❏ **Email – james.desoza@cignexneighbourhood.com**
- ❏ **Company – CIGNEX Technologies**
- ❏ **Street – 2350 Mission College Boulevard**
- ❏ **City – Santa Clara**
- ❏ **State – California**
- ❏ **Zip – 95054**
- ❏ **Country – USA**
- ❏ **Phone – 408-273-6785**
- ❏ **Shipping Address**
- ❏ **Same as Billing – Checked**

5. Click on the **Continue** button. The system will display a confirmation screen as shown in the following screenshot:

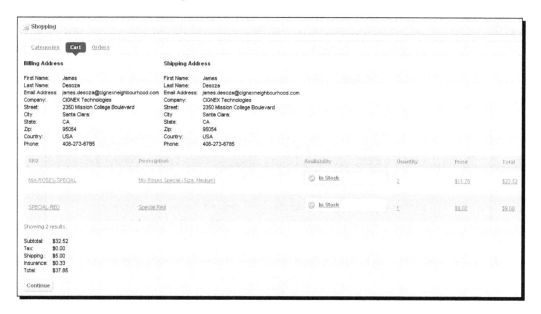

6. Click on the **Continue** button. The system will redirect to the `http://www.sandbox.paypal.com` site. On the left-hand side of the page, the system will display the order summary. From the right-hand side of the page, click on the **Have a PayPal account?** link. The system will show the PayPal sign on the right-hand side of the page as shown in the following screenshot:

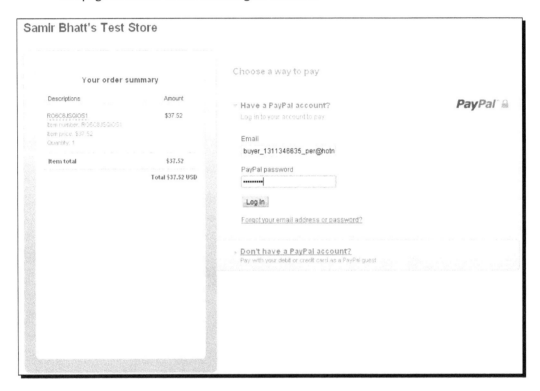

After clicking on the **Continue** button, if you see a page showing a message indicating login to sandbox environment then possibly you forgot to check the **Keep me logged in** checkbox when we first logged in to the `http://developer.paypal.com` website during the payment method configuration. No worries, we now need to log in to `http://developer.paypal.com` and check the **Keep me logged in** checkbox. Use the credentials you defined during the payment method configuration. Once you have logged in start from step 1.

7. Enter the buyer credentials which we noted down while configuring the payment method. The system will display shipping address and other order information as shown in the following screenshot. Now click on the **Pay Now** button to make the payment:

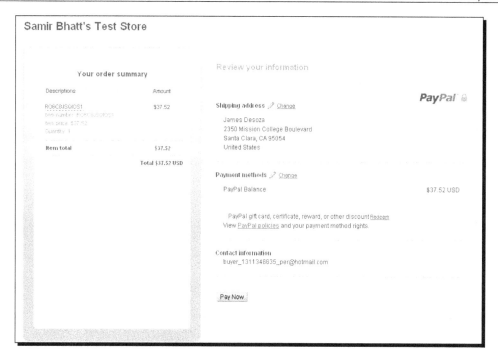

8. The system will show you the payment confirmation screen. Now click on the **Return To <Your Name in developer.paypal.com>'s Test Store** link as shown in the following screenshot. The system will redirect back to Liferay Portal and show a success message along with the order id:

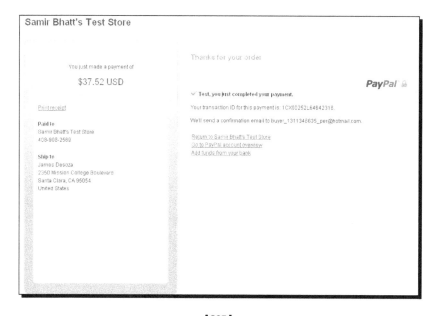

What just happened?

We just completed our shopping and made the payment for our purchase. We first checked out our shopping cart and provided billing and shipping addresses. The system then presented a confirmation screen with complete details of our order. We found the details were proper and continued to make payment.

As our Shopping portlet is integrated with PayPal sandbox environment, the system redirected us to `http://sandbox.paypal.com`. The system presented the store's home page. We then entered our buyer PayPal credentials and then confirmed to pay. Then we clicked on a link to go back to our shop's page. The system displayed a confirmation message with our order number.

If the mail server is configured on the CIGNEX Neighborhood website then the system must have sent an order confirmation e-mail to the signed in user (customer).

Let's look at the details of each view involved in the checkout process.

Address details

As we have seen when we click on the **Checkout** button, the system presents this view to us. In order to deliver, the order merchant will need billing address and shipping address. Billing address is used to send a printed invoice to the customer. Shipping address is the address where the merchant ships the items. In most cases, both the addresses are the same. To avoid entering the same address in both places, the system provides a checkbox **Same as Billing** in the shipping address section. If we enable this checkbox, the system will use the billing address as the shipping address.

This view also provides an extra comment field. This field provides an opportunity to enter some extra information related to the order. For example, the customer can provide extra comments indicating when the merchant should deliver items to the shipping address.

Entering address details for purchasing something every time is boring, isn't it? But Shopping portlet is intelligent enough and stores the address details of the user. So when we shop next time, we can use the same address. We still have an opportunity to provide new address details.

Order confirmation

As seen previously, before initiating the payment process the system displays order confirmation page. This page provides an opportunity to the customer to review order information. This view provides the following information to the customer:

- **Billing Address** – This section displays the billing address entered by the customer in the previous step.

- ◆ **Shipping Address** – This section displays the shipping address entered by the customer. If the user has enabled the **Same as Billing** checkbox, then the billing address and shipping address will be same.

- ◆ **Item List** – The system displays items that are a part of the order. Item list provides the following information:

  - ❑ **SKU** – The system displays SKU field of the item. Here it doesn't display small image

  - ❑ **Description** – Item description

  - ❑ **Availability** – This column highlights availability of stock for this item. If stock is available then a green message is displayed. If stock is not available then a red message is displayed

  - ❑ **Quantity** – Ordered quantity

  - ❑ **Price** – Unit price of item

  - ❑ **Total** – Total price of items (that is, *Quantity * Unit Price*)

- ◆ **Subtotal** – Sum of total column in the item list.

- ◆ **Tax** – Sales tax for the items. It is calculated by tax percentage set in the **Payment Settings** configuration and subtotal field.

- ◆ **Shipping** – Total shipping cost. It is the same cost which we can see in the shopping cart page.

- ◆ **Insurance** – Insurance cost. If we selected insurance in the shopping cart then this field contains the same value.

- ◆ **Total** – Total order amount. This is the amount the customer has to pay. It is the sum of the subtotal, tax, shipping, and insurance fields.

Have a go hero – verifying PayPal accounts

Using our PayPal sandbox buyer account, we paid the order amount to the PayPal sandbox seller account. We configured the seller e-mail id in the payment method configuration. So check both the buyer and seller accounts to verify the impact of the aforementioned transaction.

You need to log in to `http://www.developer.paypal.com` with the credentials that you set during the payment method configuration steps. Then click on the **Test Accounts** link and select buyer account, and then click on the **Enter Sandbox Test Site** button. Once you verify the buyer account, sign out and then do the same step for the seller account.

Order management

Once an order is placed by the customer, the merchant must ensure the order is delivered on time. This activity is called order management. The Shopping portlet provides a way to perform various order management activities such as changing order status, sending a shipping confirmation e-mail to the customer, updating payment details, printing invoice details, and so on.

Time for action – processing the order

Let's complete our first online order:

1. As the admin, navigate to Around the Corner community from Dockbar.

2. Now click on the **Orders** tab. The system will display the order listing page. We can see our first order placed by our customer James Desoza.

3. Click on the **Action** button of the order and then click on **Edit action**. The system displays the edit order page as shown in the following screenshot:

4. Now click on the **Send Shipping Email** button at the bottom. The system will show a success message and return to the same screen.

5. Now update values in the PayPal section as mentioned next:

   ❑ **Status – Completed**

   ❑ **TXN ID** – <Enter the PayPal transaction id>

   ❑ **Payment Gross** – <Enter the payment amount>

   ❑ **Receiver Email Address** – <Enter the seller's PayPal login id>

   ❑ **Payer Email Address** – <Enter the buyer's PayPal login id>

6. Now click on the **Save** button. The system will come back on the same page with a success message.

What just happened?

We signed in to our online shop as the admin or merchant. We then located our first customer order from the **Orders** tab. We then opened the order in edit mode. We first sent a shipping confirmation e-mail by clicking on the **Send Shipping Email** button. Then we changed the order status to completed and also updated information from the PayPal transaction.

Order management interface is mainly used by the merchant or order management team of the online shop. They keep track of online orders. Merchant can ensure smooth delivery of online orders with the help of order management interface. We briefly used this interface and managed our first customer order. Let's understand other attributes of the order management views in detail.

Order listing

When the user clicks on the **Orders** tab at the top of the shopping portlet, the system represents the order listing screen. We can navigate to a specific order from this screen. Let's learn about all the attributes/actions of this screen as shown in the following screenshot:

- **Searh Section** – It becomes very difficult to locate a particular order when we have so many. To solve this problem, **Shopping** portlet provides a search functionality. We can search an order based on any of the following fields. We can choose whether to use the *And* condition or *Or* condition between multiple search fields:

  - **Order Number**
  - **Status**
  - **First Name**
  - **Last Name**
  - **Email Address**

- **Order Listing** – All the orders or the order search result is displayed in this table. Following attributes are displayed in the order listing table:

  - **Number** – Auto generated order number
  - **Date** – Order date
  - **Status** – Order status
  - **Customer** – First name and last name of a customer
  - **Action** – The user can perform following actions from this action button:

    - **Edit** – The user can edit order by clicking on the **Edit** button. The user can click on the hyperlink on the ordered item to perform the same action.

    - **Delete** – The user can delete a particular order by using this action button. To delete multiple orders, user can choose the checkbox shown in the first column of one or many order item and then click on the **Delete** button available on top of the order listing.

Order details

When the user clicks on a particular order from the order listing page, this page is displayed. As seen previously, we used this screen to change the status of our first order. Let's understand the various other attributes and actions available on this page:

- **Order Information** – This section displays basic order information. The following attributes are displayed in this section:

  - **Order #** – Order number
  - **Order Date** – Order creation date
  - **Last Modified Date**

- **Address Information**:
    - ❑ **Billing Address** – Billing address of the customer that is specified by the customer while making the payment.
    - ❑ **Shipping Address** – Shipping address of the customer which is specified by the customer while making the payment.
- **PayPal**:
    - ❑ **Status** – Merchant can use this field to change the status of the order. It can have five different values: **Checkout**, **Completed**, **Denied**, **Pending**, and **Refunded**. By default, each order will be in **Checkout** state. If **Instant Payment Notification (IPN)** is enabled in the PayPal seller's account and the notification URL of **Shopping** portlet (`http://<domain>/ c/shopping/ notify`) is set as IPN, then status of the order can be automatically be changed to **Completed** once the payment is successful.
    - ❑ **TXN ID** – PayPal transaction id. As mentioned, if IPN was correctly set then this field is also automatically populated on successful payment.
    - ❑ **Payment Gross** – The amount paid by the customer for the order. It can also be populated automatically through IPN.
    - ❑ **Receiver Email Address** – Seller e-mail id. It can also be populated automatically through IPN.
    - ❑ **Payer Email Address** – Buyer e-mail id. It can also be populated automatically through IPN.
    - ❑ **Complete order link** – If IPN is properly set, then on the clicking of this link Instant Payment Notification is again sent to the **Shopping** portlet to complete the order.
- **Item Listing** – Items of the order are listed in this section. Each row contains the following attributes:
    - ❑ **SKU**
    - ❑ **Description**
    - ❑ **Quantity**
    - ❑ **Price**
    - ❑ **Total**

- **Order Amount** – This section displays the different order amounts. They are the same as what we see in the payment confirmation screen:
    - **Subtotal**
    - **Tax**
    - **Shipping**
    - **Total**

- **Save button** – We can save the changes made to the order by using this button.

- **Invoice button** – This button opens the invoice screen in a new window without any theme, header, and so on. This will allow us to print the invoice. The invoice screen is the replica of the order details screen. It does not include any action buttons.

- **Send Confirmation Email** – The merchant can send an order confirmation e-mail with this button. Once the e-mail is sent, the button's label is changed to **Resend Confirmation Email**.

- **Send Shipping Email** – The merchant can send a shipping confirmation e-mail with this button. Once the e-mail is sent, the button's label is changed to **Resend Shipping Email**.

- **Delete button** – The merchant can delete a particular order with this button.

Promotion offers

So far, we have completed an online shopping lifecycle. But for a merchant, it is very important to attract more and more customers to his/her shop and increase sales. Promotion offers are the best way to attract customers to the shop. Shopping portlet provides an in-built feature to configure promotion offers.

Time for action – promoting offers

So let's configure promotion offers for our customers:

1. As an admin, navigate to the Around the Corner community from the Dockbar.

2. Now click on the **Coupons** tab from the top of the shopping portlet. The system displays the **Coupons** listing page.

3. Click on the **Add Coupon** button. The system will show an edit coupon page.

4. Enter the values as shown in the following screenshot and then click on the **Save** button:

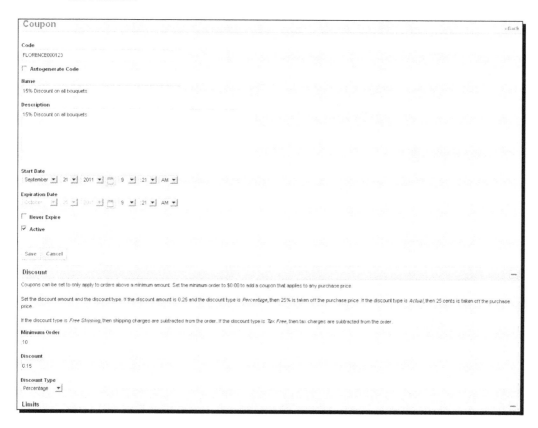

5. The system will go back to the **Coupons** listing page.

6. Now click on the **Categories** tab from the top of the shopping portlet.

7. Enter **Special Red** in the search input box and click on the **Search** button. The system will display the **Special Red** item in the search result.

8. Click on the **Special Red** item. The system will display the item details view.

9. Click on the **Add to Shopping Cart** button. The system will display the shopping cart page.

10. Change the quantity of the item to 3 and **Coupon Code** field value to **FLORENCE000123**. It is the same code which we used for our discount coupon. Click on the **Update Cart** button.

11. The system will show the shopping cart page with a success message and **Coupon Discount** element with the discount amount.

What just happened?

We just added a promotion offer in our shop. We configured our offer with a 15 percent discount on the total order amount. We configured one month's validity for our offer. We have assigned a unique coupon id to our offer. To opt for this offer, the customer has to enter this coupon ID in the shopping cart page. We added three **Special Red** bouquets in the shopping cart and updated coupon ID in the shopping cart. As we entered a valid coupon ID in the shopping cart, the system gave 15 percent discount on the total.

Let's understand the different attributes of coupon management functionality.

Coupon listing

When we click on the **Coupons** tab from the top of the shopping portlet, the system opens the coupon listing page:

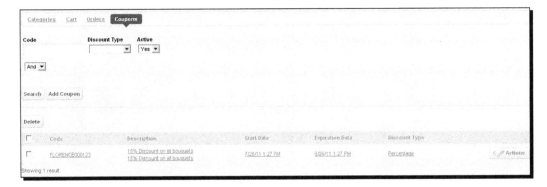

As shown in the preceding screenshot, the coupon listing page is divided into two sections:

- ◆ Search section– Search section provides a way to search coupons. Search section allows user to search coupons based on the following fields. The system also allows user to select *And* or *Or* condition between two criteria:
    - ❑ **Code (Coupon Code)**
    - ❑ **Discount Type**
    - ❑ **Active (Status)**
- ◆ **Add Coupon** button – The user can add a new coupon by using this button. When this button is clicked, the system opens the edit coupon view.
- ◆ **Coupon Listing** section – By default, this section displays list of all coupons. After performing search operation, this section displays search result. This section displays the following attribute/actions for each coupon:
    - ❑ **Code (Coupon Code)**

    ❑ **Description**

    ❑ **Start Date** – Starting date of the offer

    ❑ **Expiration Date** – End date of the offer

    ❑ **Discount Type** – Type of discount offered by the coupon

    ❑ **Action** – The system allows two actions for each coupon row. Edit coupon action and delete coupon action

- **Delete** button – User can delete one or many coupons with this option. To use this button, the user has to select one of many coupons.

Edit coupon details

This view is used to add or edit a coupon. We added our first percentage discount coupon using this view. There are different types of coupons that we can create using this view. Let's learn about all the attributes and actions of this view:

- **Code** and **Auto Generate Code** – If we enable the **Auto Generate Code** checkbox then the system locks the **Code** field and generates auto generated coupon code when we save the coupon. For our first coupon, we used our own coupon code.

- **Name** – Descriptive name for the offer.

- **Description** – Detailed description of the offer.

- **Start Date** – Starting date of the offer. We can also provide a time along with the date.

- **Expiration Date** – Expiration date of the offer. We can also provide a time along with the date.

- **Never Expire** – If it is enabled, then the coupon will never expire and the expiration date will not be used. If it is disabled, then the expiration date will be used to calculate coupon discount.

- **Active** – This checkbox is used to indicate whether the coupon is active or not.

- **Discount Section** – This section is used to define discount formula for the coupon.

    ❑ **Minimum Order** – This attribute indicates the minimum order amount to opt for the discount offered by this coupon. For example, if it is set to 10 then coupon discount will be applied only if order amount is 10 or greater than 10.

    ❑ **Discount** – Discount value. The value is used by the system with respect to the type of discount. If discount type is percentage then value of this field becomes discount percentage. If discount type is actual then the value of this field becomes discount amount.

- **Discount Type** – There are four different types of discounts supported by coupons:

  - **Percentage** – It is the same that we used for our first coupon. The system calculates coupon discount based on % value

  - **Actual** – It is used to define flat discount. For example, if discount type is **Actual** and the discount field is set to 15, then the system will provide $15 as a coupon discount amount

  - **Free Shipping** – If this discount type is selected by the user then the system will not charge anything for shipping

  - **Tax Free** – If this discount type is selected then the system will not add sales tax to the total

- **Limits** – User can provide comma-separated category list or SKU list to limit the discount offered to specific items. If comma-separated categories are provided in limit then the system will calculate discount for only those items that belong to those categories. If comma-separated SKU list is provided in limits then only those SKUs are applicable for discount.

Have a go hero – advertising

We created an offer but how do we inform our customers about the offer? We need to advertise. There are various ways to do so. We learned about creating web content in *Chapter 7*. So recap what we learned from *Chapter 7* and add a web content display portlet on the **Welcome** page. Add web content for advertising our offer. You may use the following HTML code for your web content:

```
<div style="background-color:yellow">
  <h1 style="text-align: center; ">
    <span style="font-size:72px;">15% OFF</span></h1>
  <h2 style="text-align: center; ">
    On All Flower Bouques</h2>
  <h2 style="text-align: center; ">
    Florence Flower Shop</h2>
  <h2 style="text-align: center; ">
    Coupon ID <span style="color:#ffa07a;">FLORENCE000123</span></h2>
</div>
```

 You need to log in as the admin user. Then you need to add web content display portlet and configure the web content using HTML source.

Pop quiz

1.   Which of the following statements are true?

   a.   We can re-send order confirmation e-mails and order shipping e-mails

   b.   We can remove an order from the system

   c.   Order status cannot be changed manually

   d.   Invoices can be sent through e-mail from the shopping portlet

2.   Which of the following information do we have to provide before making payment through PayPal?

   a.   Billing address

   b.   Shipping address

   c.   Communication address

   d.   Comments

3.   What are the different types of coupon discount formulas supported by shopping portlet?

   a.   Percentage

   b.   Actual

   c.   Buy X Get Y Free

   d.   Free Shipping

   e.   Tax Free

Summary

We covered almost everything you need to know about the shopping portlet. With this knowledge, you can easily set up your shop within any Liferay-based website. We learned how to configure the payment method (PayPal), tax rates, shipping rates, insurance calculation, e-mail formats, and so on, for an online shop. We also learned how to configure shopping items. We learned how our customer will shop through our online shop, how a shopper will manage orders, invoices, and promotions.

After learning about the Shopping portlet and online shopping concepts, let's get ready to learn about Liferay server administration.

10

Liferay Server Administration

In the previous chapter, we learned how to configure the online shop in Liferay. Using the shopping portlet we configured a flower shop in the Around the Corner community. We learned how to integrate the shopping portlet with PayPal, how to manage orders, how to manage shopping items, and so on. So far in all of the previous chapters, we have learned about many features useful for the end user or portal administrator.

When we launch any website to the world, it is very important to make sure our website is up and running all the time. These activities are normally done by the system administration team. In this chapter, we will learn about different Liferay server administration features.

By the end of this chapter, we will have learned how to:

- Monitor and manage Liferay server resources
- Configure log levels to troubleshoot production issues
- Configure various file upload limits and file formats
- Monitor portal sessions
- Configure multiple portals on a single Liferay Portal server
- Configure virtual hosts for communities or organizations
- Set up a staging environment within the same Liferay Portal server

Getting started with server administration

Before starting this chapter, the following steps should be performed:

◆ Liferay Portal server is installed as explained in *Chapter 2, Installing a Liferay Portal Instance*

◆ Around the Corner community is configured

◆ Games and Sports community is configured

◆ Apache web server is configured as explained in *Chapter 4, Tips and Tricks—Advanced Configuration*.

Monitoring and managing server resources

It is very important for any server administrator to monitor server resources and take necessary actions to avoid any outage. The most important resource is server memory. The server will crash if memory usage goes beyond the limit. In this section, we will learn how we can monitor the Liferay Portal resources. We will also learn about resource management activities to control resource usage.

Time for action – monitoring and controlling Liferay resources

Let's access Liferay's resource management functionality:

1. Start the Liferay Portal server if it is stopped.

2. Sign in to the Neighborhood portal using the admin credentials.

3. Now open the **Control Panel** by selecting **Manage** | **Control Panel** option from Dockbar.

4. Now from the **Server** section, click on the **Server Administration** link. The system will open the server admin portlet as shown in the following screenshot. By default, the **Resources** tab will be automatically selected.

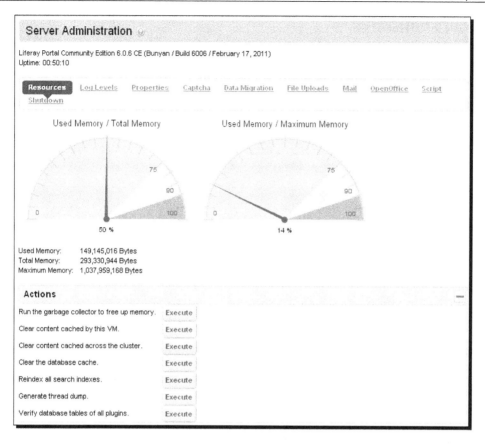

5. Now, click on the **Execute** button just beside the **Run the garbage collector to free up memory** label.

6. The system will display the same screen with a success message and changed meter charts.

7. Now click on the **Execute** button just beside the **Clear content cached by this VM** label. The system will again display the same screen with a success message and changed meter charts.

8. Now click on the **Execute** button just beside the **Clear the database cache** label. The system will display the same screen again.

We just used a few of the resource management features provided by the admin portlet. Now let's look at all the resource management features provided by the admin portlet.

Memory utilization

We have seen how Liferay Portal visualizes memory utilization. As shown in the previous section, the **Resources** tab of the admin portlet displays two meter charts to show memory utilization. There are three different measures used to generate these charts:

- **Allocated Memory**—This represents memory that is allocated to the Liferay Portal server JVM at a particular time
- **Used Memory**—This represents actual memory consumed by the the Liferay Portal server from the allocated memory
- **Maximum Memory**—This represents the maximum memory that can be allocated to the Liferay Portal server JVM

Used Memory versus Total Memory

This meter chart is a gauge that points out the **Used Memory** on a range of **0** to **Allocated Memory**. It displays the level of current used memory by objects. If it goes beyond the range of total memory, JVM will allocate more memory, up to the maximum memory.

Used Memory versus Maximum Memory

This meter chart is a gauge that points out the **Used Memory** on a range of **0** to **Maximum Memory**. The maximum memory can be configured using the Xmx JVM parameter. If the used memory goes beyond the maximum memory then JVM will throw OutOfMemory exception.

Memory management operations

The Liferay resource management functionality provides four different memory management operations:

- **Run the garbage collector to free up memory**—This button explicitly invokes the garbage collector to free up memory. We have seen that when we clicked on this button, both the meter charts reflected decreases in used memory. Garbage collection normally happens automatically by JVM. JVM decides when to do garbage collection. However, with this option we can ask JVM to perform garbage collection. Garbage collection normally finishes within milliseconds. But it is important to know that during the garbage collection process, the system may become unresponsive for some period.

- **Clear content cached by this VM**—The Liferay Portal provides a built-in feature to cache the content in memory and the file system. Sometimes, it is required to clear this cache. This option allows the admin to clear the content cache. By clearing the content cache, we can free up a certain amount of memory. However, it is important to understand that the purpose of this option is not to free up memory and improve the performance, as content cache actually improves performance of the portal. It is possible to configure a clustered environment by connecting multiple Liferay Portal nodes. This option clears the cache only from the connected Liferay node.

- **Clear content cached across the cluster**—This option is very similar to the previous option. With this option, the admin can clear content cache from all connected Liferay nodes.

- **Clear the database cache**—Liferay internally uses the Hibernate framework for the persistence layer. By default, various persistence objects are cached using the **Ehcache** framework. With the help of this button, we can clear the persistence objects from cache. Again, the purpose of this option is not to free up memory and improve performance.

General maintenance operations

Other than the memory management operations, the **Resource** tab provides the following options to perform general maintenance tasks:

- **Reindex all search indexes**—The Liferay Portal provides an indexing service to portlets. With the use of this button, we can invoke re-indexing operations for all the portlets that support indexing. Normally, portlets create index entries when relevant data is created or updated by them. However, sometimes indexes become corrupt. With the use of this option, admin can re-index all the portlets.

 This operation may take hours, if the amount of data is huge. If the requirement is just to re-index data of a specific portlet, then we can perform the re-index operation on the specific portlet from the plugin installation function.

- **Generate thread dump**—On clicking this button, the Liferay Portal generates a thread dump on the standard output. A thread dump is a vital tool to debug issues related to performance.

- **Verify tables of all the plugins**—This button checks tables of all the portlets against indexes. When portlets are developed using service builder, this option can be used to check tables against indexes.

Managing log levels

Logging is one of the most important tools for troubleshooting issues in any application. Liferay uses Log4j framework for logging. Using log4j, we can log messages for different levels. Using configuration files, we can set the log level. It is a normal feature in most of the applications but Liferay provides a way to configure the log level at runtime.

Time for action – configuring the log levels

Let's change log levels on our Neighborhood portal and learn about this feature in detail:

1. Sign in to the Neighborhood portal using the admin credentials.

2. Check if there is a debug message from the file `LoginPostAction`. There will not be.

3. Now open the **Control Panel** by selecting **Manage | Control Panel** option from the Dockbar.

4. Now from the **Server** section, click on the **Server Administration** link. The system will, by default, select the **Resources** tab. Click on the **Log Levels** tab.

5. The system will, by default, open the **Update Categories** sub tab.

6. Now enter **com.liferay.portal.events.LoginPostAction** in the **Search** textbox and press the **Search** button.

7. The system will display one result as shown in the following screenshot:

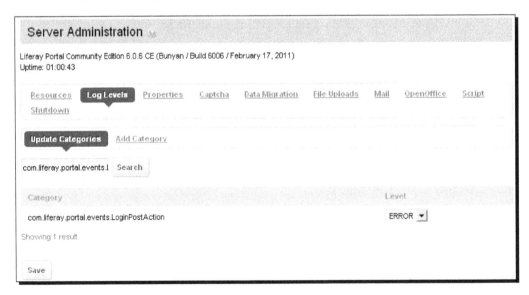

8. Now change the **Log Level** drop-down value from **ERROR** to **DEBUG**. Press the **Save** button.

9. Now click on the **Sign Out** link from the Dockbar to log out from the portal.

10. Now, again sign in to the Neighborhood portal using the admin user credentials.

11. Check the server console. You will now find a line similar to the following one. Only time and number after the `Running` label might be different:

```
21:40:39,265 DEBUG [LoginPostAction:48] Running 2
```

12. Now, stop the Neighborhood portal and start again.

13. Again, sign in with the admin user credentials and check the console. Now you will not find a line which we saw in the Step 11.

What just happened?

We just changed the log level of the `LoginPostAction` class to `DEBUG`. Every time the Liferay Portal invokes a method of this class after a user signs in. In this class, there is a debug statement to display a remote user attribute from the HTTP request object. It is logged by the Liferay Portal using log level `DEBUG`. When we first signed in to the Neighborhood portal and checked the console, we didn't find any such log message. The log level of this class was configured to `ERROR`. We then changed the log level of this class to `DEBUG`. We were then able to see the log message on the console. When we restarted the Liferay Portal server again, the debug message was not there on console.

As we have seen, we can on the fly change log levels of liferay portal classes and troubleshoot problems by monitoring the log file. We also observed this log-level change remains effective till we restarted the Liferay Portal. Now let's understand some of the other aspects related to the log-level configuration.

What if the class or package entry is not found?

To change the log level of the `LoginPostAction` class, we first located the log-level entry using the **Search** option. However, what if the class or package does not comes up in the search result? This normally happens for custom plugins. By default, there is a log-level configuration file within the portal. So, if the entry of class or package does not exist in portal's log-level configuration file, then we cannot locate the log-level entry using search.

However, we don't need to worry as Liferay provides a way to add a new entry for a class or package and configures the log level. When we navigate to **Contro Panel | Server Administration | Log Levels**, the system by default opens the **Update Categories** sub tab. We have already used the options and changed the log level of an existing class. To add a new entry, we need to open the **Add Category** sub tab as shown in following screenshot:

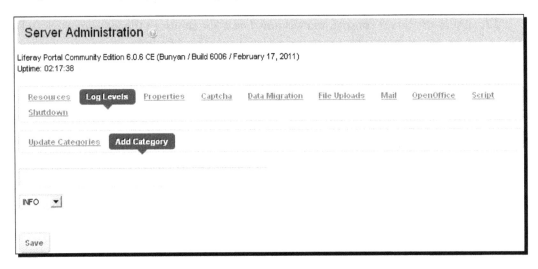

To configure the log level for non-existing class or package, we need to enter the fully qualified class name or the package name and set the log level from the drop-down. When we press the **Save** button, the Liferay Portal adds the entry in the runtime log-level configuration. We can again change the log level using the **Search** option until we restart the server.

Configuring the log levels permanently

Sometimes it is required to change the log levels permanently. Liferay defines the default log levels in a configuration file called `portal-log4j.xml`. In the previous section, we have overridden the log levels defined in this XML at runtime. But once we restarted the Liferay Portal, those changes were lost. Liferay provides a way to override default log levels permanently by creating another configuration file.

Time for action – changing log levels permanently

Let's change the log level of `LoginPostAction` permanently:

1. Stop the Liferay Portal server, if it is running.

2. Now, locate the `liferay-portal-6.0.6\tomcat-6.0.29\webapps\ROOT\WEB-INF\classes` directory from the root directory where you installed the Liferay Portal bundle.

3. Create a new directory called `META-INF` in the `classes` directory.

4. Copy `7003OS-chapter-10\code\log4j.dtd` from the downloaded code to the `META-INF` directory created in the preceding step.

5. Create a new file called `porta-log4j-ext.xml` in the `META-INF` directory we just created and copy the following code and save it:

```
<?xml version="1.0"?>
<!DOCTYPE log4j:configuration SYSTEM "log4j.dtd">
<log4j:configuration xmlns:log4j="http://jakarta.apache.org/log4j/">
    <category name="com.liferay.portal.events.LoginPostAction">
      <priority value="DEBUG" />
    </category>
</log4j:configuration>
```

6. Start the Liferay Portal server.

7. Sign in to the Neighborhood portal using the admin credentials.

8. Check the server console. You will now find a line similar to the following one. Only the time and the number after the `Running` label might be different:

```
21:40:39,265 DEBUG [LoginPostAction:48] Running 2
```

What just happened?

We created a new `log4j` configuration file in the Liferay Portal server installation. We configured the log level for our `com.liferay.portal.events.LoginPostAction` file to debug. We then tested the configuration. It worked even after we restarted the :iferay portal server.

As discussed in the beginning of this section, Liferay defines the default log levels in `portal-log4j.xml`. It is placed in the `portal-impl.jar` file of the Liferay Portal. We can override entries of `portal-log4j.xml` using `portal-log4j-ext.xml`, which we did in the previous section. During startup, the Liferay Portal first loads `portal-log4j.xml` and then overrides entries of loaded configuration from `portal-log4j-ext.xml`.

Managing file upload size and types

In *Chapter 6, Managing Pages, Users, and Permissions*, we learned various features of the image gallery and document library portlets. As we know, using these portlets we can upload image files or documents to the Liferay Portal server. It is very dangerous for any production application to allow end users to upload very large files. This can make production servers unresponsive. Liferay provides a way to configure these settings.

Time for action – configuring document library file settings

Let's learn this feature by actually using it:

1. Sign in to the Neighborhood portal using the admin credentials.

2. Now open the **Control Panel**.

3. Now from the **Content** section, click on the **Document Library** link. The system will display the **Document Library** portlet.

4. Now from the right-hand panel of the **Document Library** portlet, click on the **Add Document** link. The system will display the document upload page.

5. Now, click on the **Browse (You can select multiple files.)** link. The system will open the file selection dialog. Select any file which is around 4 MB or more in size.

6. The system will display the document upload page as shown in following screenshot:

7. The system doesn't allow adding the file because the default maximum size of the file for **Document Library** is set to 3 MB.

8. Now from the **Server** section, click on the **Server Administration** link. The system will, by default, select the **Resources** tab. Click on the **File Uploads** tab.

9. The system will display the file upload settings page.

10. In the **Document Library** section, the system displays **3072000** value for the **Maximum File Size** file. Change the value to **5242880**.

11. Now repeat steps 4 to 6. After step 6, the system will display the file upload screen as shown in the following screenshot:

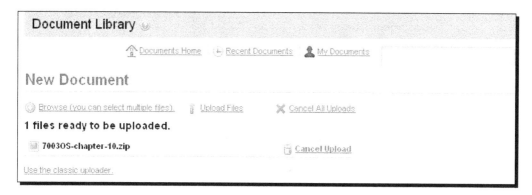

12. The system will allow finishing the upload by clicking on the **Upload Files** link. Click on the **Upload Files** link and finish the upload.

What just happened?

We first tried uploading the file in the **Document Library** portlet, which is larger than the maximum size defined by the Liferay Portal. The system didn't allow uploading that file. We then increased the maximum file size limit for the **Document Library** portlet. The system then allowed us to upload the large file.

As you might have noticed on the file upload functionality, there are so many other options. Let's understand those options in detail:

- **General**
  - **Overall Maximum File Size**—Liferay has a generic upload functionality which is used by various portlets. We can configure the maximum file size that can be uploaded using this field. We need to set the maximum bytes of a file that can be allowed using this generic upload functionality.
  - **Temporary Storage Directory**—We can define the temporary directory in which server will used to store the uploaded file temporarily. If nothing is defined then the system will use the directory defined by `java.io.tmpdir` JVM system property. In Tomcat, by default, this property points to the `temp` directory of the Tomcat root directory. You can change the location by modifying the `catalina.sh` or `catalina.bat` file.

- **Document Library**
    - **Maximum File Size**—It defines the maximum file size that will be allowed to upload using the **Document Library** portlet. The size must be provided in number of bytes.
    - **Allowed File Extensions**—This option provides a way to restrict only a certain file type to be uploaded in the **Document Library** portlet. We can define comma-separated file extensions, which should be allowed in **Document Library**.

- **Image Gallery**
    - **Maximum File Size**—It is similar to that in **Document Library**. We can define the maximum image file that can be uploaded in the **Image Gallery** portlet.
    - **Allowed File Extensions**—It defines the allowed files extensions for the **Image Gallery** portlet, the same as in the **Document Library** portlet.
    - **Maximum Thumbnail Dimensions**—We learned about using the **Image Gallery** portlet in *Chapter 6, Managing Pages, Users, and Permissions*. The **Image Gallery** portlet displays thumbnail images on an image listing page. These thumbnail images are actually scaled down to be displayed on the image listing page. Using this option, we can define the maximum height or width of a thumbnail in pixels.

- **Web Content Images**
    - **Maximum File Size**—We learned in *Chapter 7, Creating and Publishing Content*, that we can upload images in web content. Using this field, we can configure the maximum file size of these images.
    - **Allowed File Extensions**—With this option, we can control which type of images can be uploaded to web content.

- **Shopping Cart Images**
    - **Maximum File Size (Large Image)/ Maximum File Size (Medium Image) / Maximum File Size (Small Image)**—We learned in *Chapter 9, Setting Up an Online Shop*, that we can upload three types of images for any shopping item. Using this option we can configure the maximum file size of each type of image.
    - **Allowed File Extensions**—With this option, we can control which type of images can be uploaded through the Shopping portlet.

- **Software Catalog Images**
    - **Maximum File Size**—It defines the maximum image file size that can be uploaded in the **Software Catalog** portlet.

- ❑ **Maximum Thumbnail Height**—The **Software Catalog** portlet displays a thumbnail of the product image. Using this option, we can control the maximum height of this thumbnail image.

- ❑ **Maximum Thumbnail Width**—The same as the preceding option; with this we can control the maximum width of the thumbnail image.

- ◆ **User Images**

- ❑ **Maximum File Size**—As we learned in *Chapter 6, Managing Pages, Users, and Permissions*, a user can upload his/her photo to his/her profile. With this option, we can restrict the maximum file size of the user's photo.

Monitoring portal sessions

It is often required for the portal applications to monitor active sessions from users. Liferay provides a feature to monitor live sessions.

Time for action – monitoring live user sessions

Server administrator of the Neighborhood portal decided to configure live session monitoring. So let's configure live session monitoring:

1. Stop the Liferay Portal server, if it is running.

2. Locate the `liferay-portal-6.0.6\tomcat-6.0.29\webapps\ROOT\WEB-INF\classes\portal-ext.properties` file in the root directory where you installed the Liferay Portal server.

3. Open the `portal-ext.properties` file in text editor and add the following property at the end of the file and save it:

   `live.users.enabled=true`

4. Now, start the Liferay Portal server.

5. In one of the browsers, open the portal and sign in to the portal using the normal user that we created in *Chapter 9, Setting Up an Online Shop*, (**james.desoza@ cignexneighbourhood.com / test**).

6. In another browser, sign in to the Neighborhood portal using the admin credentials.

7. Now in the browser where we signed in as admin user, open the **Control Panel**.

8. Now from the **Portal** section, click on the **Monitoring** link. The system will display the current **Live Sessions** as displayed in following screenshot:

9. Now, click on the link for the **James Desoza** user. The system will display the session details screen.

10. Scroll down to the bottom of the page and click on the **Kill Session** button.

11. The system will go back to the **Live Sessions** listing page and now it will show only one session.

12. Now go to another browser where we earlier logged in as **James Desoza**.

13. Click on any page link (for example, **Shopping**). The system will show the page but as a guest user. You can see the **Sign In** link now available in the header.

What just happened?

By default, live session monitoring is disabled in Liferay. So, we first enabled it by adding a configuration property in Liferay's configuration file. We then opened two browsers. In one of the browsers, we logged in as normal user and in another browser we logged in using the admin user credentials. We then used Liferay's live session monitoring functionality. We found there were two sessions. One session was for the admin and another was for normal user. We then browsed details of normal user session. We killed the normal user session. Then we again moved back to another browser, where we logged in as normal user, and we found the session was lost and the system logged out the normal user. This is because we killed the normal user session using the admin user credentials.

So in practice, it may sometimes be required to either kill the session of a particular user or maybe we will need to monitor the details shown by the live session monitoring feature. As we observed, there is so much information presented by the live session monitoring functionality. Let's understand briefly what kind of information we can get from this functionality.

As shown in the preceding screenshot, the system displays the following information for each live session:

- **Session ID**—This column displays the JSESSIONID used by the server. It uniquely defines the user session.

- **User ID**—This column displays the ID of the Liferay user. This ID is automatically generated by Liferay at the time of user creation.

- **User Name**—Just beside the user ID, the system displays the full name of the user.

- **Screen Name**—This column displays the screen name attribute of the Liferay user and who is associated with the session.

- **Last Request**—This column displays when the last HTTP request was made by the user, who is associated with the session.

- **Number of Hits**—This column displays the total number of requests made by the user.

As we have seen, when we clicked on a particular session the system presented a screen with more details specific to that session. Let's understand what these details are:

- **Live session Details**—The system first displays the same session information which was displayed on **Live Sessions** listing page.

- **Browser/OS Type**—The system displays the browser type and version that the user is using. It also displays the operating system details of the user's machine.

- **Remote Host/IP**—This field displays the remote host and the IP of the client.

- **Accessed URLs**—This section displays a list of URLs accessed by the user associated with the session.

- **Session Attributes**—This section lists all the session attribute names that are there in the associated user session.

Configuring multiple portals on the same Liferay server

We created our portal for CIGNEX Neighborhood. Now, imagine that we get a requirement to create a Liferay Neighborhood portal. We need to then install another Liferay server and configure it, right? Is there any other way? Yes, we can also use our existing Liferay server to configure another portal which does not share any of the CIGNEX Neighborhood portal information. Without using a separate database, application server/servlet container, and other resources, we can easily set up another portal on Liferay.

Time for action – configuring another portal instance

Let's create a Liferay Neighborhood portal on the same Liferay Portal server:

1. Locate the host file from your machine and open it in a text editor.

 On a Windows machine, first open the **Run** dialog from the **Start** menu. Then enter **drivers** in the **Run** dialog and press *Enter*. The system will open Windows Explorer. Now, open the etc folder from the opened explorer. There you will find the host file. On linux, the host file normally exists in the /etc/ directory.

2. Now in the host file, add the following line at the end of the file and save:

   ```
   127.0.0.1 neighborhood.liferay.com
   ```

3. In *Chapter 4, Tips and* Tricks—*Advanced Configuration*, we have configured the Apache server using the httpd.conf file. Now open the same httpd.conf file in a text editor.

 We can locate the httpd.conf file in the conf directory of the Apache web server installation root directory.

4. Remove the following lines added in *Chapter 4, Tips and Tricks—Advanced Configuration*, with the following lines:

   ```
   ProxyRequests On

   ProxyPass / http://localhost:8080/
   ProxyPassReverse / http://localhost:8080/
   ```

5. Add the following lines in the `httpd.conf` at the end of the file and save:

```
NameVirtualHost *:80
<VirtualHost *:80>
  ProxyPreserveHost On
  ProxyPass / http://localhost:8080/
  ProxyPassReverse / http://localhost:8080/
  ServerName neighborhood.cignex.com
</VirtualHost>
<VirtualHost *:80>
  ProxyPreserveHost On
  ProxyPass / http://localhost:8080/
  ProxyPassReverse / http://localhost:8080/
  ServerName neighborhood.liferay.com
</VirtualHost>
```

6. Now restart the Apache web server.

7. Start the Tomcat server, if it is stopped.

8. Sign in to the Neighborhood portal using the admin credentials (URL: `http://neighborhood.cignex.com` / **User Name** / **Password**: **test@liferay.com** / **test**).

9. Now open the **Control Panel** (by selecting **Manage | Control Panel** option from Dockbar).

10. Now from the **Server** section, click on the **Portal Instances** link. The system will display the current portal instances as shown in the following screenshot:

11. Now from the **Portal Instances** screen, click on the **Add** button. The system will display the **New Portal Instance** form. Enter the details as shown in following screenshot:

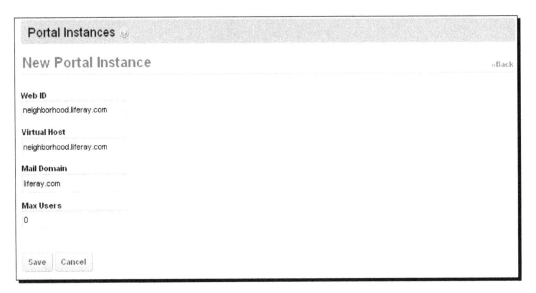

12. Now save the instance by pressing **Save**.

13. Now open another browser and enter the following URL:

    `http://neighborhood.liferay.com/`

14. You will notice that the system shows a different home page than what was displayed after step 8. Now sign in to the Neighborhood portal using the admin credentials.

15. The system will ask you to set password reminder question and answer. Enter the details as you want and press the **Save** button.

What just happened?

We just configured new domain for the Liferay Neighborhood portal mapped to the local machine IP. For a live environment, we need to register the domain. For testing, we used the local machine's host file to do so.

We then reconfigured the Apache web server. In *Chapter 4, Tips and Tricks—Advanced Configuration*, we configured the Apache web server to send all the requests to the Liferay Portal Tomcat server. However, now as we want to have two virtual hosts mapped to two different domains (`neighbourhood.cignex.com` and `neighbourhood.liferay.com`), we modified the settings. We used Apache's `mod_proxy` connector to connect Tomcat and the Apache web server. We can also connect to Tomcat and the Apache web server using another popular connector called `mod_jk`. This connector works on AJP13 protocol.

We then created a new portal instance in Liferay with the virtual host as `neighbourhood.liferay.com`. We then signed in to the portal using this virtual host. We found that the admin user was treated as a first-time user and was asked to enter the password reminder question and answer. Also, we found that the home page was different from what we had before these changes. This is because internally Liferay created a virtual instance. It has its own copy of users, content, and so on.

So now if you access the portal using `http://neighbourhood.cignex.com/`, then you will get data of the CIGNEX Neighborhood portal which we have used in the book till now. And, if you access the portal using `http://neighbourhood.liferay.com/`, we will land to a new portal instance.

With this feature of Liferay, we can easily configure many different portals on the same infrastructure.

This feature can also be used to implement database sharding. The database sharding feature allows us to scale database horizontally. This allows us to dynamically split the data into multiple databases based on an algorithm. This can be achieved by connecting each portal instance to a separate database. You can read more about Liferay's database sharding feature at following wiki page:

`http://www.liferay.com/community/wiki/-/wiki/Main/Database+Sharding.`

Virtual hosting of communities and organizations

In the previous section, we learned how we can configure multiple portals on the same Liferay Portal server. We configured virtual hosts for two different portals configured on the same Liferay server. Now suppose we have a requirement to allow accessing the Games and Sports community directly with a URL like `http://sports.cignexneighbourhood.com/`.

Time for action – virtual host configuration

Let's configure virtual hosting for the Games and Sports community.

1. Locate host file from your machine and open it in a text editor. It is the same host file which we edited in an earlier section.

2. Now in the host file, add the following line at the end of the file and save:

   ```
   127.0.0.1 sports.cignexneighbourhood.com
   ```

3. Again, we need to configure Apache configuration for new settings. So please open the `httpd.conf` file in a text editor. This is the same file which we edited in the previous section.

4. At the end of the file, add the following lines of code:

   ```
   <VirtualHost *:80>
     ProxyPreserveHost On
     ProxyPass / http://localhost:8080/
     ProxyPassReverse / http://localhost:8080/
     ServerName sports.cignexneighbourhood.com
   </VirtualHost>
   ```

5. Stop the Apache web server and start again.

6. Start the Tomcat server, if it is stopped.

7. Sign in to the Neighborhood portal using the admin credentials (URL: `http://neighborhood.cignex.com` / **User Name** / **Password**: **test@liferay.com** / **test**).

8. Now navigate to the Games and Sports community by selecting **Go To | Around the Corner** menu option from the Dockbar.

9. Now, navigate to the **Settings** functionality for the Games and Sports community by selecting the **Manage | Settings** menu option from the Dockbar.

10. The system will open the **Settings** functionality. As shown in the following screenshot, enter the details and press the **Save** button:

11. Now sign out from the portal and open the `http://sports.` `cignexneighbourhood.com` URL in the browser. We will directly land on the Games and Sports community home page.

12. Now browse other pages of the site and observe the URL pattern.

What just happened?

We first configured the `sports.cignexneighbourhood.com` domain entry in our host file. This was similar to what we did in the previous section. We then re-configured the Apache web server to add one more virtual host for the `sports.cignexneighbourhood.` `com` domain. We finally configured the virtual host settings for the Games and Sports community in Liferay.

Then, when we accessed the portal using the new domain, the system landed us on the home page of Games and Sports. Then, we browsed other pages and found the URL pattern to be different. Normally, when we access the pages without the virtual host configuration URL pattern for public pages is as follows:

```
{http/https}://{domain name/host IP}/web/{friendly url of community
or organization}/{friendly url of page}.
```

However, when we configure the virtual host for public pages, the URL will become shorter, as follows:

```
{http/https}://{domain name/host IP}/ {friendly url of page}.
```

We configured the virtual host only for public pages. It is possible to configure the virtual host for both public and private pages.

Let's understand the **Settings** functionality in detail. As shown in the preceding screenshot, we have the following fields available in the **Settings** functionality:

- **Public Virtual Host**—We already configured this field. If we want to provide a virtual host for the public pages of a community or organization, we need to provide the domain name here. So when we access the Liferay Portal using that domain name, Liferay internally forwards the request to the respective community or organization. Virtual host name must be unique across the portal, that is if we configure the virtual host for portal instances, communities, and/or organizations, then all of them must have a unique virtual host name.

- **Private Virtual Host**—This field defines the virtual host name for private pages. Its use is exactly the same as the **Public Virtual Host** field.

- **Friendly URL**—This field defines a friendly URL for community or organization. When a virtual host is defined either for public or private pages and the portal is accessed by the virtual host, this field will not be used to compose the full URL as explained above.

The **Settings** functionality is exactly the same for both organizations and communities. It can also be accessed from the **Manage Pages** portlet. It is the same portlet which we have used in *Chapter 6, Managing Pages, Users, and Permissions*, to configure pages. There is a **Settings** tab which displays the same settings functionality which we have used in this section.

Implementing the staging environment

As we have experienced throughout this book, the Liferay Portal is very flexible and allows us to configure the website and content on the fly; imagine if we make our CIGNEX Neighborhood portal available to everyone. We will still use these features regularly, maybe to add new content, configure new pages, and so on. In practice, we usually have a staging environment for the website. The staging environment is normally a replica of the production environment. Before adding content or applying content changes, we perform them on staging. If that is successful then only we apply the same changes on the live environment. Liferay provides in-built feature to configure staging environment for any community or organization.

Time for action – configuring staging environments

Let's learn about staging environment configuration by implementing it for the Around the Corner community.

1. Sign in to the Neighborhood portal using the admin credentials
   (URL: `http:// neighborhood.cignex.com/`).

2. Now navigate to the Around the Corner community by selecting the **Go To | Around the Corner** menu option from the Dockbar.

3. The system will display the **Florence Flower Shop** page.

4. Now navigate to the **Settings** functionality for the Around the Corner community by selecting the **Manage | Settings** menu option from Dockbar.

5. The system will, by default, open the **Virtual Host** tab. Click on the **Staging** tab.

6. The system will open the **Staging** tab with only one drop-down. Select the **Local Live** value from the **Staging Type** drop-down.

7. The system will then show the **Staged Portlets** section and the **Advanced Options** section as shown in the following screenshot:

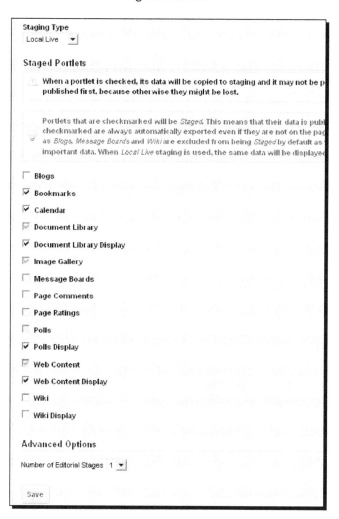

8. Keep the default values on the screen, and press the **Save** button. The system will ask you for confirmation. Press **OK** in the confirmation dialog.

9. The system will create a staging environment. Now, we can observe that the page is highlighted with a yellow border. The yellow border indicates that this is a live page of the Around the Corner community. The system has also an additional menu **Staging** in the Dockbar. Now, click on the **Return to Full Page** link from the top-right corner of the **Settings** portlet's border.

10. Now navigate to the staging environment page of Around the Corner community by selecting **Staging | View Staged Page** menu option from the Dockbar.

11. The system will display the same page with a red border around the page. The red border indicates that it's a staging page. You can also observe the URL in the address bar of the browser. The system has appended -staging in the community-friendly URL (around-the-corner).

12. Now, open the add application dialog by selecting **Add | More...** menu from Dockbar. Expand the **Tools** category and drag the **Language** portlet on top of the **Shopping** portlet as shown in the following screenshot:

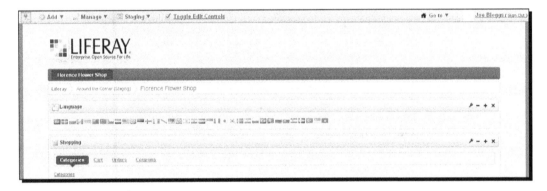

13. Now navigate to the live version of the page by selecting **Staging | View Live Page** menu option from the Dockbar. Check if the **Language** portlet is there on the top of the **Shopping** portlet. It will not be there.

14. Now navigate back to the staged version of the page by the selecting **Staging | View Staged Page** menu option from the Dockbar.

15. Now click on **Staging | Publish to Live Now** menu option from the Dockbar. The system will open the **Publish to Live Now** dialog as shown in the following screenshot:

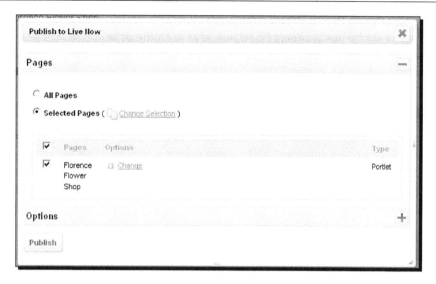

16. Keep the default values on the screen and press the **Publish** button.

17. The system will open the confirmation dialog. Press the **OK** button.

18. Again, navigate to the live version of the page by selecting the **Staging | View Live Page** menu option from the Dockbar. Check if the **Language** portlet is there on the top of the **Shopping** portlet. It should be there now.

What just happened?

We just enabled a staging environment for the Around the Corner community. Internally, Liferay has created a replica of the Around the Corner community, which is called the **staging community**. The original Around the Corner community is now referred to as the live community. All configuration changes like adding a new portlet on a page are now allowed only in the staging community. In other words, the staging community is a read/write kind of community while the live community is a read-only kind of community. Both live and staging communities are linked to each other internally.

As we discussed, the system added a new menu called **Staging** in the Dockbar once we enabled staging. Using this menu, we navigated to the staging version of the Around the Corner community page. The system allowed us to add a new portlet on the staged version of the page. We then checked if the system also added that portlet in the live version of the page. As we never published the changes from the staging community to the live community, we did not find the **Language** portlet on the live community page. We then published the changes from the staged version to the live version page. We chose to immediately publish the changes to the live version. After we published the changes from staging to live, we verified the changes on the live version of the page. It was there.

So we learned how we can use liferay's staging feature to implement a staging environment within the same liferay portal server. So far, we have used the default options either to enable the staging environment or to publish the changes to the live environment. Let's learn about these features in detail.

Staging configuration

We have used the **Settings** option from the Dockbar to configure the staging environment for the Around the Corner community. The same option is also available for organizations as well. We can also configure staging from the **Manage Pages** functionality. The **Manage Pages** portlet provides the **Settings** tab under which we can locate the same staging configuration options.

In the previous section, we kept the default values in the staging configuration. Let's look at the details of staging configuration options:

♦ **Staging Type**—Liferay provides two flavors of staging environment—local and remote. We have chosen the local staging environment in the previous section. In the case of the local staging environment, as we have seen, Liferay creates a replica of the community or organization. All the changes are allowed to be made in the staging version of the community or organization. We can then publish these changes. If we want to set up the staging environment on a completely different Liferay Portal server then we need to choose the remote live option. This setting needs to be done on the staging server. Once we choose remote live options, we need to provide some more details related to the remote live environment as shown in following screenshot:

- ❑ **Remote Host/IP**—We need to provide the IP of the remote Liferay Portal server on which we have our live environment.

- ❑ **Port**—We need to provide the live Liferay Portal server's port here.

- ❑ **Remote Group ID**—We need to provide the group ID of the live community/organization. When we publish the changes from the staging server, they will be published to the organization/community mentioned through this field.

- ❑ **Use a Secure Network Connection**—This checkbox defines whether the staging functionality should use HTTPS or HTTP based on the web services to publish the changes on the live environment.

- ◆ **Staged Portlets**—This section displays all the portlets which can be staged. We can choose which portlet's data to be maintained in the staging environment. For all the checked portlets in this section, Liferay will not allow changing the data in the live environment.

- ◆ **Number of Editorial Stages**—This field defines how many levels of approvals we need before we publish the changes to the live environment. We chose **1** as we did not want any approval for publishing the changes to the live environment. If we choose multiple stages then the system will ask us to define which role can approve the changes at each stage. Suppose we select **3** stages from this drop-down; then the system will ask us to select the roles for each stage as shown in the following screenshot:

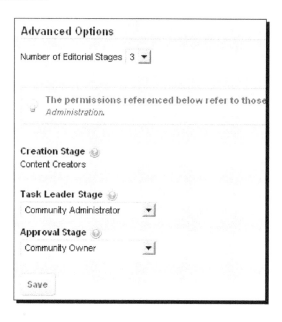

As shown in the preceding screenshot, there are three stages in the staging workflow. The first stage is the **Creation Stage**. In this stage, the users with **Content Creators** role can make the changes in the staging community and submit their change proposal for approval.

The second stage is the **Task Leader Stage** where the user can select the role for task leaders. The users with selected role can assign reviewer for the proposal.

The third stage is the **Approval Stage**. The user has to select the role for the approvers. The users with the selected role can approve the proposals and publish the changes to live. So this way, we can implement the staging workflow with multiple stages.

Publish to Live Now

In the previous section, after completing the changes in the staging environment, we published those changes to the live environment using the **Publish to Live Now** function. We did not change any default values in the form. Let's look at the details of each field available in this function:

* **All Pages**—If this radio button is checked, the system will publish the changes made in all the pages of the staging environment.
* **Selected Pages**—With this option, we can selectively publish the changes of only certain pages. When this checkbox is enabled, the system displays a hyperlink **Change Selection** to choose the pages.
* **Page Option**—This option will be available for each selected page. We can choose whether we want to publish the changes of a page to live or delete a page from live.
* **Options**—This section provides various checkboxes to select what kind of data should be published to live. It also provides a way to define the amount of data to be published to live.

Scheduled publication

As we have seen in the previous section, if we use the **Publish now** option, Liferay immediately publishes the changes to the live environment. In practice, we wish to publish changes from the staging environment to the live environment during the non-pick hours. So, if we use the **Publish now** option, then we will need somebody to actually perform this activity during the non-pick hour. Just to click a couple of buttons, we will need to request somebody to perform this activity. Fortunately, Liferay provides a better way. We can actually schedule publication of changes at some time in the future.

Time for action – scheduling publication of portal changes

Let's make changes in the staging environment of the Around the Corner community and schedule the publication of these changes to the live environment:

1. Start the Tomcat server, if it is stopped.

2. Sign in to the Neighborhood portal using the admin credentials (URL: `http:// neighborhood.cignex.com/`).

3. Now navigate to the Around the Corner community.

4. The system will display the live version of the **Florence Flower Shop** page.

5. Now open the staged version of the **Florence Flower Shop** page by selecting the **Staging | View Staged Page** menu option from the Dockbar.

6. We will now change the configuration of the **Language** portlet. Click on the **Configuration** mode of the **Language** portlet. The system will open the **Configuration** mode dialog box as shown in the following screenshot:

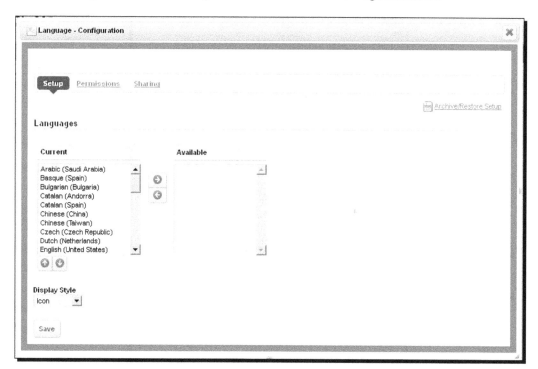

7. Change the value of the **Display Style** field to **Select Box** and press the **Save** button. The system will save the changes. Now, close the configuration mode dialog box.

8. The system will again go back to the staging version of the **Florence Flower Shop** page. We can now see the display of the **Language** portlet.

9. Now, navigate to the live version of the **Florence Flower Shop** page by selecting the **Staging | View Live Page** menu option from the Dockbar. Check if the same changes are there on the live version page. They will not be as we haven't yet published the changes on live.

10. Navigate back to the staged version of the page by selecting the **Staging | View Staged Page** menu option from the Dockbar.

11. Now, open publication to the live functionality by selecting the **Staging | Scheduled Publication to Live** menu option from the Dockbar. The system will open the **Scheduled Publication to Live** dialog as shown in the following screenshot:

12. Enter the **Language Portlet Change** value in the **Title** field. Change the value of the **Start Date** field to the current date plus five minutes. Keep the default values in other fields.

Enter the time and date in GMT format as default date and time is configured in GMT.

13. The system will add the scheduled event and display the event listing pages as shown in the following screenshot:

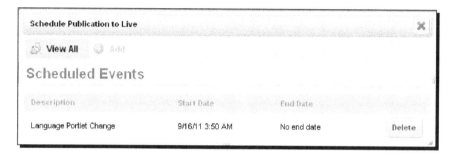

14. Now, close the **Schedule Publication to Live** dialog. Navigate to the live version of the **Florence Flower Shop** page by selecting **Staging | View Live Page** menu option from the Dockbar. Check if our changes in the staging version applied to the live version of the page. If the current time is before the **Start Date** value then the system will not reflect the changes. Once the time mentioned in the **Start Date** field is passed, refresh the page. The system will reflect the changes in the live environment.

What just happened?

We just used another way to publish the changes to the live version, the scheduler. First, we made the changes in the staging version of a page. We then double-checked whether the changes were published to the live version of the page. They were not. We then used the **Scheduled Publication to Live** function to schedule the event. We have given a name to the event. We configured the start time of the event. We then double-checked if the changes were already applied to the live version. Again they was not. We refreshed the page once the start date of the scheduled event was reached. We then checked the live version of the page. We found that the changes made in the staging environment were published.

The scheduled publication to live functionality provides the same features as publish to live now functionality. Additionally, it provides a way to configure the time when the publication should happen. We can also configure recurrence of this publication event. For example, if we want to publish the changes from staging to live automatically every seven days. We can configure this by providing start date, end date, and repeat method (Weekly) as shown in step 11 of the previous section. We can also delete any future publish events as shown in step 7 of the previous section.

Summary

We learned most of the key features which will be useful to administer the Liferay Portal server. We learned how to manage and monitor the memory usage and CPU usage, how to troubleshoot problems with logging features, how to monitor and manage user sessions, how to configure multiple portals on the same Liferay Portal server, how to configure virtual hosting, and how to configure the staging environment within the same Liferay Portal server. With this knowledge, you can easily administer the Liferay Portal server.

PayPal Test Account Configuration

This appendix provides a step-by-step guide to configure the buyer and seller accounts on the PayPal's Sandbox environment. The PayPal's sandbox environment provides a way to test the payment workflows without affecting the actual bank accounts.

Let's configure the test buyer/merchant accounts on the PayPal's Sandbox environment:

1. Open `https://developer.paypal.com/` in a browser and then click on the **Sign Up Now** button.

2. Enter the details in the sign up form as follows. This will create a test PayPal account. Remember the e-mail address and password which you provide. Click on the **Agree** and **Submit** buttons.

    - **First Name**: Enter your first name
    - **Last Name**: Enter your last name
    - **Email Address**: Enter your valid e-mail address
    - **Password**: Enter valid password
    - **Confirm Password**: Enter valid password
    - **Security Question**: Select security question of your choice
    - **Security Answer**: Set security answer for your security question

3. PayPal will show you the confirmation screen. PayPal will also send an e-mail with the e-mail verification link. PayPal will send an e-mail on the same e-mail ID which you specified in the preceding step.

[It is not very likely but sometimes this mail can go to the junk mail folder.]

4. Once you receive the e-mail from `service@paypal.com` with the account activation link, click on the link. PayPal will show you the confirmation screen as shown in the following screenshot:

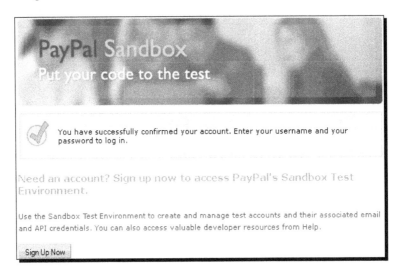

5. On the same page, you will find the **Member Log In** area as shown in the following screenshot. Enter your e-mail ID and password, which you have set in step 2. Also, enable the **Keep me logged in** option. Then click on the **Log In** button.

6. Now from the user home page, click on the **Preconfigured account** hyperlink under the **Test Accounts** section.

7. PayPal will show you the **Create a Sandbox Test Account** page. Enter the following details as mentioned and then press the **Create Account** button:

  ❏ **Country: United States**

  ❏ **Account Type: Buyer**

  ❏ **Login Email: buyer**

  ❏ **Password: buyer@123**

□ **Add Credit Card**: Visa

□ **Add Bank Account**: Yes

□ **Account Balance**: 50

8. PayPal will show you a listing page with the buyer account available on the list. Now click on the **Preconfigured** hyperlink to add a merchant account. PayPal will again show the **Create a Sandbox Test Account** page. Enter details and then press the **Create Account** button:

□ **Country**: United States

□ **Account Type**: Seller

□ **Login Email**: seller

□ **Password**: seller@123

□ **Add Credit Card**: Visa

□ **Add Bank Account**: Yes

□ **Account Balance**: 0

9. Now from the account listing page, click on all three disabled links one by one to make them enabled. Also, keep note of the buyer and seller account log-in e-mail addresses as shown in the following screenshot:

Log-in Email		Payment Review	Negative Test Mode	Reset
◉ seller_1311347213_biz@hotmail.com		Enabled	Enabled	Reset
Business	Verified			
▣ View Details				
○ buyer_1311346635_per@hotmail.com		Enabled	N/A	Reset
Personal	Verified			
▣ View Details				

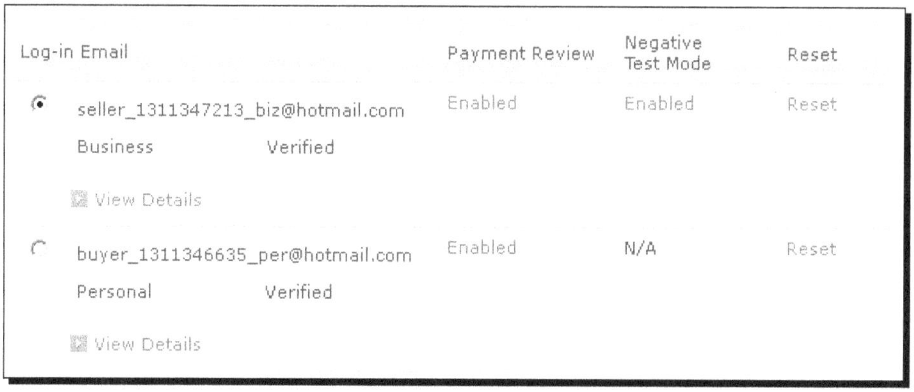

By following the preceding steps, we configured the test accounts in the PayPal Sandbox environment. Whenever there is a need, we can use the buyer or seller account with the following credentials:

- Buyer account
    - **User ID**: Enter the e-mail ID displayed after performing step 9. We need to use the e-mail ID which starts with the word **buyer**.
    - **Password**: **buyer@123**

- Seller account
    - **User ID**: Enter the e-mail ID displayed after performing step 9. We need to use the e-mail ID which starts with the word **seller**.
    - **Password**: **seller@123**

B
Pop Quiz Answers

Chapter 1, Planning your Portal

Section	Answer
1. Pop quiz – multiple choices	1. c 2. b
2. Pop quiz – watching Liferay Portal portlets in action	b
3. Pop quiz – checking the OpenOffice service	b

Chapter 3, Understanding Portal Basics and Theming

Section	Answer
1. Pop quiz – true or false	1. False 2. True 3. False 4. False

Section	Answer
2. Pop quiz – select the correct answer	1. d
	2. b
	3. b
	4. e
	5. b
3. Pop quiz – accessing a portal with a normal user account	1. b, d
	2. a, b
	3. b
	4. a, c, d
	5. a, c
	6. b
	7. a

Chapter 5, Building your First Liferay Site

Section	Answer
1 Pop quiz – true or false?	1. False
	2. False
	3. True
	4. False
	5. False
	6. True

Section	Answer
2. Pop quiz – true or false?	1. True
	2. False
	3. False
	4. True
	5. True
	6. True
3. Pop quiz – multiple choice	1. c
	2. c, d
	3. c

Chapter 6, Managing Pages, Users, and Permissions

Section	Answer
1. Pop quiz – true or false?	1. False
	2. True
	3. True
	4. False
2. Pop quiz – disabling the Register option for a guest user	1. d
	2. c
	3. b
3. Pop quiz – defining permissions for a bookmark entry	1. d
	2. c
	3. a
	4. c

Chapter 7, Creating and Publishing Content

Section	Answer
1. Pop quiz – uploading an image	d
2. Pop quiz – migrating static content from an existing site using the web content portlet	1. d 2. d 3. d 4. d 5. d
3. Pop quiz – populating the registration page	d
4. Pop quiz – uploading a PDF file	d
5. Pop quiz – embedding a link for a PDF file	c
6. Pop quiz – enabling comments for content	c
7. Pop quiz – displaying documents	d
8. Pop quiz – using the web content list portlet	c
9. Pop quiz – adding the asset publisher portlet	d
10. Pop quiz – adding a file conversion feature	d

Chapter 8, Exploring the Communities

Section	Answer
1. Pop quiz – multiple choice	c
2. Pop quiz True or false	1. a 2. a
3. Pop quiz – multiple choice	a

Chapter 9, Setting up an Online Shop

Section	Answer
1. Pop quiz – configuring the e-mail templates	1. c 2. c 3. a, b 4. a, d
2. Pop quiz – item creation	1. b, c 2. c 3. a, c, d
3. Pop quiz – adding items to the shopping cart	1. a, b 2. b
4. Pop quiz – promoting offers	1. a, b 2. a, b 3. a, b, d, e

Bonus Chapter, Exploring Social Collaboration

Section	Answer
1. Pop quiz – multiple choice	d
2. Pop quiz – multiple choice	1. d 2. d 3. d 4. d
3. Pop quiz – multiple choice	1. d 2. d 3. d
4. Pop quiz – multiple choice	d

Index

M

Magic Quadrant for Horizontal Portals report 10
mail server
  about 9
  steps, for enabling 115, 116
manage option, Dockbar
  about 71-73
  page layout option 72, 73
  page option 72
  settings option 73
  sitemap option 73
manage pages interface
  community pages, managing 156
  current logged-in user pages, managing 156
  current pages, managing 156
  menu items 156
  organizations pages, managing 156
manage pages interface, menu items
  export/import 157
  look and feel 157
  pages 157
  private pages 157
  public pages 156
  settings 157
maximum memory
  about 322
  vs. used memory 322
member role 182
memory
  allocated memory 322
  general maintenance operations 323
  management operations 322, 323
  maximum memory 322
  used memory 322
  vs. maximum memory 322
  vs. total memory 322
meta tags, page level attributes 161
monitoring option 73
my entries link 252
MySQL
  used, by configuring Liferay 58

N

Name, page level attributes 160
Neighborhood Congress
  sub-organization, adding 133

Neighborhood Prosperity public page 158
Neighbors Congress
  documents, displaying 221
number of editorial stages option 345

O

offers
  promoting, for customers 312-314
Omniadmin role 182
online content management 196
online game
  setting up, Flash Portlet used 230-232
Online Games public page 158
online order
  listing 309, 310
  processing 308, 309
online shop
  checkout process 302-306
  configuring 270, 271
  e-mail templates, configuring 279-282
  insurance cost, configuring 278, 279
  page, configuring 270, 271
  payment, configuring 272
  payment, making 302-306
  payment method, configuring 273
  shipping cost, configuring 277
online store
  prerequisites 270
  setting up 270
OpenID
  SSO with 99
  using, for authentication 100-102
OpenOffice
  installing, steps 27, 28
  integrating 112
  integration, enabling 112, 113
  service, checking 29, 30
  service, starting 29
Open Social API
  URL 246
Open Social Gadgets
  integrating 247, 248
open source portals
  vs. commercial portals 12
Oracle WebLogic
  about 39

Thank you for buying
Liferay Beginners Guide

About Packt Publishing

Packt, pronounced 'packed', published its first book "*Mastering phpMyAdmin for Effective MySQL Management*" in April 2004 and subsequently continued to specialize in publishing highly focused books on specific technologies and solutions.

Our books and publications share the experiences of your fellow IT professionals in adapting and customizing today's systems, applications, and frameworks. Our solution based books give you the knowledge and power to customize the software and technologies you're using to get the job done. Packt books are more specific and less general than the IT books you have seen in the past. Our unique business model allows us to bring you more focused information, giving you more of what you need to know, and less of what you don't.

Packt is a modern, yet unique publishing company, which focuses on producing quality, cutting-edge books for communities of developers, administrators, and newbies alike. For more information, please visit our website: www.packtpub.com.

About Packt Open Source

In 2010, Packt launched two new brands, Packt Open Source and Packt Enterprise, in order to continue its focus on specialization. This book is part of the Packt Open Source brand, home to books published on software built around Open Source licences, and offering information to anybody from advanced developers to budding web designers. The Open Source brand also runs Packt's Open Source Royalty Scheme, by which Packt gives a royalty to each Open Source project about whose software a book is sold.

Writing for Packt

We welcome all inquiries from people who are interested in authoring. Book proposals should be sent to author@packtpub.com. If your book idea is still at an early stage and you would like to discuss it first before writing a formal book proposal, contact us; one of our commissioning editors will get in touch with you.

We're not just looking for published authors; if you have strong technical skills but no writing experience, our experienced editors can help you develop a writing career, or simply get some additional reward for your expertise.

Liferay Portal Enterprise Intranets

ISBN: 978-1-847192-72-1   Paperback: 408 pages

A practical guide to building a complete corporate intranet with Liferay

1. Install, set up, and use a corporate intranet with Liferay—a complete guide

2. Discussions, document management, collaboration, blogs, and more

3. Clear, step-by-step instructions, practical examples, and straightforward explanation

Liferay Portal 5.2 Systems Development

ISBN: 978-1-847194-70-1   Paperback: 552 pages

Build Java-based custom intranet systems on top of Liferay portal

1. Learn to use Liferay tools to create your own applications as a Java developer, with hands-on examples

2. Build your own Social Office with portlets, hooks, and themes and manage your own community

3. The only Liferay book aimed at Java developers

Please check **www.PacktPub.com** for information on our titles

www.ingramcontent.com/pod-product-compliance
Lightning Source LLC
Chambersburg PA
CBHW080147060326
40689CB00018B/3882